Tim Bradford

was born and brought up in Li
University of East Anglia and ha
A large proportion of his adul
players with very short legs for the football
Saturday Comes. He has fused together a philosophy of life
based around Epicurian socialism, astral projection, bacon
sandwiches, Victorian domestic architecture, Leeds United,
traditional brewing practices and country music.

www.jayzus.com

More from the reviews:

'An irreverent and funny book which will have you laughing
into your Guinness'   *What's On*

'The title is taken from a chance encounter at Camden tube
station with a man whose death has been greatly exaggerated
and yet fervently expected. This tempts Bradford into making
an odyssey of sorts around Ireland. A book like this could
so easily slip into whimsy, but Bradford's book is good-
humoured, clever and well written. He takes on Ireland on its
own terms, never patronises nor indulges his subject matter.
He breaks Ireland up into imaginary zones. Dublin is Viking
Town, the Midlands, for reasons best known to the author, is
Orange County; the south is Maryland after the moving statues
at Ballinspittle. The book is interspersed with animations,
which will make you laugh out loud – like the map of Ireland
depicting areas of heavy rainfall – the entire island, of course.
It's worth buying for his hilarious and accurate descriptions of
Oirish theme pubs alone. Enjoy.'   *ri-ra*

'Determinedly and flatulently funny.'   *Irish Bookseller*

'Bradford sets himself up as a cod Kerouac and his ambitious and spumily garrulous, itinerary takes in the mystical garages of Youghal, the Curragh of Kildare, a cultural tour with a female Gaelic footballer and a spot of sticking out the thumb with the spottiest hitchhiker in Europe. Much of quintessential Ireland, of course, isn't in Ireland, and Bradford does the Kentish Town and Kilburn pub crawl too.' *Glasgow Herald*

'Okay, before we go any further, it's honesty time: do you know who Shane MacGowan is? If you do, you may well love this bizarre book. If you don't – or if you think that a Pogue might be an outsize bouncy ball or some sort of Irish potato pancake – then this might be for you but only if you are in the mood to expand your range of cultural references . . . The real reason for Bradford's journey is a desire to drink large amounts of Guinness, kiss the Blarney stone – and any passing female – to put his finger on the essence of Irishness and live to tell the tale. (As, indeed, has Shane MacGowan. Just.) . . . There are plenty of reasons to read *Is Shane MacGowan Still Alive?* He's funny, for a start and his love of drinking makes him perfectly suited to explore at least one time-honoured aspect of Irish culture. In the end though, as Tony Hawks before him in *Round Ireland with a Fridge*, Bradford turns his eye just as well to things beyond the bar.' *Sunday Times*

'A rambling, tongue-firmly-in-cheek look at Ireland, Irishness beyond Ireland and nationality in general . . . rampant and funny.' *BBM*

'A good (and pertinent) odyssey in search of the authentic Ireland.' *Venue*

'A superb and positively hilarious book which adds a liberal helping of cynicism to the portrayal of folk singers in bars, vomiting tourists, and moving statues. As much fun as a night's pub crawl round Dublin. Well, almost.' *Manchester Evening News*

Is
Shane MacGowan
Still Alive?

TRAVELS IN IRISHRY

Tim Bradford

Flamingo
An Imprint of HarperCollinsPublishers

The author and publishers are grateful to the following for permission to
reproduce material: Kinky Music and R&E Music for permission to quote
from 'Before All Hell Breaks Loose' by Kinky Friedman and Panama Red
and 'When the Lord Closes the Door (He Opens a Little Window)' by Kinky
Friedman and Jeff Shelby; Warner/Chappell Music for permission to quote
from 'Hit Me With Your Rhythm Stick' by Ian Dury; BMG Music for 'I Should
Be So Lucky' words and music by Mike Stock, Matt Aitken and Pete Waterman
© BMG Music Publishing Ltd/Mike Stock Publishing Ltd/Sid's Songs Ltd/All
Boys Music Ltd (All rights reserved. Used by permission); Leeds United FC
for permission to quote from *The Leeds United Book of Football*. Thanks to
Pogue Music Ltd and Perfect Songs Ltd for permission to quote from '
A Rainy Night in Soho' by Shane MacGowan.

Every reasonable effort has been made to contact copyright holders for
all the extracts reproduced in this volume. The publishers apologise for any
omissions and are happy to receive any emendations from copyright
holders at the address below.

Flamingo
An Imprint of HarperCollins*Publishers*
77–85 Fulham Palace Road,
Hammersmith, London W6 8JB

www.**fire**and**water**.com

Flamingo is a registered trademark of HarperCollins*Publishers* Ltd

Published by Flamingo 2001
3 5 7 9 8 6 4 2 1

First published in Great Britain by Flamingo 2000

Copyright © Tim Bradford 2000

Tim Bradford asserts the moral right to
be identified as the author of this work

ISBN 000 655168 8
Photograph of Tim Bradford © Tony Davis 2000

Set in Postscript Linotype Hiroshige by
Rowland Phototypesetting Ltd, Bury St Edmunds, Suffolk

Printed and bound in Great Britain by Clays Ltd, St Ives plc

Contents

ORANGE COUNTY

SHANEWORLD

MARYLAND

List of Illustrations

Acknowledgements

To start with, I have to thank Annie, the real traveller, for years of encouragement and belief (even when I lived in Walthamstow), and without whom none of this would have happened.

Next, at the risk of coming over all Tom Hanksish, there are countless others who've helped me along the way. I'd like to thank various people in Ireland for their hospitality and help – Deidre, Rachel, Jackie, Bernie, Ted, Declan and the gang, Sarah for her knowledge of 'culture', The Balinteer-St Johns women's Gaelic Football team for showing me the benefits of dedication and strong thighs, Arthur Guinness for a clever invention, Michael for his knowledge of hurling, Marie McCraith for advice, Ronnie Matthews for his time, Tom Matthews (no relation) for his art, Seamus McGonagle (even if it's probably not his real name) for being there red faced and plastered that day in Dublin back in '88. Thanks to Bill and Helen for putting me up (and up with me) for so many years. And also to those who preferred not to be mentioned (whether for tax, moral or emotional reasons) – thanks anyway.

Closer to home: thanks to Terry for an overall creative vibe and telepathic transference of ideas (and the crossword), Pat, also for the crossword, Sarah, Lady Blathery, for help with Irish pubs, Spizz and Karen for feeding me as I strained to finish the first draft, Ian Plenderleith for years of inspiration and for words of encouragement at crucial times, my parents Rhona and Tony for setting me on my way (and Tone for passing on his great knowledge of Irish accents over the years), my brothers Toby and Matt (Snake) for travels we've shared, Dom and Seth Weir and Jo Ackerman for the all-important Finty & Rollo project, Brendan for putting it all in perspective, Alan Marshall, Jane Rylands-Bolton, Rob Conybeare, Julie Taylor, Gordon Thorburn, Justin Mullins and Michael

Donaghy for coaching and guidance over the years, Tony Davis for making me look like an alcoholic U-Boat captain, Rich for the lend of the coat, Elaine in Paris for help and advice, Philip Gwyn Jones for his belief, Georgina Laycock for her help (and her interesting name), Richard Hawkes, an early cartoon patron, Mike O'Donnell from the Institute of Celtic Studies. I am ever grateful to Andy Lyons and Doug Cheeseman at *When Saturday Comes* for continuing to give me bits of work even while I was off on my travels. Plus all my friends – genuine Irish and Irish by osmosis – who threw ideas my way over the years.

To Cindy for her love and support and for picking me up at the lowest points and washing the ink off my hands. And finally, thanks to Cathleen, for getting me up in the mornings and helping me realise that the rest of it is just 'stuff'.

To the Irish people who
have changed my life

But Leeds taught me something else – that
work and will to win are just as vital as any
instinctive skills you may possess.

JOHNNY GILES, *Leeds United Book of Football*

Today I decided not to think of you
But was betrayed by a lazy pub window.
I saw a slim tree whose delicate red leaves
Rose and fell in the Thames breeze –
A mixed-up drinker, at this time of year,
I can taste Yeats in the beer.

ROBERT GAINSBOROUGH, 'Maude Gone Fishing'

Preface

This book is based on journeys I made to Ireland in 1998, and on various forays back to previous visits, or (in one or two cases) into an alternative reality. It's divided into a series of ancient mythical areas, which I've made up. Some names have been changed, some have stayed the same. I'd like to think that you can start at whatever point you want in the book. Think of it as a rambling pub conversation about all kinds of trivia such as What is Irishness? What is Englishness? What is nationality? Who are we? Who are you? Are you staring at my leprechaun? Ah, so many questions and so little drinking time . . .

WELCOME TO IRELAND

Is Shane MacGowan Still Alive?

Camden Tube to Camden Lock

I came out of Camden Town tube, badly in need of a piss, and crossed the road to Barclays bank. There was just enough in there to get me through the evening – I was thankful that I'd kept the account at the little village in Suffolk where I'd worked for a while years ago. They knew I was a hopeless case but, because of that, they always made sure I could somehow get hold of money – perhaps they liked the fact that they had an impoverished London-based slob on their books rather then the usual farmers, shopkeepers, salesmen and village idiots. No, not very likely at all, it was probably just a computer error that kept giving me access to cash.

I was going to an Evan Parker gig at Dingwalls. Not my usual midweek fare, atonal improvised alto saxophone (is it anybody's?), but I was meeting my old schoolfriend, Plendy, and Martin, a mad Welsh mate of his who worked at the BBC World Service Monitoring Centre in Reading, and who was the kind of bloke who'd make witty one-liners that referred to Anglo-Saxon poetry and Russian revolutionary film makers. You had to be on your toes with Martin all the time.

I started walking quickly in the direction of Chalk Farm, then saw a figure heading towards me at about 0.5 mph. I instinctively slowed down to get a good look at him. He was wearing a baggy, dishevelled black suit with an open-necked shirt and he looked as though just keeping upright was taking up all his energy. At one point he staggered into the road and kicked a half-full black dustbin bag, then zig-zagged back onto the pavement. I tried to catch his eye as he passed me, but he was staring straight ahead, at some point in the pavement or the future which might keep him going. I turned and watched him disappear into the night, then carried on to the club.

'Guess what?' I said to the lads a few minutes later, as Evan Parker went 'eeeeeaaooooo a bleedeblee doooOOOWWaaapooopopopo'.

'What?'

'Shane MacGowan is still alive.'

And before Martin had time to make a witty connection between 'Rum, Sodomy and the Lash' and *Beowulf*, I went to the bog.

IRISH MYTHS & LEGENDS 1
How to be Irish

1 Why you Need to be Irish

Gone are the days when being English opened doors for people around the world. Now Irish is where it's at culturally, economically, sexually and politically. The Brits have been jealous of the Irish for centuries because of their ability to drink, their nice singing voices, their straight-armed dancing style (which is so much sexier than Morris dancing) and their ginger hair.

2 Positive Affirmations

You *can* be Irish. You *can* leave behind the English world of semi-detached houses, garden gnomes and Freemasonry. It's simple. Just repeat one or more of these simple phrases every day after getting home from the pub and in no time at all you'll find yourself on the fringes of the Irish football squad for the next World Cup.

Every day, in every way
I'm becoming Irishyer and Irishyer

Feck me
I am Irish

England 0–Ireland 1, Euro '88

3   Diet

The way to a man's nationality is through his stomach. The Englishman needs two vital foodstuffs to keep him going – roast beef and baked beans – while the Irishman can survive on just one, the simple potato. It is the most versatile form of nourishment on the planet and only Guinness has more vitamins and minerals and less calories.

4   Exercise

Football and darts are the national sports in England, and everyone in the country knocks a ball around in the road after work then goes down the pub, sinks fifteen pints of lager and throws little arrows at a board. It's fun, but this regime is not great for total all-round fitness. However, there are many traditional Irish pastimes which increase strength and cardiovascular fitness, such as pub brawling, hurling, throwing the potato and that dancing where you keep your arms straight and move your feet really fast.

5   Making Friends

Irish people and English people are very similar except for slight variations in social etiquette. Without generalising *too* much, whereas the English are repressed, tightarsed cold fish with people they don't know (such as their parents) Irish people will slap a stranger on the back, shout 'How are ye?' at the top of their voices, buy them a drink then take them home and give them a damn good seeing to.

6   Sex

Sex sells. Everyone knows this. That's why I've included it in this book. The publisher will probably make sure that 'sex' is written on the cover somewhere in an eye-catching font, and then copies of the book will be put in the sex manuals' section of the big shops. And those sections are always full of eager people with bulging wallets.

Sex with English people is all messy and complicated what with condoms, Femidoms, spermicidal gel, multiple orgasms (for both partners), prenuptial agreements, and the dreaded threat of kiss 'n' tell tabloid revelations. In Ireland all these things (including multiple orgasms) are rationed by their owners, Catholic Church International Holdings plc, so people have to make their own fun.

7   Release the Leprechaun Within

English people have an inner child that has temper tantrums, plays video games and downloads pictures of famous actresses in swimwear from the internet. Irish people, in contrast, have an inner leprechaun that has a great laugh and lives in those clear plastic domes that you have to shake to make the snow fall.

8   Dye Your Hair Ginger

FINNEGANIA

London

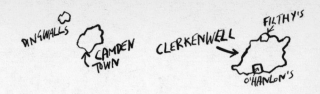

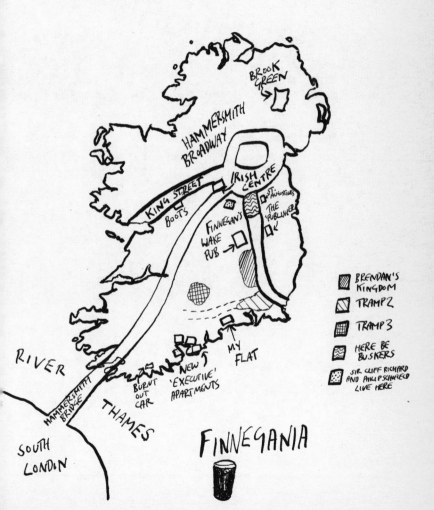

DINGWALLS

CAMDEN TOWN

FILTHY'S

CLERKENWELL

O'HANLON'S

BROOK GREEN

HAMMERSMITH BROADWAY

IRISH CENTRE

KING STREET

BOOTS

ST. AUGUSTINE'S
THE PUBLISHER

FINNEGAN'S WAKE PUB →

RIVER

HAMMERSMITH BRIDGE

BURNT OUT CAR

NEW 'EXECUTIVE' APARTMENTS

MY FLAT

THAMES

SOUTH LONDON

FINNEGANIA

BRENDAN'S KINGDOM

TRAMP 2

TRAMP 3

HERE BE BUSKERS

SIR CLIFF RICHARD AND PHILIP SCHOFIELD LIVE HERE

On a Clear Day You Can See Fulham Football Ground

Hammersmith to Ireland (in my head)

Hammersmith was fucking cold. Ice had travelled over from Scandinavia, passed across the North Sea like a self-satisfied speed skater[1] and taken the short journey along the quiet, silver river to W6, where it had formed an unhealthy union with heavy metal particles, those noxious clumps of cancer dust that float around the major capitals of the world, but particularly the Fulham Palace Road. Most people would have cheerily admitted that it was no worse than normal. If I'd talked to anyone. But I went through phrases of not talking to anyone, particularly Londoners over fifty, who would, naturally, start to bang on about 'pea soupers' and the 1950s and rationing and how the Kray twins were 'lovely fellas' really and football teams were much better in those days. They weren't, I wanted to say, actually. Better. The football teams. I knew this and had already made up an argument for the time when I would be confronted in a dark alleyway by a gang of preposterously nostalgic and assertive football-mad cockneys. Players in the forties and fifties were just a load of unfit brickies with smoking-related breathing problems who hoofed the ball from one end of the pitch to the other.

[1]Eric Heiden, say. Not Wilf Thingy, the plucky English bloke.

But despite the pollution, this part of Hammersmith is a beautiful place, full of life and noise and crap buskers and spilling-over pubs and real newspaper stalls (with more Irish papers than you can get anywhere in Ireland) and half-crazed hawkers selling six lighters for a pound ('Laydeeezz. Lighters, laydeez?'), with Charing Cross Hospital looming over everything in much the same way that St Paul's Cathedral must have dominated the old city in the late seventeenth century. Though Charing Cross Hospital isn't quite as attractive. The upside of this is that there are no Japanese and American tourists taking videos of themselves or asking you for the way to the 'Tower of London, buddy', which has to be a good thing. People – well, estate agents and puff-piece hacks in the *Evening Standard* – are always talking about Fulham Palace Road 'coming up', getting smartened out and sorted. But all that ever seems to change are the pubs, which are the only things that don't need changing.

There is nowhere in Hammersmith, to my knowledge, that you can get away from the sound of cars. Sometimes I'll lie in the bath with the windows of the flat open. I don't mind the cold. I want the noise. I listen to the traffic. It reminds me of the sea. The noise, the roaring, coughing eternal circle of Hammersmith Broadway, picking up speed towards the A4 and M4. It never stops.

I decided to do my bit for reducing air pollution by selling the car. My girlfriend Annie had bought the Vauxhall Corsa back in 1994 when we'd lived off Portobello Road and she was working in Weybridge. Now she'd been promoted and had headed off to Houston, Texas. What did I want with a car? This was my task, the one thing she'd left in my capable hands. We'd spent a day, back in November, driving around various garages trying to get a decent price. Then I remembered a conversation I'd had with a garage mechanic in Limerick at the tail end of 1992. He'd fixed the breakpads on my brother's rickety old Ford Fiesta for a fiver, and told us that if we wanted to sell the car we'd get £1,500 for it. We were incredulous. Bearing in mind that the pound and the punt were almost on a par, it seemed like a twenty per-cent mark-up at least. The thought entered my head that I could drive

"SURE, SO WHAT'S THIS SQUIGGLY BIT, THEN?"

the Corsa over to Ireland, have a holiday, sell the car and make a good deal. I'm no businessman, but the glamour of this proposition had quite an appeal.

I don't know much about cars. But I knew I needed an adventure. I had just turned 33. Thirty-three. The Lord of Lords, our Saviour Jesus Christ, had done the business by the time he was thirty-three – had a real relationship with a deity, tried to lead his people to freedom, had arguments with the leaders of an occupying army, been crucified on a big hill in front of crowds of people then reincarnated himself for his friends. I had done none of that (though there was the night of a sixth-form party in Lincoln in 1982 when, after puking most of my innards up, I recovered sufficiently inside Ritzy's night club to the extent that some people thought it was a miracle. 'Truly, that man is the son of God', said some little Lincolnshire disco girl in a John Wayne accent as I forced half a pint of cider down my throat.).

I needed to get away for a while anyway because I was becoming too set in my ways. I'd even stopped my regular habit of giving money to the bedraggled figures in the subway at Hammersmith roundabout. Well, one of them. He spoke in a Yorkshire accent but he could have been Russian, rocking backwards and forwards staring at his palm. Sometimes I used to think, sorry mate I'm just too skint, but I'm not as skint as him no matter how much I've pissed away in a pub on Archway Road. I once had to break up a fight he was in – he was about to beat up a skinny frightened guy who was trying to steal his patch. Luckily, I had a microphone stand; I was on my way to a gig in the Tut 'n' Shive on Upper Street – the British Country & Western revival we called it ('Brit cunts', said our friends), so I brandished the mike stand and told them to stop fucking about. Now I was mad at him (and really mad at myself). I was down there once with my dad and brother and was going to tell them about the incident but they were mesmerised by an appallingly drawn

picture of Bob Marley that some bloke was trying to pass off
as a poster to tourists on their way to see Sir Cliff in *Heathcliff*
at the Hammersmith Apollo.

What really annoyed me was that I wished this bloke was
a nice friendly beggar who conformed to genteel ideas of
homelessness, like the old Irish fellow further up Fulham
Palace Road who stands in a doorway near the shoe shop,
and who never wants money, just things to stare at.

My flat is, believe it or not, at the epicentre of old-fashioned
tramp activity in the South Hammersmith area. Tramps must
be descended from some ancient race that are tuned into ley
lines which converge on my flat, or are inexorably drawn
here by electromagnetic forces that we house dwellers don't
yet understand. In my more fanciful moments I think to
myself that I might be The King of the Tinkers and they have
come to claim me as their own. For much of the time I certainly look like a trainee tramp. Hair virtually down to my
shoulders, a week's worth of blotchy, sandpaperish stubble.
Crappy old clothes (I've only been shopping for clothes twice
since 1989).

My aforementioned 'favourite tramp' – whose name is
Brendan and who comes, originally, from Co. Tyrone – leans
against an electrical meter next to the newsagents nearest
Fernando's café on Fulham Palace Road. He patrols from
there down to the doorway next to Luigi's pizza place about
two hundreds yards further south.[2] I've only seen him away
from this area twice. Once on King Street opposite the Living

---

[2]In a more recent, deadline-challenging development, Fernando's greasy spoon
business has been bought out and is now another Italian restaurant.

department store (London's only Third-World shopping experience. They've got a couple of items and you never get served because the staff are always on the phone – Now gone as well. A curse!). Brendan forages locally and lives on what he can find – usually some form of superbrew extra-strong lager which, in accordance with the manufacturer's specifications, turns immediately and magically into urine as soon as it is swallowed.

Once I happened to be sitting on an eastbound Hammersmith and City Line train at the Hammersmith terminus, reading a collection of John B. Keane's essays and stories in an attempt to travel to Ireland for less than a tenner (I try to save money by applying for those cheap airline ticket offers but they seem to get booked up years in advance). I was reading a chapter entitled 'My Personal Tramp' when he – My Favourite Tramp – sat down opposite me. I wanted to say to him – I didn't know his name then – 'Well, do you know what? You, Mr Tramp, are my *favourite* tramp in all the world, and I've just found this story called 'My Personal Tramp'. And here you are on the train with me. Incredible coincidence, is it not?' I could tell from his worn-out, sad-eyed expression that he would not, in fact, find it incredible, he would simply think I was some ranting nutter and would probably get quietly off the train and move up a couple of carriages. So I didn't say it.[3] Some facts – tramps' hair goes thick because the alcohol lowers their testosterone levels. They stand in overcoats staring off into nothingness. Many tramps are like angels and think other people can't see them.

[3]A while later I was writing up the notes to this chapter on the same train and a modernist tramp sat down next to me, smelling of BO, roast kidney and special brew, and fags, his purple jeans darkened with recently squirted urine. Was I inadvertently attracting the tramps while writing about them?

Then it happened. Ideas that had obviously been kicking around in my brain for a while decided to join forces. I thought about when I was seventeen, and obsessed with Jack Kerouac, when life seemed full of possibilities, when a car was a symbol of adventure and freedom.[4] I was struck with the idea of heading off like Sal and Dean into the west, except I'd be doing it in this pretty little bright-red girl's car, with a guitar and a crate of beer in the boot.

I had a feeling my mate Terry might fancy the trip. A knackered-looking handsome Irish raconteur, Terry looks vaguely like Sean Hughes, that knackered-looking handsome Irish raconteur. Which was ironic, as he had bumped

My Great Great Grandfather Ole Horseperson

---

[4]In my mid teens I spent day after day reading my favourite authors, Jack Kerouac and George Orwell. I loved *Down and Out in Paris and London* but there was also something slightly warped about it, the sordid voyeuristic slumming of a middle-class bloke with too much time on his hands. Incidentally, how do you know if you're a tramp? Is it genetic, mapped out generations before? One of my ancestors used to head off from his Buckinghamshire village home at regular periods to pubs and clubs in the Midlands to play the squeeze box and the spoons. My great grandmother's family in Yorkshire were horse people, which was apparently a euphemism for gypsy stock. I'd seen a photo of her father, looking tall and strong with a big black Victorian moustache. I imagined him looking proud on horseback.

into Sean Hughes several times at after-hours pubs and clubs and would invariably try and get into an argument with him. Usually because Terry was about to get off with a girl who thought he was Sean Hughes, then the real Sean Hughes would come along and spoil it. Like a Brian Rix farce, really. Or a Brian Rix farce co-written by James Joyce:

What the Finlan saw a Butler sore her Mother Mary.

(Scene – late nightshite midnight black jean bar under the chip smell tourist choking Tottenhemhem Caught Road. Finoola, Assumpta, Terry in chitchat inebriation)

Terry: Wear you froming to?

Assumpta: To? To? From? Live?

Terry: Chunky fleshy Finoola.

Finoola: The beer-stained sweat of old pine, belly stubble shaved.

Assumpta: Are you Sean Hughes?

Terry: Me funny Sean. Sunny, heavy-lidded sad Sean.

Sean: No me real deal feelme funny Sean. Who are you?

Terry: Doppelganger boy. Johnny Stalker. Johnny Walker.

Assumpta: Double Sean bedfun thrusting, eh Sean?

Anyway, I put it to Terry that the trip might be a good laugh.
I said something like, 'Let's go off to Ireland for a week or so,
try and sell the car, meet people who know the truth, get
drunk, stand on mountain tops, go painting, sit in pubs
listening to old men's stories, laugh at and fall in love with
mad Irishwomen, shout on the western edge of the world,
sing folksongs, cry in the rain, puke in soft green fields, catch
a moving statue and put it in our pocket.'

Terry took a sip of his pint and smiled at me. 'Argh, yeah,
why not?'

I regularly wander through Hammersmith and see Irish faces
everywhere – heavy-set red-haired women, beautiful dark-
haired girls, old guys with lined faces and sad eyes, tiny, grinning leprechauns made of felt who sing 'When Irish Eyes are
Smiling' when you press their bellies. Hammersmith is an old
Irish area. At present around eight per cent of the population of the Hammersmith postal district is Irish born – the
figure for London as a whole is four per cent and one and a
half per cent for Britain (from the 1991 census). It's hard to
know the figures for second- or third-generation Irish, the
fresh-faced youngsters who choose to spend their evenings
bashing away on bodhrans at the wonderful and lovely
Hammersmith Irish Centre. This hive of Celticity is opposite
St Paul's church, round the back of Marks & Spencer with
a good view of the flyover and its dark underbelly and of
Coca Cola's UK headquarters. It's a yellowy brick building
built in the mid-nineties. They run music, history, language
and dance courses as well as occasional gigs and Irish music
sessions and manages to appeal to the generation who came
over after the War with stout and dance-hall music coursing
through their veins as well as the kids brought up in the

borough on hip hop and alcopops. It's at the north-west end of what I regard as the Irish village of Finnegania[6] – the spiritual centre of which is a discarded can of Guinness under the flyover which can be reached by crossing over the curve of the A4 and walking round the Apollo Theatre.

Inside the centre it's very pale and high ceilinged, perhaps in an attempt to be like a church, although the atmosphere is more akin to an English village hall, the world of amateur dramatics and pantomimes, cake stalls and tombola, prized marrows and dollies made of wicker, the tables left over from university seminar rooms. Looking at the group of lads with their great faces and lost eyes, come to hear their grand-children play the penny whistle or sing a ballad, I couldn't help thinking that this scene should be a smoky low-slung pub in the forgotten back streets of a midlands Irish country town.

The workshop was a collection of musicians of all ages and talents. Whistle players, people on squeezebox, uillean pipes, banjos, guitars. The music sounded like Irish music yet didn't really ever get going. The notes were right and the rhythm and speed were there but something was missing. A  bloke who looked like Gerry Adams, President of Sinn Féin, was sat at a table surrounded by friends and family. When a jig came on, Gerry started dancing. Do you reckon that's Gerry Adams? I said to my friends. No they said, it isn't. Well it looks like him to me. I wonder what he's doing here. Gerry Adams was dancing away with a baseball cap back to front on his head. Look at him. I'm not sure what the hard-liners of the IRA would think if they could see him now. That's not Gerry Adams, Tim. You'd think, if he's going to make a public appearance like this, that he'd have learned to dance properly. Still, I bet he can dance better than Ian Paisley. The

[6]Historically speaking, the Irish village in Hammersmith, at least in the nine-teenth century, was actually about half a mile to the north-west at Brook Green.

music workshop group started to crank it up a bit. Ffaafnaaa nfffnaa twiddleidsleeeeeeeeee ggieee doo deeed didddle dee deee did diddd ddiiiidie dieeeeiieee . . . pipes and fiddle and accordion, more relaxed this time and my foot started to tap. Then a middle-aged guy took the microphone and introduced a couple of female singers. They did ballads, one in a high-pitched and haunting style about some tragedy or other, then a slightly younger girl did 'The Raggle Taggle Gypsy' followed by something about Johnny being the handsomest in the village (it's always Johnny isn't it, never Tim. How come it's never 'but Tim was the tallest and fairest and cleverest and funniest and most talented of them all'? – if there are Tims in Irish folk songs I'm pretty sure they'll almost always be village idiots or something.)⁷

Finnegan's Wake,⁸ just round the corner, is a pub that nobody should go to, some big brewer's mangled attempt to

⁷As well as the Irish centre there's a thriving busker scene in west London, usually situated in the subway at the top of Fulham Palace Road. The best of them is known simply by his unofficial stage name Bloke with Organ in a Wheelchair. He's a fat old fellow with grey hair and glasses; a more recent addition to the scene. He rests his organ on a stand and plays Irish classics, usually with a tinny drum machine diddling away in the background. One of his better numbers is 'When Irish Eyes are Smiling', which goes something like this: Bum bh bum phh daao daaaoooo daooo daoaooo daooo daoo daooo Bum bh bum phh daao daaaoooo daooo daoaooo daooo daoo daooo Bum bh bum phh daao daaaooooodaooo daoaooo daooo daoo daooo. tinkle dee dee deeeeeeeeeee'. I once saw him stand up and pack all his stuff away and for a second I was outraged that I'd given him money not because of the music but because of his disability but then I thought it serves me right, transport is a big problem in London when you're getting to gigs.

⁸*Finnegans Wake* is the James Joyce book that nobody has read. *Ulysses* is also the James Joyce book that nobody has read, but everyone claims they have (that's why it is now the *Citizen Kane* of novels, up there at the number one spot in recent lists of the best novels of the century). *Finnegans Wake* was Joyce's last book, his mangled and messianic attempt to reinvent the language and structure of the novel and piss people off at the same time (he was probably much more successful at the latter). Of course, I don't really know what I'm talking about, not having read it.

reinvent the concept of Irish pub-going. It is a brand, a kind of corporate kit pub, except you pronounce the k as in *sh*. There are several of them dotted around London. I do know what I'm talking about here because I unfortunately am sucked into it from time to time by its possible promise of wild-haired colleens dancing on the tables. And the footy.

This Hammersmith version is like a west-of-Ireland theme park set in a grubby looking thirties building. Two towering slot machines guard the main entrance, like the giants Gog and Magog of the City of London, winking their multi-coloured lights at each magical drinking warrior who enters the establishment. There are dark brown wooden floor-boards, old newspapers and Irish posters all over the walls and ceilings. A violin case here. An accordion there. Near one of the several TV screens that pump out constant satel-lite sport is an old brown briefcase with the words MICHAEL O'MALLEY, LEGAL SECRETARY written on it in thick white paint (or possibly thin mashed potato). On the other side of the pub is a wooden shamrock (Is it, I wonder, the magic one ex-President Mary Robinson gave to Javier Pérez de Cuéllar, the former head of the UN, to ward off the evil machinations of Boutros Boutros-Ghali?). At various points there are pots and pans and *stuff* – basically all sorts of ill-thought-out cultural flotsam.

And the clientèle are just too perfect – perhaps they're actors. A group of raucous red-haired women sit at a table in the middle, carousing and eyeing up the blokes. An old fellow with bulbous red nose and the look of a noble Gaelic poet nurses a pint of stout near the door. Young couples stare into each other's eyes. A group of young Irish lads in leather jackets and real haircuts crack jokes and stare off into the distance at imaginary Nicole Kidman lookalikes running across a mountain top. The Irishness is suffocating, but it's a joke, a shell, a thin layer of treacle. I can't even remem-ber what the pub was like before it was Finneganed, but probably just some nondescript and harmless local boozer.

When I first arrived in London in 1988, it was still bursting with authentic Irish pubs – ramshackle Victorian or Edwardian edifices which dominated the village high streets and side roads of the city – Muswell Hill, Walthamstow, Shepherd's Bush, Hammersmith, Hoxton, Ladbroke Grove, Leyton. They may not have had the insignia of boozers back in Ireland – the name of the proprietor painted bright above the front window – but went by mostly prosaic English names, the Bells, Red Lions, White Harts or slightly more obscure monikers like Pelican or Green Man – but everybody knew what they were – and a high proportion of the drinkers within (or if not them, their parents) would have hailed from Ireland.

A creak of the flaky-painted door with its carved-pattern glass and you would enter into a main area of cigarette smoke, alcohol breath, crap aftershave (has anyone ever bettered Old Spice as a flowery counterpoint to the acid stink of maleness?), the crack of pool ball and blur of voices slightly rasping and off key like the trombone and baritone section of a school wind band. Decades of tobacco smoke were caked into the walls. The breathtakingly high, ornate ceilings made them seem like cathedrals of drinking, places of worship for those to whom the Sunday lunchtime pint was the spiritual high point of a week of grind. And the six other days of the week were quite good as well. The landords would either be big, farm-fed, red-faced, two- or three-chinned prop forwards, or red-haired whippet-like gone-to-seed lads with nervous darting eyes and a graceful way on the dancefloor at wedding receptions. Reddish carpet blotched with unidentifiable stains and, like the ageing clientèle, marinated in beer. Scuffed fittings, post-plush velveteen benches to the walls for the older hands to sit side by side, watch the world go by and say that they'd 'seen it all before'.

The last four years have seen a big change – theme pubs,

fun pubs, chain pubs – whatever you want to call them – have been springing up all over the place. Scruffy Murphys, Finnegan's Wakes, O'Neills, Waxy O'Connors, Bodhran Barneys, Linus the Leprechaun's Happy Shamrocks (OK, I made that one up). The Irish theme pub has not only arrived in London, it has taken over. What the marketing managers either fail to realise (or more probably don't care about) is that this has created a shift in attitudes towards Irish culture. What used to be thought of as ancient, romantic and perhaps with a bit of 'edge' are now regarded as tacky eyesores, smart-fitted commercial machines with the ubiquity of international high street brands like McDonalds. Real drinkers now eschew a visit to the local Irish pub because it suggests frivolity where once it denoted authenticity, mindless fun where once there was both pleasure and pain, shallowness where once was an almost religious need to get shit-faced. Discord where once there was close harmony singing.

Some might argue that this is a positive aspect of what is jocularly known as the Celtic Tiger, the hard-driving Irish economy of the mid- to late-nineties, that it shows Ireland has become a real country at last and not some has-been backwater, a vessel for nostalgia freaks who dwell on the past, that it is creating new (and annoying) ideas of Irishness, reinventing itself for the new millennium. For those who frequent the places and like to get off on the nuances of culture, history and habit while fulfilling their alcoholic-unit quota, this is bullshit. These pubs are a fake validation of the ridiculous chirpy good-time Oirish vibe (the ones that Americans love so much). Every pint we have in these places is an encouragement for marketing men to rip off and parody a vibrant culture and steal its images. (Pause for breath, see Appendix.)

Down the cold, forgotten warehouse road that leads to the river – past the scrappy hedges and damp walls – lay the ghost of a car, a burned-out Ford Escort of early eighties' vintage, a pagan sacrifice, a love rite to a favourite Spice Girl from some self-styled juvenile delinquent. Behind the poorly made wooden fence, idle bulldozers waited for the next morning's shift when time will move nearer another new block of viciously ugly luxury apartments with river views. I inspected the car, thinking that it used to belong to somebody but now no-one, as a police helicopter waited overhead, then somewhere a siren, then a gunshot sounded, or was it a criminally faulty gas cooker perhaps taking the heads off some eager diners at a student lager and spag bol evening?

The light was going down, reflecting warmth against the scaffolding on the Harrod's Depository. Or 'Harrods Suppository', as one of my friends used to call it in all innocence, the same friend who thought that *West Ham* played at Hammersmith. Which, when you think about it, isn't so strange. Seeing the shell of a motor made me decide that I should check the battery on the little Corsa. I didn't want it to go flat again. It would soon be going on a journey.

Hey, Mister, Got any Tayto?

Most Irish pubs worth their salt and vinegar will serve Tayto, the Irish potato crisps. To the untrained palate (i.e. mine) they taste exactly the same as any other kind of crisp. But to the rootless Irish person drifting round the world dreaming of home, they are a beautiful and rare foodstuff which transports the eater on a mystical journey back to Erin's wild shores. People buy boxloads of the stuff saying they are addicted to them. They're dry, slightly greasy and very cheese and oniony. But you don't understand, says the fat person stuffing their face with crisps. Lots of Irish food is special like that, particularly if it's hard to come by. Here's a brief selection:

Superquinn Sausages

You've got to try some Superquinn sausages, I was told. I sat down to my fry-up with these little fried rabbit droppings at the side of the plate. Mmmm, these fried rabbit droppings

SUPERQUINN
SAUSAGES
– A TASTE EXPERIENCE

look delicious. But where are the Superquinn sausages? Hey, those are the Superquinn sausages. Ah, stop messing.

Irish Butter

Irish people abroad will drive around a new city for days looking for Irish butter. I mean, butter is butter. It all tastes the same to me. But they like their traditional Irish butter – like Kerrygold. Kerrygold was actually created by Heinz magnate Tony O'Reilly for the Irish Dairy Board in the mid-sixties. But if you mention this to an Irish person, it's as if you have criticised Michael Collins or the drummer out of U2. Kerrygold is simply a recent brand with an invented fictional heritage, like the crap beer you get in many new Irish pubs. Hey, managed to get a dig in at crap Irish pubs again there. The proofreader's obviously not concentrating.

Ring Cheese

In the long-gone days when I played rugby, the concept of 'ring cheese' would have been enough to send me into paroxysms of mirth before collapsing on the floor in a soggy puddle of giggles (at least I hope that's giggles and not the product of the 'cream cracker game' – oh, never mind). Ring is an Irish speaking area in Waterford. Cheese is a dairy product made from milk and – but you probably know that already.

Chocolate Kimberleys

Ordinary Kimberley biscuits are, apparently, disgusting and taste like cardboard. But you've got to taste Chocolate Kimberleys. They're simply heaven. You're supposed to leave them in the fridge for a while. Mmmmmm. It'll be an experience you'll never forget. It's a biscuit thing with marshmallow in, a bit like Wagon Wheel but not as tasty or big.

Red Lemonade

Lemons are yellow but lemonade is red, at least in Ireland. White lemonade, or to be more precise, see-through, is for amateurs. Real drinkers take red lemonade with their tipple. Is it like Lucozade or Tizer? I asked in all innocence. Don't be silly. It's lemonade made with special red lemons. Right. But it's not really red, it's orange.

VIKING TOWN

Dublin

CROKE PARK

LIFFEY

HOLYHEAD

WALES

TEMPLE BAR

GRAFTON STREET

BRIDGE CLUB

HAMMERSMITH

DUNDRUM

VIKING TOWN

🍺 CULTURAL TOUR SPOT

🎻 BUSKER

⚜ VIKING

@ EMAIL HERE

Visions of Beer and Loathing on the Road to Holyhead

Hammersmith to Dublin

As usual I had left everything until the last minute. This was fine with me – in a way I was happier like that because it didn't give me too much time to cock things up. When other people were involved, however, it became more of a problem.[1] I had only mentioned to Terry a couple of days earlier that I was *definitely* heading off at this time. He's usually pretty spontaneous, but this was short notice even for him. I'd spoken to him earlier in the day and he said he'd call some time in the evening if he'd managed to get it all together. I smelled disaster already (it smells sweet and sickly like treacle pudding except it's also as dry as chalk on a blackboard). Why couldn't I organise anything properly? Terry would most likely be in a pub doing the crossword and thinking subconsciously about Ireland. That was something, I suppose. I sat in the little box room at the end of the flat and stared down at The Car, waiting for the phone to ring.

I had had strange fears that either mine or Terry's short-term memory tanks would give out and one of us would

[1] $o2/a \ (m) = a \times f/m - m = me$, f = fuckup quotient, a = amount of things to be fucked up, o = other people.

forget about the trip. The thing was, Terry and I had one thing in common, a dramatically deficient short-term memory system. We could both recall events which took place in the sixties, news broadcasts, the colour of the sky on a spring morning, what the three-year-old girl next door wore at her birthday party, where we were when we first heard 'Yellow Submarine', the *Radio Times* with Philip Madoc as an Indian warrior in *Last of the Mohicans* on the cover, how we felt when we could count to ten, *Thunderbirds*, *Captain Fantastic and Mrs Black*, the metallic and salty taste of Knorr soup, the lavender-water smell of great grandparents' houses, recurring dreams of flying and five-year-old girlfriends.

But ask us what we did yesterday or where we put that thing we were holding five minutes earlier, you know, the thing, and we were lost. We both had our theories about this. I felt that there was a little tank where the short-term memories were left to ferment for a while into long-term memories, after which they would progress to the much larger long-term memory tank. Our short-term memory tanks were just too small for the amount of sensory data we experienced in our frenzied lives, so it all got pushed into the long-term memory tank, which could not be accessed for at least eighteen months. The fantastic thing was that we'd be going on a trip together which neither of us would remember for a year and

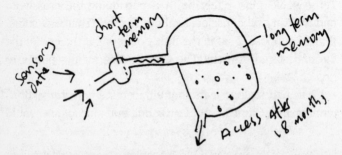

Tim's short- and long-term memory-tank system

a half. The thing was, Terry and I had one thing in common, a dramatically deficient short-term memory system.

Terry's theory (I think – my memory's not great) was that we both drank far too much, and this destroyed the synapses responsible for short-term memory. The high of drinking mirrored the positivity of childhood. This similar mood allowed us to access memories that normal people might have forgotten.

Terry's short-term memory system:

Terry is Neal Cassady and I am Jack Kerouac. He's full of energy and madness and I sort of write it all down. Or maybe I am David Cassidy and Terry is Jackanory, always telling crazy stories and appearing every evening at about 5 o'clock. Actually, this *On the Road* analogy is a bit crap, because although Kerouac did all the writing, it was Cassady who did the driving. Kerouac never drove. Ever. He bummed lifts. Either in cars or on freight trains. Terry can't drive either. Though he claims he has been able to since the age of six – he just doesn't have a licence.

Me and Terry in the car would take over some little community in the west of Ireland and terrorise the locals – annoy 'cops' and flirt with chicks in roadside tourist gift shops, just like those lads in *Easy Rider*. We were bohemians, outlaws, outcasts, in the grand tradition of mad partnerships:

- Kerouac and Cassady
- Hunter S. Thompson and his lawyer
- Fonda and Hopper
- Boswell and Johnson
- Bob Hope and Bing Crosby
- Dean Martin and Jerry Lewis
- Abbott and Costello
- John Noakes and Peter Purves
- Sandy Gall and Reginald Bosanquet
- Pippin and Tog
- Tony Blair and Gordon Brown

Using telepathy and 'special' mind powers to make Terry ring:

Deep breaths, Tim. Get comfortable. Put your memory tanks onto 'timer' mode (Economy 7 will do).

Ring ring ring ring ring. Terry Terry Terry Terry Terry.

If Terry doesn't ring

The leprechaun will sing

Ring ring ring Terry ring

I make a decision to take the singing leprechaun (that I'd bought on the Swansea–Cork ferry) with me if Terry doesn't show:

If Terry didn't show I had already had the thought that I might take my little green fabric friend with me. (He has the voice of a very squeaky Irish jockey and sings the hits of the day, particularly at Christmas. Well, no, actually, all he sings is 'When Irish Eyes are Smiling'.) My singing leprechaun comments on the action now and then but can't influence it. If I'm doing something wrong, or he wants to say 'no' he'll

sing 'When Irish Eyes are Smiling' (possibly recorded by the
wheelchair synth player of Fulham Palace Road) when I
press his belly. If he's feeling happy and positive, the singing
leprechaun stays quiet. I think. I can never be sure. The
singing leprechaun would be Jack Kerouac and I would have
to be Neal Cassady, which meant a hell of a lot more work
for me. I went out to pack the car. I must have been out for
no more than ten minutes but when I got back there was a
message on the answer machine from Terry.

The message on my answer machine from Terry:
'Hello hello. Yeah, er, hi Tim, it's Terry. Er, I'm afraid I'm
going to have to be really boring and middle-aged and blow
you out this weekend. Yeah, er, I'm just feeling really knackered at the moment. Sorry mate. Speak to you when you get
back. Erm, give us a bell sometime if you get a chance cheers
bye.'
   Terry had phoned from some pub in the centre of town.
Which meant I couldn't ring him back to try and get him to
change his mind. The singing leprechaun looked up at me
with searching eyes. I pressed his little tummy and he sang
me a beautiful version of that old Irish song. I collected the
rest of my stuff, turned off the heating and went out to the
car.

One o'clock in the morning and it was just me, the car and
the cold inky-orange streets of West London – incredibly, I'd
managed to get to the top of Fulham Palace Road without
running over a tramp or one of those pale but high-spirited
late-night youngsters who sometimes hang around outside
twenty-four-hour shops shouting at each other in cod-
Jamaican accents and looking as though they've recently
overdosed on casual sportswear.

Feeling just a little hypnotised by the enthusiastic purr of the Corsa's 1.4L engine, I shifted up and down gears with all the grace of a bull elephant doing needlestitch, then coasted up through an almost deserted and ghostly Shepherd's Bush to the roundabout, then up the A40. Hammersmith is a gateway in and out of London: big roads take you west, the tube and the A4 take you into town. It's good for country boys like me who don't know where the hell they want to be – in the city or out in the sticks. I paused for a moment to change down into second, then a manoeuvre so simple even a little kid in a pedal car could do it – get onto that motorway and head for Wales. But not me – God knows what I was playing at but I soon realised I was heading back into town towards the West End and the City. Wrong direction again. The Singing Leprechaun in the passenger seat said nothing as I came off at the next slip road at Royal Oak station, did a U-turn near some claustrophobic-looking Georgian town-houses then back out onto the road underneath the A40. Is it left or right? Left or fucking right? 'When Irish Eyes are Smiling', sang the Singing Leprechaun, which I took to mean a left. I had another three hundred miles to go along the A40, M6 and loads of other Ms and As. I knew I was bound to get lost now and again and didn't really care, but if I fucked up like this every three or four miles I wouldn't make it to the ferry for at least another couple of days.

I've never liked driving much. Not in cities anyway. I've never really trusted myself with all that metal and glass. When I was seventeen my parents give me a choice of driving lessons or a record player for my birthday. To have a car was a passport to success in Lincolnshire, particularly with women. The more sought-after girls lived out in the back of beyond, the daughters of farmers or village schoolmasters.

By choosing not to drive I was also choosing the town girls (or, in reality, choosing no sex), choosing fresh air, choosing two feet, choosing music.[2] While some of my friends got into wing mirrors, exhausts, turbo brum-brum camshaft wheelie gauges etc., I was into free jazz, new-wave pop, electro and Northern industrial music. In a way it was still an attempt at pulling – a girl would come round and I'd leave my Teardrop Explodes French import EP, Ornette  Coleman Atlantic albums, or Cabaret Voltaire and Afrika Bambaata twelve-inch singles somewhere obvious for her to see (like on the front doorstep, or perched on the toilet bowl). A not very successful technique, naturally. Perhaps I should have hung them from the ceiling.

If there was a party somewhere out in the sticks you had to befriend a gang which had a designated driver. Gangs were like little tribes and were made up of different character types who had specific roles to play. You'd have the son of a respected teacher or lawyer who might know some of the local cops and sweet-talk them. You'd have a hard nut in case your gang was challenged by another gang (particularly from another town) – he was a sort of champion. You'd have a good-looking babe magnet who would lure the females or act as a frontman when the gang went hunting as a pack. You'd have a leader, the charismatic brains, a talker and ideas man who would say let's go here, let's go there. You'd have a hippy drop-out alternative culture kind of guy who would be the comedy character. And finally, and most importantly, you'd have a driver. The driver was a monklike figure who had eschewed the pleasures of alcohol in return for approval amongst a group who otherwise might not have

[2] Does this make me sound like some romantic delta blues guitarist or Gram Parsons figure who rejected his family's wishes for him to become respectable?

given him the time of day. It was a social transaction. The driver got camaraderie and social acceptance. The gang got someone to ferry them from village pub to town pub to party to nightclub. There was a small group I knew who would occasionally let me hang around on the periphery and smile inanely at their antics, who had a driver known simply as 'Driver'. We'd all be completely plastered and he'd just drive, with a big happy grin on his face. I never understood it. Never got inside his head. Perhaps I never really worked out the rural vibe. It exists in Ireland too, that need and importance to have a car (like horses would have been to my great grandmother's people). If you're out in the country and you don't have a car you're fucked. Or, in the case of trying to get off with the daughters of village schoolteachers, not fucked.

The Great Lincolnshire Graphic Novel

ON A CLEAR DAY YOU CAN SEE LINCOLN CATHEDRAL, 20 MILES AWAY, FROM THE TOP OF WILLINGHAM HILL...

ON MOST DAYS LIKE THAT, THE ONLY SOUNDS ARE DOGS BARKING AND THE CHUG OF OLD TRACTORS

YING BEAST

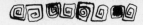

I adjusted the mirror, got into cruise mode, got comfortable. A straight run, give or take a few confusing motorway exits in the West Midlands. Undeterred by my dysfunctional directional sense, I put some lachrymose alternative country sounds onto the stereo and turned up the volume as much as I could without the dashboard vibrating out of its position and the car falling to pieces. First up, 'Windfall', by Son Volt, 'Houses on the Hill' by Whiskeytown, 'Snow Don't Fall' by Townes Van Zandt, 'Oh Sister' by Dylan. I got a tingly feeling at the romanticism of it all, until I remembered I was still inside the M25. As the car rumbled out of west London towards Hanger Lane, then through the tunnel as though escaping from some concrete nightmare and out onto the motorway and freedom, the harmonies got richer ('Both feet on the floor, two hands on the wheel, let the wind take your troubles away').

Driving through England on motorways is not an exciting thing to do. Driving through England on motorways at night is incredibly boring. Like Phil Collins singing about watching paint dry on a continuous tape loop on the radio. I sometimes wonder what proportion of the countryside you can see from a motorway *is* actually attractive. Motorways were specially designed so the country would look shit and people would think the motorway is more attractive so they should build more of them. I accept that the country hasn't been completely covered in motorway and concrete. After all, when you're lost in the countryside you can drive around for days looking for a way out – you won't even find a pub or shop or person who speaks with a recognisable accent, never mind a motorway. But when you *are* on the motorways it does seem as though that's all there is. Especially around Birmingham. Everything is motorways and junctions, lights

of the road, lights of cars, more junctions, road signs, concrete, cars, tarmac, more cars and more lights, that reach into
the distance like a vicious, never-ending torch-carrying mob,
a mob that wants to kill the monster but you want to protect
him something in his eyes suggests a vulnerable tortured soul
they're getting nearer no stop aarrrghh . . . Anyway, after
Birmingham I started to fall asleep at the wheel. As you do as
soon as you get anywhere near Birmingham.[3] I came off a
slip road and stopped for petrol at a little garage. The lanky
spotty floppyhaired nineteen-year-old creature behind the
counter looked at me with the doomed sad eyes of one too
used to sickly bright lights and the smell of petrol. I was feeling very tired so bought some Lucozade,[4] that sickly sugary
drink with the eerie nuclear fall-out orange glow.

Back on the road, I came off at a roundabout near
Shrewsbury and took the first left turn. Standing at the side
of the road was a hitcher. I was nearly asleep again and
lolling backwards and forwards, half dreaming about rural
Ireland, the sea, mountains and curly-haired Australian
actresses. Picking up a hitcher is an instinctive decision. You
don't have time to analyse them or hand out a questionnaire.
In an ideal world none of us would be in a hurry and we'd
have time to interview a prospective hitcher over coffee in
some transport café:

Driver: So, where do you see yourself in five hours' time?
Hitcher: I think London is the place for me, all things con-
sidered.
Driver: What skills can you bring to a car drive?
Hitcher: I can put tapes into the cassette player and can
make light conversation peppered with the occasional witty
but shallow observation.

[3]And there goes the lucrative Brummie market.

[4]Product placement cash might offset the costs of reproducing song lyrics.

Driver: Well, thanks for spending time talking to me. I've a few more candidates to see and I'll let you know in a few hours' time.

Hitcher: Great, thanks very much. Bye.

Driver: Bye then.

An alternative would be to swipe a smart card into a hitcher checkpoint and an upcoming driver can check to see if you're compatible.

Of course, the reality is SCREEEEEEEEEEEEEEECHH quick get in mate. It's only when it's too late that you find you've picked up some crazy looking bloke with specs and wild hair like a crazed tinker in a blue waterproof jacket. Or, more commonly, an overweight, spotty type with a moustache. But I needed someone to keep me awake. I've fallen asleep at the wheel before and you get a bit of a shock when you suddenly realise you've either been driving for twenty minutes in a daze or you've driven off a cliff and you're fifty feet underwater.

I cleared the shite – including the Singing Leprechaun – from the passenger seat onto the floor and told the hitcher to screeeeeech quick get in mate. He was an overweight, spotty type with a moustache and was up and running almost immediately.

'I didn't think I was going to be picked up. I've been waiting here for two hours. Loads of people went past, then you turned up.'

I did, it's true. I told him I just needed someone to keep me awake.

'Feel free to just jabber away,' I said, carelessly.

He told me he was looking for work. At two in the morning outside Shrewsbury!? He'd hitched over from East Anglia, where he'd been working as a panel beater and putting up marquees and thought Wales might be the land of milk and honey. Zilch and no money more like, I suggested. I told him

I was going to Ireland so could drop him off anywhere on the way. He had a sort of bristly squaddie tash with skin so 'crazy' he was an exact fifty-fifty cross between Nigel Mansell and Manuel Noriega – if Noriega had had the Jeff Goldblum role in *The Fly* and Mansell was Geena Davis and they'd both got caught in the 'pod' and merged.[5] It wasn't just acne it was something . . . more sinister.

So, a panel beater eh? That means you get to give World Cup pundits a good kicking then? I asked.

'No, it's cars and that,' he said. His accent was hard to place – maybe half Brummie, half Norfolk.

But it was the marquees thing that was great, he said. He put them up for car races and that, cash in hand. Now the work was gone and he'd had to give up his bedsit. I asked him where he was from. His parents were Irish. His mother still lived in Mayo. That's where Oasis are from, I said. What? he asked. Mayo. Their mother is from Mayo. They used to go there on holiday. Hmm he said. Anyway, they moved over to Birmingham when he was a kid and he was small and got bullied because of his accent, so decided to lose it and become a Brummie. He'd hated being a kid, he said. Hmm, I said. His father had recently died of a heart attack. He was out of work. He'd got bad skin. It was heart-breaking stuff. I asked him to stick on another country tape. The first song was Patti Loveless's 'We Ain't Done Nothin' Wrong'.

---

[5]Actually it was as a fly that Goldblum became one with not Geena Davis.
Thinking about it, Nigel Mansell would have made an interesting dictator and Noriega a great racing driver – Emerson Fittipaldi and Mario Andretti had similar skin conditions. They also might have made a great double act – Morecambe and Wise, Abbott and Costello, Mansell and Noriega.
The 'I Love Nigel' show:
Noriega: Let's have some cocaine!
Mansell: Mmm – that's *interesting*.
(Cue laughter and curtain call)

'This is a bit sad isn't it? Have you got any happier stuff?' No, I said, indignant that he had overstepped the mark with his lack of hitcher etiquette. He started talking about never being able to settle down, always on the move and I asked him if he'd read *On the Road* by Jack Kerouac. No, never heard of him. I've got a copy somewhere in my bag, I said. Want to borrow it? I was coming on all Henry Higginsish here. Nah, it's OK, he said. I wouldn't ever read it anyway. I started to nod off again as he droned on.

Hitcher: Life is so sad.
Me: Uh huh. Hmmm.
Hitcher: Marquees bluh bluuuh bluuuh bluuhhh marquees bluuuh bluuuh bluuuuh.
Me: Car keys? Uh huhh! Hmmmmm!

I stopped at a garage somewhere in Wales and bought us both a sandwich (he didn't have any money, he said). When we set off again I asked him when he'd last seen his mother in Ireland.

'Oh a long while,' he said. 'But I've got cousins in Dublin who I saw a couple of years ago.' I suggested to him that, since Wales seemed pretty quiet jobwise (although, admittedly, it *was* the middle of the night) and the Celtic Tiger[6] was still so rampant, he should go with me on the ferry and get off in Dublin. It wouldn't cost him anything. He pursed his lips and thought about it. OK, he could go and see his mother. And his cousins would put him up for a while, until he got a job. But he still wasn't happy. Think about it, I said. We agreed he'd go as far as Holyhead and then make his mind up.

How many are like him, I thought? Most of the Irish people of my age in London all came over ten years or so ago for the money because there wasn't anything for them at home[7] (though now, of course, things are different). So many people around the world claim Irishness (seventy million apparently). They or their ancestors have all had to leave and the sentimental myths are built up. There's often a dream of returning. But to what? Sometimes all that's there is a memory of Irishness, a semi-fictional home, a country they carry in their hearts to salve the rootless detachment. I thought of the folk songs which must have been written by people missing home, like the 'Fields of Athenry', or 'Spancel Hill'. I thought about asking the hitcher to press the Singing Leprechaun's belly for me. His soulful rendition of 'When Irish Eyes Are Smiling' would have been the perfect sound-track to my mind's sleepy wanderings.

Being brought up in England in the early seventies meant that Ireland was a constant but not always apparent factor in my life. It began naturally with those crap jokes which always involved an Englishman, a Scotsman and an Irish-man – the Irishman naturally always being the fall guy. The Englishman was never anything but maddeningly sensible – you didn't care what he said or did – the Scotsman sort of sat on the fence, unsure whether to be daft or boring, and the Irishman, the kind of fellow you'd probably get on with if you met him in a pub, would happily humiliate himself, shoot himself, jump out of an aeroplane without a parachute, or refuse to get off with Raquel Welch, in the interests of the narrative. For a while I had a theory that the Irishman in the Irish jokes was actually taking the piss out of the Englishman's caution (the subvert-from-within philosophy).

---

[7]Imagine if all these Irish-born people who've left Ireland could vote, like British expats can. The political landscape would be turned on its head.

But I suppose that wasn't what got the laughs on Saturday evening TV shows like *The Comedians* where blubber-necked walruses in dinner suits with big lollipop microphones and accents like gravy would entertain a nation (or rather pander to our prejudices), a nation moreover still stuck somewhere in the late 1950s (apart from those few lucky fuckers who actually had a shag and an acid tab in 1967).[8]

And then, of course, there were the bombs that I'd hear about on the news and not quite understand, bombs that were to do with Ireland. Why England was at war with Ireland (and 'Ulster') I could never work out (I knew it was war because the British army were always there in the TV pictures – I read all the war comics so knew the score). In many people's consciousness bombs and Ireland thus became synonymous. Years later, at the end of the eighties, a paranoid mad distant relation tried to stop me going on a weekend jaunt to Dublin with my mates saying, pleadingly, 'Them Paddies'll bomb yer if yer don't watch out!'

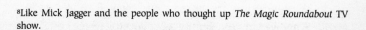

---

[8]Like Mick Jagger and the people who thought up *The Magic Roundabout* TV show.

At Holyhead, in the cold flinty early morning light, we were one of the first cars in the queue. We both stared out at a shard of fading orange in the clouds. Go and see your family, I said, seemingly on some kind of repatriation mission. We got out of the car and went to check the ferry times. It would cost him a tenner to come back over. He waddled over to the phone to call his sister, who lived down in the southwest, to see if she would wire him twenty pounds to a bank somewhere in Dublin. It all sounded a bit elaborate to me. But the sister wasn't there, only the husband, and he didn't want to do anything until the sister came back. I didn't understand. Someone in your family asks you for twenty quid – is it that big a decision? (Mad Relation: 'Yeah but Tim, what if the IRA got their hands on the money, they'd be using it to buy missiles from Libya and that.') I walked around Duty Free while he sat in the car trying to think what he should do. I got back in and handed over twenty quid, obviously expecting never to see it again. He must have read my mind.

'You think you'll never see this money again don't you, but I promise you as soon as I get in touch with my sister I'll get her to wire me some money and I'll send you it straight back – Yeah, I'll send you it in a couple of weeks, if you give me your address.' I scribbled it on the back of an envelope and gave it to him.

On the ferry we went down to the front. It was like a big shopping centre with huge cathedral-like windows and an American-style cocktail bar with a Budweiser neon sign. Whatever happened to boats that actually looked like boats, I thought. In the gift shop were some of the Singing Leprechaun's captive brothers and sisters. I pressed the belly of one of them and a sweet tune rang out. It seemed somehow familiar – where had I heard it before? Then it came to me – it was the famous old ballad, 'When Irish Eyes are Smiling'. The Hitcher wandered off and I tried to get some kip, thinking of garages, Irishwomen and Terry (I hoped he was regretful but guessed not – not his style, he'd be tucked up in bed sound asleep with a bellyful of good beer and a head full of crosswords).

About an hour later the Hitcher came back, I bought him a coffee and we discussed his plans. He hoped he'd never go back to England now. He was feeling positive. We stopped in Dún Laoghaire and he phoned his cousins in Tallaght to tell them he was coming. I then drove to Dundrum in south Dublin and stopped outside the big 60s-style shopping centre where busy consumers were going about their business. What are you going to do now? he asked. I'm going to have breakfast with my friends. He asked me about them. Oh they're just a family of crazy and beautiful single women who live near the foot of the mountains and talk a lot, I laughed, sadistically. He looked at me pleadingly but I said he'd better go. Get a bus or something, I said. No, I'll save my money he said, it can't be more than five miles or so. I pointed him in the direction of Tallaght and waved goodbye. I knew I'd never see him again. Normally in these circumstances you feel some sort of sorrow after the bond that's been forged. OK, there was a bit of that but I was also rather glad to see the back of the miserable bugger. Not much like Kerouac in *On the Road*, is it? I'd like to know how he got on, though. I hope he did stay in Ireland, maybe working in a pub in Mayo or even earning a bit of dosh on the back of the Dublin boom. Chances are, though, that he was lured back to England by the promise of a chilly bedsit and semi-regular employment, and the possibility of forgetting his dreams and just surviving on his own.

Notes on a Cultural Tour of Dublin

Dundrum to Temple Bar

After arriving in Dublin the plan was to have a quick wash and a bite to eat with my friends, the Macs, then start going through the Yellow Pages looking for Opel (the Irish brand of Vauxhall) dealers. I already had a few leads to check up on, people I'd spoken to in London before I left. Then Sarah Mac looked me in the eye and said, 'Do you really want to spend all afternoon driving around Dublin trying to sell that car?'

(Of course I did. That was why I was here.)

'Nah, not really. What I'd like to do is a cultural tour, and maybe work out a plan of action for the car later on.'

I took the bus with Sarah from where they lived in Dundrum into the centre of Dublin. During the journey we worked out the best way to do a cultural tour and give ourselves time to discuss the car. We decided we would go round a few pubs and have a pint in each one. Every pint we drank would represent a different aspect of Irish culture. I told her about one of my previous visits to the city when along with friends I had trawled around looking at the Book of Kells.

'Well,' she said, 'we'll start there then.'

'What a great idea,' I said.

(The following tour is a mental and physical assault course of culture and Guinness. I moved around Dublin like a terrified blind man being led by a sadistic, hedonistic guide dog, hearing strange amplified urban voices, following the smell of cheap tourist perfume and beer-stained wooden floors, my fingers caressing the smoothly polished bar-tops and tables of grand pubs, my mouth bitter from the black stuff and the salty taste of laughter's tears. I thought about writing some of it down, but instead relied on memory. With no particular plan in mind except to imagine I was no longer some East Midlands Kerouac-lite sad bastard but a latter day Dr Johnson-style cleverperson, sitting in pubs and watching people, learning this and that and writing things down then stuffing it all into my rucksack like some kind of demented memory snail. Some of the places we went to have simply disappeared forever. These are the ones that remain.)

The Book of Kells

This seemed like a logical choice for our first cultural stop-off point. The big pub with glass partitions, somewhere off Grafton Street, was quite austere and formal, perfect for viewing a thousand-year-old manuscript that had been illuminated by monks. As the first pint of the day, the Book of Kells was always going to be popular. There was a bit of a queue at the bar (bloody tourists) and we then had to wait to let the pints settle. It was worth the wait. The Book of Kells was just the right temperature and very smooth. You have to keep thousand-year-old manuscripts that have been illuminated by monks at the right temperature. We talked a bit about people we knew and I hoped the car would be all right.

The Martello Tower at Sandycove

This was an interesting pub, with two levels and lots of strange pictures on the wall.

Maud Gonne

This was a quiet old pub on a side street. It was Sarah's idea to name it after the great Irish heroine, Yeats' lost love. I'd first met Sarah out in the west of Ireland in the early nineties. In those days she was into karate and was a rumbustous hard-drinking wild woman with mad long hair. Now she had slimmed down to become a slinky hard-drinking wild woman with fashionable long hair, pierced bellybutton and celtic tattoo on the small of her back. She was a Gaelic footballer and also well-versed in ancient Irish history and modern Irish politics. Her grandmother's family had been old republicans – the grandfather had been De Valera's driver for a while and had also worked for John McBride, husband of Maud Gonne. I'd talked to her grandmother about all this just after Neil Jordan's *Michael Collins* had been released. Being an old anti-Treatyist, Granny Mac wasn't quite so rosy and sentimental about the likes of Boland and Collins as Jordan's film. She had also met Maud Gonne. I won't tell you exactly what she said, but you won't read about it in the history books.

Charlie Haughey

There was racing on the telly and I was dying for a piss.

The Divorce Referendum

A serious, dark pub. We got into a big talk about Irishness and what it means. From the point of view of someone living in London who goes to pubs a lot, Irishness could be a marketing man's creation, the vision that is Heritage Ireland, the fake Irish pubs.

But there's the cold-eyed heavily moral and religious Irishness, which has ruled more or less since the twenties. Some of that pious moralism must come from the impeccable double standards of the Victorian English, and has attached itself to a devout Catholicism. But, I'm reliably informed, the church and state thing is already well on the way out, or at least becoming just a part of the heady cultural mix. Travelling in the west a few years ago I found myself in a B&B which was stuffed full of religious icons, lifesize statues of Mary and Jesus scattered around, making the place seem as though it was full of people. In our room, along with a bleeding heart painting of Jesus and another giant statue of Our Lady, was a well-fingered German porn mag. You could have cut the juxtaposition with a knife.

And yet younger folk probably don't give two craps about all the old-style stuff. Irishness is no longer Collins and Dev, Willie MacBride and Yeats, but Boyzone, Roy and Robbie Keane, Bono and Sinéad O'Connor. Behan and Kavanagh? Zig and Zag!

Bored with that one, we swapped coats, swigged down the last dregs of the Divorce Referendum, took a couple of pictures and headed off in search of more culture.

Gate Theatre

I tried to remember Jockser's speech about
the stars in *Juno and the Paycock*, but was
already starting to lose it. We had to stand
up because it was so popular. Sarah showed me her tongue
stud and talked about Gaelic Football. From what I understand, having a tongue stud (and other piercings) is now the
rule for anyone who wants to join the official Gaelic Athletic
Association (the GAA) and I had this image of all these old
lads with nipple studs and Prince Alberts, along with their
broken noses and false teeth.

Sharon Shannon and Donal Lunny

Music pub. We start to get mystical
and Sarah talks about her dad in the
west. We wonder what it's all about.
None of the cosmologists currently
writing today believe in the universe as a swirling bazaar gov-
erned by market forces. But if we see the universe as being
like a business what were the conditions needed for it to
exist? A gap, a *need* for a universe for a start. Until the idea
of existence became real. But where did the funds come
from? What bankrolled this fledgling business? Was it a
loan? There was nothing. The question is, did it happen
spontaneously like, say, the craze for rock 'n' roll heart
tattoos, or did it come from above, like Coke or Barbie?

The Peace Process

Noisy boozer. Drank very quickly and
flirted with each other a little.

Ireland 1–Italy 0 World Cup '94

A real dodgy backstreet boozer. Guys in football shirts and littles 'taches, red faces, little
slit eyes. A tall old man at the bar looked
different. In a suit. Heard us talking.

'Where are you from?'

'I was born in Louth.' I think I'm so clever.
It's true and makes some people think I might be Irish.

'I presume that's Louth in Lincolnshire.'

A smart one. It turned out he had been stationed in
Lincolnshire in the RAF. He started asking me questions and
knew more about Lincolnshire than I did. I went to the bog.
A fat bloke in a Man United second strip (the blue and white
one – by the time this comes out that will probably be ten
second strips ago) came in and said I'm lovely and would I
like his limited edition plate then he says I'm not really lovely
I'm a daft bastard. Back out in the pub he confronted the
RAF lad in a mock fight and they put on English accents.

My head was going, but me and the RAF lad (who by now
could hardly stand) then got into a mad conversation which
went something like this:

RAF lad: Ah, you English fucker.

Me: I'm not surprised by your reaction. Any conversation
I have with certain friends in pubs about Irishness and
Englishness eventually leads someone to expressing their
distaste at eight hundred years of English rule in Ireland. In
some ways it's a tricky conversation for me, because I still

haven't really got a handle on what it means to be English. I mean, who are the English? What do they stand for? Some would say that's obvious. The English are the British.

RAF lad: You daft bastard.

Me: Right – the English may have created the idea of Britishness for their own ends. After all, it suits the English power base if an Ulsterman, a Welshman and a Scot all claim allegiance to the British crown. This doesn't mean that the English don't exist, but they are perhaps more likely to admit to being British than anyone else in the 'British' Isles.

RAF lad: British? Ha!

Me: And there's another thing. It really pisses off some of my friends when people say the 'British' Isles. Ireland isn't in the British Isles. It's a geographical term which has become a geopolitical term. And an outdated one at that. I read somewhere a suggestion that they be called the Celtic Isles. After all, as well as Ireland, Wales, Scotland and Cornwall, a large proportion of the people in England must be descended in some way from the Celts, or even further back is more likely.

RAF lad: Ah you.

Me: Yes, although I look like a mangy German or Scandinavian, my mother's family are all short, dark-haired and sallow-skinned. Anyway, the culture of the so-called British countries is obviously non-Anglo-Saxon. But all this stuff about ancient races. What on earth *is* 'Anglo-Saxon' culture? In the context and history of Ireland, Anglo-Saxon culture represents a centralised blanding out of traditional folk culture as a way of damping down Celtic nationalism. Exactly the same thing happened in England. Over the centuries we seem to have lost so many of the things which make a culture rich – like music, dress, language, food. Much of the local traditions have been lost because of centralisation. In Ireland, Anglo-Saxon culture has generally meant Protestant culture. It wasn't always like that. When Henry II invaded Ireland he wasn't introducing Protestantism. But he wasn't an Anglo-Saxon, he was a Norman.

RAF lad (to Manchester United bloke): Hear this fellah.

Me: So when did the Anglo-Saxons take over in Ireland? I mean, they invaded England in about the fifth and sixth centuries. Can it be true that it wasn't until a thousand years later that Anglo-Saxon culture came to the fore. I've always felt that this Anglo-Saxon thing is a bit of a problem. The English are as much to blame as anyone because we like to see ourselves as Anglo-Saxon. But in reality when people talk about the Anglo-Saxon race they are referring to a total mix of Anglo-Saxon, Jute, Norman, Dane, Norwegian and Celtic, plus 'Wessex' Culture and the Beaker People. And now add some Afro-Caribbean, Asian, Turkish, Jewish. Englishness must always have threatened to take on multifarious forms. But up until now, Englishness has been confined to what the ruling elite choose to portray it as. Is there a general malaise afflicting people in their thirties? Maybe we are the new lost generation like Kerouac and his mates, not knowing what the hell our core values are or where we want to go (for instance, like the two-headed god Janus we straddle the cultural divide of punk and dance music, but we sit in neither camp, with our balls being tickled by the new romantics). Politically we are the last of the passionate left wingers, left high and dry by the New Labour experiment, left to thrash about in a muddy sea of irony.

I'd describe myself as English, but not in some pastoral, village-green sort of way. There are many forms of Englishness. You can take your pick. Mine is an expressive, multi-racial socialist humanist hedonism. Manifested by something like Glastonbury, Ken Livingstone, William Morris, John Cooper-Clarke. I'm a fucking hippy do-gooder.

RAF lad: Well, yer a cunt at any rate.

Dana

Couldn't fit any more Guinness into my belly if I tried. Sarah was still going strong and laughing at my pathetic attempts to keep up. Music playing. Started to sway. This one was Dana – had to finish it.

'James Joyce and we'll be half-way there.'

'No, we've already done the Martello Tower,' she smiled.

I started going on about the car, how I had to get back and start driving it around. That's the last I remember for a while. We apparently got a cab home. Later, Sarah showed me some Gaelic football moves.

This seemed like a logical choice for our first cultural stop-off point. The big pub with glass partitions, somewhere off Grafton Street, was quite austere and formal, perfect for viewing a thousand year old manuscript that had been illuminated by monks. This was an interesting pub, with two levels and lots of strange pictures on the wall.

This was a quiet old pub on a side street. It was Sarah's idea to name it after the great Irish heroine. I'd first met Sarah out in the west of Ireland in the early nineties. There was racing on the telly and I was dying for a piss. A serious, dark pub. We got into a big talk about Irishness and what it means from the point of view of someone living in London who goes to pubs a lot. Irishness

Maud Gonne Charlie Haughey Dana jockeys Gaelic football tongue studs music Guinness Dublin cars petrol money Celtic Tiger help falling mountains Yeats Maud Gonne Charlie Haughey Dana jockeys Gaelic football tongue studs music Guinness Dublin cars petrol money Haughey Dana jockeys Gaelic football tongue studs music Guinness Dublin cars petrol money Celtic Tiger help falling aaaargh mountains Yeats Maud Gonne Charlie Haughey Dana jockeys Gaelic football tongue studs music Guinness Dublin cars petrol money Celtic Tiger help falling aaaargh mountains Yeats Maud Gonne Charlie Haughey Dana jockeys Gaelic football tongue studs music Guinness Dublin cars petrol money Charlie Haughey Dana jockeys Gaelic football tongue studs music Guinness Dublin cars petrol money Celtic Tiger help falling aaaargh mountains Yeats Maud Gonne Charlie Haughey Dana jockeys Gaelic football tongue studs music Guinness Dublin cars petrol money Celtic Tiger help falling aaaargh mountains Yeats Maud Gonne Charlie Haughey Dana jockeys Gaelic football tongue studs music Guinness Dublin cars petrol money Celtic Tiger help falling aaaargh mountains Yeats Maud Gonne Charlie Haughey Dana jockeys Gaelic football tongue studs music Guinness Dublin cars petrol Charlie Haughey Dana jockeys Gaelic football tongue studs music Guinness Dublin cars petrol money Celtic Tiger help falling aaaargh mountains Yeats Maud Gonne Charlie Haughey Dana jockeys Gaelic football tongue studs music Guinness Dublin cars petrol money Celtic Tiger help falling aaaargh mountains Yeats Maud Gonne Charlie Haughey Dana jockeys Gaelic football tongue studs music Guinness Dublin cars petrol money lose it. We had to stand up because it was so popular. Music pub. We start to get mystical and Sarah talks about her dad in the west. We wonder what it's all about. Noisy boozer. Drank very quickly and flirted with each other a little. A real dodgy backstreet boozer. Guys in football shirts and little tashes, red faces, little slit eyes. Couldn't fit any more Guinness into my belly **and then I woke up**

The Informal Urchin-gurrier Choir of Hill 16

Gaelic Sports

Gaelic football is very much like rugby except the players' bodies are smaller, their legs are bigger and their hair curlier. Until these travels, my only experience of the sport had been from fading posters in pubs showing hard-looking blokes with big squashed noses and heavy shoulders staring at the camera in the way they would if someone was eyeing up their wife or their tractor. All I could tell about the tactics was that one of the big lads would get hold of the football, belt it upfield, a crowd of big lads would chase after it and jump up in the air trying to catch it. The biggest lad would achieve this, to a great roar from the crowd, then boot it between the posts for a point.

Actually, the tactics and various styles of Gaelic football are far too numerous to mention here – sometimes, for instance, they will *hand tap* the ball to a teammate who then kicks it upfield to the big lad, roar from crowd, boot, point etc. Like Americans at baseball and gridiron, the Irish are world champions at all Gaelic sports. No-one else can touch them because no-one plays the stuff. So the All-Ireland champs could call themselves the World champs but, un-like their American cousins, the Irish are naturally more modest. In the last few years, however, this Gaelic monopoly

has been challenged by a sleek, fast, tight-trousered new opponent in the shape of Australia. The method? The Gaelic Football–Australian Rules hybrid called Compromise Rules.

The games started up in 1984 (and a mini series is played regularly now) as a means of addressing the obvious similarities between Gaelic Football and Australian Rules. The latter, a late-eighteenth-century invention, takes many of its elements from Gaelic Football. In GF you get three points for a goal – i.e. in the net – and one for kicking the ball between the posts – like a combination of football and rugby. Hand passing is allowed but the mainstay is kicking a round ball. No tackles are allowed but you can block. In AR it's three between the main posts, one for the outer sticks. Tackles are allowed. Marks (free kicks) are made when you catch the ball cleanly. It's an oval ball. Compromise Rules seems to be 80–90 per cent Gaelic Football.

Sarah once took me to one of these compromise games at Croke Park, the cathedral of Gaelic sports. We walked from O'Connell Street then down Parnell Street in the north side, past flats and small seen-better-days terraced houses, kids sitting on steps with skinny dogs, little inflatable plastic footballs by their side. People were staggering around in the streets, shitfaced drunk and with huge grins on their faces. Most of the crowd I was following got in as students, although they looked as if they hadn't seen the inside of a classroom for at least ten years. Inside I marvelled at the faces – thick-set, dark-browed, big noses, broken noses or wiry and ginger. Dublin shirts were prominent but there were also Galway, Clare, Ofally, Kilkenny and Waterford fans there too. It was a blustery afternoon and I was near the back left corner of Hill 16, the most celebrated terrace in Ireland.

Gaelic footballers dress in normal sports gear. Aussie Rules players wear underpants and tight fitting disco vests. 'It's so no-one can grab them and pull them over,' said an Australian doctor I talked to.

'No, it's so they can show off their muscles to the crowd, isn't it?'

'No, no, no, you're wrong, it's a very practical outfit for contact sports.'

'Like picking up dockers in backstreet gay bars?'

'Hey, don't knock it.'

Disappointingly for the crowd, the Aussie players weren't wearing their trademark swimming trunks and skin-tight T-shirts but were in regular gear. The Irish players all had little bodies and big red legs – the Australians were all shapes and sizes, some stringbean, some squat, some normal, some athletic, some brawny – with a few surfer haircuts around.

The game started at a madly fast pace. Everyone agreed it

was exciting to watch. Ireland dominated and, when they went twenty points up, the feeling was that it was going to be a bit of an embarrassing final scoreline. Behind the canal end, which at the time of writing has been knocked down, I could see rows and rows of terraced houses and behind that the Dublin mountains. It was a beautiful urban scene. Many big sports stadiums are now being moved to out-of-town sites, but their constituency will always be the heart of the city.

As the wind blew in our faces, the sounds of Irish voices came drifting down from the back of Hill 16. An informal Gurrier Choir, an ensemble made up of local grubby-faced urchins and midget wiseguys (though some of them might have been out-of-work jockeys) had perched itself high at the back of the stand and was responding to any Australian resistance in that part of the ground like a highly effective and ruthless military unit. Two portly Australian fans just a few rows further down had been spotted.

'Skippeeeeee, skippeeeeeeeee Skippeeeee the bush kangaroo. Skippeeeee, skippeeeeeeeee Skippeeeee my friend and yours too.'

One of the Aussies shouted 'Come on Australia!' Quick as a flash an urchin shouted out in a mangled *Neighbours*-style accent, 'Cam on Awwstayyylyah . . . h aha ha ya fat Aussie bastard!' As the Irish Tourist Board might say, one hundred, thousand welcomes.

Ireland were thrashing them. I'll admit I started to get quite excited. All I can recall about Australian sportsmen over the last few years is them pummelling English rugby and cricket teams into the ground. Now they were getting pummelled. I thought about the losses at sport and the stereotypes of national characteristics. The English are Anglo-Saxon, slow-moving, cautious but well organised and focused. (If sport is, as some commentators suggest, a metaphor for warfare, is that how the Angles and Saxons fought their battles?) The

Irish are ferocious and gung-ho. The Scots fast, skilful and angry. The Welsh pessimistic but mercurially skilled. The Australians ultra-competitive and athletic. And I suppose, if we're going to really follow this through logically, the French are seductive and the songs they sing in the showers after the match don't scan properly.

After the end of the second quarter, the refs made love. They must have done – and the gestation period for a young ref[1] must be about fifteen minutes – because by the third quarter there were four refs on the pitch. Either they rubbed up against one another and went for it big time or maybe they are like those one-celled organisms which simply split in two to carry out the reproductive process. If the game had gone into fifth and sixth quarters the number of refs would no doubt have increased exponentially. This is the reason why these games have to stop after the fourth quarter. Also, refs do go on reproducing. This means that at the end of every game there has to be a ref cull. Refs are given a lethal injection in the dressing room. The danger for Irish society is if these refs escape into the wild and start to over-run the hillsides, bogs and plains.

Word before the game was that there would be a huge scrap at some point. Apparently this is par for the course in Aussie Rules. The Aussie lads had been sticking the boot in or putting in late tackles for a while, niggling the Irish. Then it all kicked off – some innocuous little challenge near the Canal End and two players started lashing into each other. I got the feeling it must have been staged. Within a second or two, half the players had joined in and after three or four more seconds it was a total free-for-all. All the trainers and subs came chasing out onto the pitch like when you're at school and someone shouts 'scrap!' with one eye on the staffroom, waiting for the teacher to come along and pull you

[1] Called 'Reflings'.

apart, cuff you and take you to the headmaster while the onlookers will sit in the lessons for the rest of the day with stupidly large grins on their faces. It was handbags at three paces – hardly a punch seemed to connect, they were sort of waffing thin air with their eyes closed – you could imagine them rolling around on the floor pulling each other's hair and scratching.

Meanwhile the crowd were going completely mental – grown men were jumping up and down like kids and clapping their hands with glee. Then I realised I was doing it too – jumping up and down from foot to foot, clapping my hands together and shouting 'Whhhoooooooooaaaaaaaaaaaaaa!!!!!!!' at the top of my voice. When the fight finally petered out it was the end of the third quarter and the crowd gave both teams a standing ovation – the Irish walked off the pitch in a tight little huddle and I could imagine them shouting 'Join on the gang' or 'Does anybody want to play aaarrmmmmyyy? No girls – only boys.' Whatever else happened in the game, this was guaranteed to put bums on seats for the next encounter a week later. Very clever.

The Irish have a reputation for fighting. They even go on about it themselves. In America too, they're called the 'fighting Irish'. But they certainly don't seem to fight any more than the English. In fact, blokes out and about drinking in the centre of towns seem a lot less aggressive. Whatever, the Australians would treat them with respect now, said the bloke standing next to me. They perhaps see the Irish as a sort of madder version of themselves, the pure source of the idiosyncratic Aussie spark, and they'd be united in their hatred of whingeing Pommie bastards. But it seemed to me that the fight was not a sign of mutual respect but a deliberate tactic to throw the Irish out of rhythm. They may have won the scrap but would they win the match?

In the fourth quarter a man in luminous lime green overalls ran onto the pitch at various intervals. At first I wasn't sure if everyone else could see him. Could it be the drink? I discussed it with a few other fans and we decided he was the team gossip because he kept running over to players and chatting to them. He fancies your wife. Did you see *Eastenders*? Your investment portfolio is doing well, etc. An on-pitch information service, perhaps?

The urchin gurrier choir, quiet for a while, opened up in full voice once more, with an old battle ballad.

'Aussie Aussie bastards,' they sang. 'Aussie Aussie bastards.' Then the Kylie Minogue song, 'I should be so lucky, lucky, lucky, I should be so lucky in love.'

A bit of Rolf Harris: 'Tie me kangaroo down, sport, tie me kangaroo down.'

'Come on Australia,' said the bravest of the two Antipodeans nearby.

'Stick it up your arse, you fat Aussie bastard!' sang the choirboys. 'You fat bastard, you fat bastard! Youse is all a load of women!'

There was a big countdown by the crowd, then the hooter went for the end of the game. The final score was 62–61 to Australia. The winners were delighted, leaping around and hugging each other. It had been a terrific, hard-fought match, sporting heaven for those who like blood, guts and a lot of skill.

Then one of the little Hill 16ers began a solo refrain – 'You'll never beat the Irish, You'll never beat the Irish – except,' he went on, deadpan, 'maybe at soccer, rugby, snooker, cricket, darts, Compromise Rules . . .' His mates fell about laughing.

Dublin, Fair City of Vikings, Buskers and Soaring House Prices

(and the Celtic Tiger is rather unimaginatively mentioned too)

Twenty-four quietish hours in Dublin

2 am

I'm trying to get to sleep in O'Shea's Hotel, between O'Connell Street and the railway station, while downstairs in the '24-hour bar' a dreadful singer/accordion player is murdering a few classic tunes and I'm praying that he'll shut up soon. No such luck – 'Rivahhhssss roon freeeeeeeee-hhhhhhrrr', 'Dirrdi ooooooohl taaaaaaaaahhhhhhhhhhn', 'Fffffeeeeeeeellllzzzzz ovathenraaaiiiiiiiiiiiiiii' etc., etc., come piling one on top of the other. I'd popped in earlier for a quick half.[1] There were a mixture of local people with cold, pinched faces and skint and harassed looking tourists sitting around fondling their itchsome facial hair, their tongues lolling into fizzy yellow pints of lager. Next to me were some lively 'Europeans', who seemed to know all the words to all the songs. Their leader, a Eurotourist archetype, was a big-boned man with non-designer stubble, in a Luftwaffe-issue lumberjack shirt and a post-post-post punk hairdo – bald at

[1] An old Lincolnshire word meaning 'pint'.

the front, brown and greasy at the back. He seemed extremely upset by the plight of most of the protagonists of the songs – his face was one of absolute concentration and conviction as he listened to the music. I decided he was called Klaus, even if Greek. The Erinese, the brandy-buttered maudlin sentimentality of it all was too much for me after half an hour or so. It reminded me of a Paddy's Day in London a few years back, red-faced folk with tears in their eyes bawling out songs – this was Dublin for Christsakes, what had they got to be nostalgic about? I got up to leave and, after a few whispers and hand signals, one of the Euro-group parked their big, denimed backside in my seat.

'Noit?' said the pretty dark-eyed receptionist, meaning-fully, as I headed for the stairs.

Back up in my rooms I turned the light out and tried to get

some sleep, but the singer seemed to have taken my disappearance as an affront and belted it out louder:

Singer: Let's put the speakers up in the corridor outside the miserable git's room, hey ladies and gentlemen?

Klaus the Possibly Greek Eurotourist: Ha ha, yesss, zat iss good johke! 'Ze Vild Rover', jah?

I flicked the TV on – the film *When Saturday Comes*,[2] starring Sean Bean and Emily Lloyd, was showing. In many respects the singer downstairs was a lot more entertaining than this terrible piece of British cinema.

'Begorrah Jimmy,' said Emily Lloyd's character in a really crap Dublin accent and I just burst out laughing, though they were nearly tears. I wished I was more drunk, then it might seem more entertaining. By the end I realised I am perhaps unique in the world, having now seen the film twice.

I don't know what happened to Emily Lloyd. She seemed to sort of disappear after being superb as the young girl in *Wish You Were Here*. Sean Bean was eerily watchable, though. He's like one of the sleazy blokes who'd stand on the back of dodgems when you were a kid, never smiling, catching girls' eyes. Perhaps one of his family was a horse person. The balladeer downstairs seemed to have turned it up another notch with Wild Rover (annoyspentarlmaemooniaaaahhwehssskkeeeeeunbbbbbeeeeeeeehhhhhhrrr), with the audience joining in now.

Klaus: Und itz no nay never vill I plahh ze vild rover jah?

Finally, as the music fades and the punters wander off to their beds, I drift off to sleep, day-dreaming of the pretty dark-eyed receptionist wearing a bikini made out of an Irish

---

[2]Nothing to do with the magazine *When Saturday Comes*. If you stay to the end of the film, the last credit says that. But who in their right mind is going to stay until the end of the credits unless they work for the football magazine and are anxious to see that there's a disclaimer somewhere.

flag, singing the 'Fields of Athenry' to me while doing the back stroke in a gigantic pint of yellow lager, while Klaus is chained to some rocks below the surface ('Help achtung, Englander, I cannot breathe ... arrrrggghhhh ... blob-babubblblblblbbl').

9 am

I wake up feeling good. I immediately try to plug my laptop into the phone lines. No chance. I don't really want a newspaper but it seems like too much hard work not to get one. But what if something incredible has happened overnight, like God has proven that He exists, or there's been a General Election on the quiet? I hate newspapers for the way they play on your emotions like this. Make you scared to miss out.

9.15 am

Outside it's a typical summer's day. Cold and windy with a promise of rain. Across the street an old man stands in a doorway, with an old black beret on, watching. He has a long nose and ears that drop down to his elbows. He's got a proud look in his eye. I imagine that he's been a ferocious Republican warrior in his life. I walk down the street and suck in the damp air. Saturday morning. The most perfect feeling. Kids in last season's Man United shirts are playing with a half-inflated football in the street, bouncing the ball against the wall of a kebab shop. They never stop playing, even when someone walks past. Sometimes people get the ball blasted in their ears, and the lads are all apologetic. They stop occasionally, such as when a car turns into the street.

Further up, a small bald man tries to start his car, which sounds like an old asthmatic, or a faulty chainsaw. Or a car that won't start. In the newsagents I ask the fat guy with the shaved head and 'tache behind the counter if there are any *Guardians* left. No, he says. It's the *Irish Times* again. He's got a few odds and ends of food, soup, mouldy fruit, packets of cereal. Like the old grocers I used to frequent, who stocked only a few tins of Oxtail soup, a couple of bread rolls, Quaker Oats (not Scotch Porridge Oats, only Quaker) and a Battenburg cake. Is that from the house of Battenburg, I wonder? Were they like the Hapsburgs? Perhaps that's why the Hapsburgs declined, because they hadn't got a fancy cake named after them.

10 am

I pop into an Internet café on O'Connell Street to pick up my e-mails and send some stuff back to Andy, Editor at *When Saturday Comes*. It's run by a posse of young cybervixens (the cafe, not WSC – more's the pity), equally adept at making espressos and using Internet Explorer. There's a queue so I get a cappuccino and flick through the *Irish Times*. Five minutes later one of the girls shouts my name and I'm on. I have an Internet e-mail account with Hotmail – irishtim@hotmail.com. It means you can pick up messages on any machine wherever you are in the world. It's busy, so I tap in a number that I remember saving. I get in. A dopey-looking guy with a goatee beard wearing shorts is sitting next to me, cursing. He looks over.

'Hey meean, like how dja git inta hartmayerl?'

I tell him.

'Coooooool!'

The place is full of young Americans, Spanish, Germans, Italians and Australians. I appear to be the oldest person there by at least five years. I think of Dublin changing, then I get an image in my head of the singer from last night appearing on one of the computer screens singing 'Ring a ring a roses, on my ISDN line, I remember Dublin in the rare old times'. Really cooooooooool!

10.45 am

The Dublin sky is a milky yellow grey. Drizzle dashes against my cheeks as I stand at a street corner near the Liffey, watching a gaggle of schoolgirls in bright blue uniforms next to the Pádraig ō Síoláin (Patrick Sheehan) monument as they chatter excitedly about 'stuff'. As the rain comes down harder I stand near the window of the Virgin Megastore and listen to the 'Real Ibiza' trance house CD while staring out at the clouds and the water hitting the glass.

11 am

I wander, inevitably, towards Temple Bar. When I first came over to Dublin with my Lincolnshire mates Plendy, Dukey and Ruey (Mad Relation: 'If you take them out first, they can't hurt you, Tim. Through that window – SMASH – then buddabuddabuddabuddabudda. Arm round the neck, block the windpipe with the blade of the hand, push head forward. Snap. It's the only way.'), we'd stumbled across Temple Bar, a ramshackle haunt full of scaffolding and secondhand clothes shops. We got caught up in a demo for the Birmingham Six. It was 1989 – they were heady days. The world seemed to be changing so quickly.

Things *have* changed, but not necessarily in the way we thought back then. Temple Bar has altered out of all recognition. Glitzy restaurants, themed superpubs, trendy clothes shops, designer tat emporiums. The Dublin Viking Experience Museum – a tourist attraction for the worst kind of heritage junky saddos – money changes everything, like love. Like those ecstatic lottery winners who share tales of house extensions and bright red sports cars, the jealousies of friends and ruined love lives and values gone haywire, Ireland has, since the mid-nineties, undergone an upheaval the like of which it's never experienced before. A country transformed. Have we seen the last of the old Ireland, Dev's

Ireland? Ireland is letting go of the past, in the way that Britain did in the sixties and the US in the fifties.

In the little square, flocks of dark-haired Euroteentourists are sitting on the steps in their brightly coloured waterproof gear, staring down balefully at maps of the city. Short-haired trendy buggers loll around the tables outside trendy cafés, not caring a jot for anything except being trendy. Thick-armed bald boyos in corporate polo shirts stand guard out-side the grand and glitzy looking superboozers which are the new temples, turning away non-believers and large English stag parties. Skinny, frowning girls wearing too much make-up rush about with carrier bags full of shopping.

I sit down next to a mapless Euroteentourist who, due to the absence of props, is simply staring balefully into the middle distance. I get out my notepad. Just at this moment a mad, hard-faced pensioner in black zip-up flying jacket, flared jeans and trainers hoves into view, spitting expletives. He sees me watching him and shouts across the cobbled street 'Ye bollix!' I avert my gaze, but he walks (no – not quite the right word – he lurches and sways) right up to me and shouts again 'Ye bollix!' I look up at him and say 'Sorry?'

'Bollix. Yer book is bollix!' If this is meant to be some kind of sign it's not a very auspicious one. He crawls off in the direction of the Viking museum.

When I first met Annie and her Irish friends ten or more years ago they said there was something typically English about me. No there isn't, I said. What is it? Tell me, tell me. There was something placid about me, they said. You could see it in the eyes. Irish blokes, they said, have mad eyes. I can do mad, I said. I can have mad eyes. Look. Arrrgh. I'm mad, me. Grrrr. Yeaaah suuuuuuuuuure, they said. I took to

practising in my shaving mirror, having
mad eyes. (You have to make them a bit
slanty as well as wide.) Arrrrrrghhhhh
... I'm maaaaaaaaad. I had always
equated mad eyes with the actor
Malcolm McDowell.³ You can easily
do a Malcolm McDowell – just pull
the corners of your eyes until you

look like one of those crappy 1970s comedians doing a version of a Chinese person. Go on, it's easy. One minute you're
you, the next, your nearest and dearest is screaming blue
murder that Malcolm McDowell has got into bed with them.
I had my floppy hair cut shorter and started wearing contact
lenses which made me stare a lot without blinking. But keeping my eyes wide open like that was hard work. My eyes are
sensitive and get dry very easily. This would make me blink
a lot. This is a sort of mad look, the blinking thing, but it's
more Anthony Perkins in *Psycho* rather than the 'sexy' mad
look I was aiming for.

Irish women's eyes are not so much mad as soulful. I tried
soulful but it's much more difficult than mad. Soulful made
me look like a soppy kids' TV presenter, or sort of David
Cassidyish. I decided to stick with mad. I carried this mad
thing a bit far on my first meeting with some real Irish
parents. They're Irish, I thought, they'll appreciate that I'm a
madcap lad. At Sunday lunch I asked for the bone from a
shoulder of lamb⁴ and started to gnaw away at it like a frenzied puppy, grunting quietly to myself and now and then

---

³I just know here that some readers will be thinking of the kindly Roddy
McDowell, and saying to themselves, 'What's this guy talking about – he's got
lovely eyes.' Roddy McDowell is another famous actor with Irish roots. Roddy
was *How Green was My Valley?* Malcolm was *A Clockwork Orange* – if Andi
McDowell had been in a production of *The Woman in White* we'd have ourselves
an Irish flag. As it is, she was in *Green Card* so my little theory is scuppered.

⁴Ah well – there goes the wealthy 'vegan' market.

looking up to check the admiring glances. This didn't seem too outrageous an act of madness. I'd done it for years in my parents' house, where the ability to eat like a dog, drink like a fish, piss like a horse and shit like a bull elephant was positively encouraged and seen as a sign of manliness in me and two brothers.

Father, in a put-on voice, said 'You have the manners of a Viking.' I acted mock hurt, but took it as a compliment. The Viking thing gave me a little niche, especially as the Parents lived near Waterford, an area of continuous Norse invasion in the ninth and tenth centuries. I saw myself as a one-man rape-and-pillage unit, though without the rape. A sort of sensitive Viking, who would only pillage after asking nicely first. And, being a nice English lad, I'd queue for it, of course.

11.30 am

The Dublin Viking Experience and Feast. Ah, well, I just couldn't resist. Plus I was curious to see what the Flying-Jacketed Soothsayer thought of it – alas, he is nowhere to be seen. The entrance is via a gift shop. I go into a very dark lecture theatre. A film is showing about the Vikings, narrated by that deep-voiced bloke who did the public information films in the seventies. There are only two others there. Then a real-life Viking appears on the bow of a ship, and starts shouting at us, telling us to row. It starts to get windy and spray is flying about. Someone offstage has just thrown a bucket of water over me. The little Viking (because he *is* very little – looks like a schoolboy bass player from a Deep Purple tribute band) carries on ranting as the 'ship' begins to move up and down. Then we dock at Dublin harbour and get out. The ferocious Viking is even smaller up close. He also seems quite shy. Maybe it is his first time. Or perhaps he is just disconcerted to only have three people on the tour. His speech is tailored for children and he doesn't seem to be able to ad lib. Yeeeessssss. Eeerrrrrrrm. Weeellllllll. Errrrrrm.

Yeeeeeeees. I can't imagine that the Vikings would have been very successful with this line of unassertive communication.

Celtic chieftain: What do you want from us, oh fearless Viking?
Viking: Yeeeees. Errrrrrm. Weeellllll. Yeessssss.
Celtic chieftain: Bloody wimp. Let's kill the bastards lads!

He asks where we are from. The couple say that they are from Lincoln.

'Yeeeees. Errrrm. And where is that?'

'In Lincolnshire. England.'

'What about you?' the Viking says to me.

'I'm from Market Rasen.'

'And where is that?'

'In Lincolnshire as well.'

We are an advance force from another Viking area, the Kingdom of Mercia.

'Do you know Peter Rhodes?' the bloke asks me.

'Yeah – I got my hi-fi system off him back in the early eighties.' (The one that should have been my driving lessons.)

'He's a bit of a character, isn't he? Is he related to the bloke who used to have the leather shop there?'

The all-powerful Viking warrior is feeling a bit left out at this point and tries to win us back into his make-believe Norse world by being more Vikingy,[5] but he's already lost us. He points out this and that in the facsimile Viking town of Dublin in which we are standing – like how they made houses or ground corn – and meanwhile our conversation is all, 'Do you know that pub on the hill in Lincoln?', 'Have you

[5] He needed some 'Arrrrghhh' and some mad eyes. I could have given him a lesson or two.

ever played that old Lincolnshire game Spin the Weasel?'
and, 'Have you been to . . .' etc. We are introduced to some
miserable Celtic bird called Maeve who shows us round her
house. You can tell by the look in her eye that she thinks this
job is demeaning and that she's a proper actress and should
be working with Liam Neeson or Gabriel Byrne rather than
trying to impress three poxy tourists from the East Midlands
of England. Then a camp skinhead Celtic priest appears and
starts shouting at us.

12.30 pm

I stand on the Ha'penny Bridge overlooking the Liffey. On
the *Irish Times* website you can look at one of the Dublin
bridges every two minutes. Ineffably sad, just pedestrians
and cars. The river is gentle and more like a canal when compared to something like the Thames in the centre of London.
The sounds all around are of drills and sanders, of never-
ending building and reconstruction work. I decide to head
back again through Temple Bar. In the little alleyway a
septuagenarian harmonica player does 'Danny Boy' amidst
the hubbub of voices. He's way off the tune, but I throw
some pennies into his scruffy hat. I just stroll – past the Tailor
of Taste, Dunstan's carpet shop, Eddie Rocket's. Two Aussie
girls with pierced everything stop me and ask if I'd like to
buy their environmental magazine. I chat for a while then
they ask whereabouts in their own country I am from.
Miraculously, they make the sale.

I go into a pub full of skinheads with a big picture window
and, while slowly sipping a Guinness, watch people walking
about outside (it's a similar feeling to sitting and staring at a
slow-moving river). A man with a large bunch of sunflowers
stops and stares back at me. A dispatch rider waits at the
traffic lights and whistles happily. An old man in a silver
puffa jacket staggers slowly past, talking to himself. Then a
hand touches my shoulder as a woman's voice says, 'Are you

Mary O'Mannion?' I turn around slightly, to give her a quick flash of oversized chin and five days' growth and she stands rooted to the spot. 'Oh . . . sorry.' A group of lads nearby laughs then put their faces back down to their pints with serious expressions when I look at them. Hmm. It dawns on me that not having had your hair cut for a year can cause problems. There's me thinking I now look like a Viking warrior and someone thinks I'm a blonde Irishwoman.

I wonder, though, if Mary O'Mannion is a celebrity of some kind. Although Ireland is roughly the same size as England, it has only about a tenth of the population. So those who do become famous are quickly household names. There are two different categories of celebrity Irish person – Past-it Musicians and Populist Politicians.

Past-it Musicians
The most famous past-it musicians are Bono, The Edge, Adam Clayton and that other one, the drummer, whose name I can never remember but who looks normal – like the sort of bloke you'd meet down the pub. Back in 1980 when U2's first album, *Boy*, first came out, loads of my friends were into U2 and played them incessantly round at their houses. That's what we'd do for entertainment. We'd invite mates round, make them instant coffee and play them our latest records in the hope of increasing our social standing (or something) and to get feedback on the chick-seducing quali-ties of various albums ('Tim, I feel that Ornette Coleman is not going to get you anywhere with Helen Butterworth').

U2 sounded a bit overeager and pompous – I didn't like Bono's *faux*-operatic vocal style nor the Edge's histrionic guitar sound. The rhythm section was good, though. Their songs seemed to really pump and chug along. Bono and The Edge have become part of the Irish Celtocracy, mercurial wizards with idiosyncratic glasses, street hairstyles and amusing clothes. Adam Clayton, as an Englishman, is a kind of Lord of the Blow-ins. Which leaves the drummer whose name I can't remember. He doesn't seem to have changed much. My favourite Past-it Musician.

Populist Politician
One of Ireland's most successful cash crops of recent years has been the Populist Politician. Charles Haughey. He's an interesting fellow. Everyone seems to know he's a chancer, yet it goes with the territory. A modern version of some myth-ical wily old Celtic chieftain. Even though old strains die out, new ones appear to take their place – Dessie O'Malley, Bertie Ahern. However, my favourite is Proinsias De Rossa, simply because of his name.

1 pm
I go to a Chinese restaurant, where there is a buffet – all you can eat for £9.99. The dining room is decorated in pink-flocked wallpaper with pictures of lions, and is empty except for two blokes discussing house prices over a pot of Chinese tea. I have a bowl of soup then pile my plate high. The thing is, you never really want to have a second helping. I'm star-ing at the over-cooked noodles, trying to force myself to slurp them into my mouth, as the two blokes chatter on about mortgages and interest rates. Going back down the pink stair-case, I feel like I'm coming out of an MSG-flavoured womb, being reborn, and there are lots of black and white pictures of famous Irish people who have eaten in the restaurant, none of whom I recognise, except for Eamonn Andrews. Eamonn smiles down in his big-chinned way and says, 'Good luck!'

2.10 pm
An old man stares at the near-naked mannequins in a clothes shop window. He smells like he's just pissed himself.

2.20 pm

I wander into a little history bookshop crammed with goodies about the Civil War, Independence, Irish factionalism, local Dublin history, some antique books, run by a very dapper middle-aged gent in a dark suit, whose eyes follow me around the shop in the way Hawkeye Marwood used to do when we'd muck about in his sweetshop aged seven or eight holding 2p and trying to decide what to have. 'Get yer hands off them midget gems,' he'd snarl. And that was him on a good day. 'Passing trade' – that was his motto.

I sniff around for a while looking eggheadish. Another customer enters – high excitement – in the brown cords, rumpled jacket and straggly haired uniform of a university lecturer. He wants some obscure textbook about Wolfe Tone – the early years, and Darksuit seems to think he is a better catch than me, hovering around him like a shy debutante with his hands held together. They get into a discussion of contemporary accounts of the 'Rising' of 1798 and Darksuit nearly manages to tempt the customer with the juicy morsel of a pamphlet of Fenian poetry. But then Lecturer says he'll take the phone number down and ring again in a few weeks, to see if anything has turned up. The cad! That's the sort of behaviour fourteen-year-old boys display at discos – Oh yerr, give us yer number love, I'll phone yer, honest.

I eventually buy a reference book entitled *Jack B. Yeats – His Watercolours, Drawings and Pastels*. Jack B. is my favourite Yeats of the Yeats brothers (sounds like a late-seventies country combo). Former Liverpool defender Ron Yeats is my favourite Yeats of all time. The atmosphere of learning and dry-as-dust academia is slightly suffocating and it's nice to get outside again. I wander around in the fresh air for a while flicking through my new book and looking at the pictures.

3 pm

For a minute or so I follow the greeny-brown and excited chatter of two Spanish girls, elegant and birdlike (them not me), walking up O'Connell Street in long black coats, nice hair clips, shiny shoes. I press the button at the pedestrian crossing – the device makes a beep-beep-beep sound like a hospital life-support machine (well, the ones on the telly, at any rate) or something from *Star Trek*. The drizzle comes down again and mixes with the sweet smell of car fumes. A group of old men watch transfixed as a Kit-Kat lorry is unloaded. Two newspaper sellers, like something from a Hulton Picture Library shot from the twenties – a bloke with a big beard and a skinny bloke, both in flat caps – sit in a doorway with a pile of *Evening Heralds* in front of them, shouting 'Eeeerenaarrrrugh'. A traffic warden with a big nose and a moustache sniffs the air, in the way of a hungry ferret, for illegally parked vehicles. Why is it that people in uniform in Ireland always look as though they've stepped straight out of another, much older, era?

3.30 pm

Ah, I'm such a tourist. Down on the river again it feels like Paris – a babble of different accents, German, Italian, Japanese, American, Scandinavian. Many – the Scandinavian and German ones especially – are skinny blonde girls in jeans staggering under huge backpacks, like brightly covered snails in the afternoon rain. But there are also lots of gaunt, pinched, knackered looking folk chainsmoking away, for whom life looks to be a struggle rather than a pleasant Eurotourist excursion – locals still hoping for the Dublin economic juggernaut to pick them up. Fat lads with 'taches and baseball caps on back to front stand in doorways waiting for their evening bus. A group of Dutch or Belgian tourists waddle down the pavement in tracksuits and cameras, the men with beards, the women all sporting northern-European-style Attack Breasts.

4 pm

I go to another bookshop, the Flying Pig. Lots and lots of great second-hand books there and cartoons on the wall, a couple by Tom Matthews the *Irish Times* cartoonist. I pick a few old books, including a first edition copy of *The King of the Tinkers* by Patricia Lynch, then go up to the counter where two burly, sort of hard-looking lads with fuzzy goatee beards – slightly overweight old punks at a guess – are filling up space.

Me: Hi. I was wondering, have you got a book called *The Last Mandrax Butterfly*?

Burlyboy 1: *The Last Mandrax Butterfly*? Have we got that?

Burlyboy 2: Have we? I don't know. What's it about?

Me: It's about blow-ins in West Cork.

Burlyboy 1: Blow-ins? What are they now?

Me: (earnest expression) Well, Some villages in the west Cork area are completely inhabited by English and German hippies who run art galleries and have alternative lifestyles and stuff like that.

Burlyboy 2: English!? . . . and Germans!? Living in West Cork? No!

Burlyboy 1: Are there a lot of English in West Cork then?

Me: Er, erm, well, I think so yes.

Burlyboy 1: Oooh, no-one told me.

Burlyboy 2: Who told you there were Germans in West Cork? I've never heard anything like it.

Me: Ummm . . .

Burlyboy 1: Is it good then, this book?

Me: I, er, don't know. That's why I'd like to read it.

Burlyboy 2: Well we haven't got it.

Burlyboy 1: But we'll have to go down to West Cork to check up on all those Germans!

I buy my books and leave.

5 pm

The buskers on Grafton Street appear to have been given pitches according to their musical style. First drummers, a few skinny student types with wispy beards and Traveller clothing getting a funky circular rhythm going. People stand around tapping their feet, a few sway, two middle-aged women wiggle their lovely big backsides. Next one along, about twenty-five yards, a sincere-looking young guy belts out Bob Dylan's 'Like a Rolling Stone', then further along a red-haired fellah with a full beard sings nasally ballads on his own, then a skinny black guy playing some unheard-of reggae number and finally a forty-something bloke with long hair and flying V guitar gives it the full-on Hendrix thrash. Like anglers, they seem to stick to the pitch they are given. This stops any of the busking battles which often take place in other cities, particularly when the musicians are not only moving about but playing similar styles of 'busk' ('I'm John Lennon!' 'Ooh, no, it's me, it's me!'). Dublin Corporation should be applauded – or rather their Metropolitan Busking Coordinator should. London Transport Police take note.

6 pm

I go to a taxi rank to get a cab to Wickham Park. The driver is a podgy snub-nosed guy with a big smile.

'Is this my cab?'

'No it isn't ha ha ha yes it is really I'm only joking. You'll have guessed,' he says, turning to look at me, 'that I'm a bit of a joker. I like to have a bit of a laugh with people.'

'Uhuh,' I say.

'Are you Australian?'

'No, I am not.'

'Ha ha, anyway, there was this old couple telling me they wanted to go to the Sheraton Hotel and I said all serious like oh no I'm sorry that burned down a couple of days ago and you should have seen their faces ha ha and I go ha ha only joking it didn't really burn down it was a *joke.*'

'Did they laugh?'

'Well the old fellah did a bit but she obviously hadn't got much of a sense of humour because she never said a word after that the whole journey. Another trick I have is to flash me lights and point at people's wheels – other cabbies, like – or at the back of their cars. Watch this.'

He drives at speed up to the back of a cab that's carrying two passengers and flashes his lights. The other cab slows down and pulls into the left-hand lane. Snubnose then points at the back of the cab. The other cab slows down, and Snubnose sticks his thumb up and grins. The other cabby shakes his fist in cartoon fashion and goes Grrrr.

'Ha ha ha ha HA!!'

Oh fucking hell, I think.

'You gotta have a sense of humour in this life or you've had it,' he continues, then goes quiet. Ah, lovely. This lasts for quite a while. We drive through suburbs that seem just like London. So many similarities. Eventually the silence is too much for him. He turns on the radio and the DJ is advertising a concert by the recently-reformed eighties funk-pop band ABC.

'I fancy going to that,' says Snubnose. 'They're my favourite band – I love all them New Romantics: Human League and Duran Duran. How did that song go' (sings in high-pitched voice), 'Tears something or other?'

'Are not enough,' I say.

'What?'

'"Tears Are Not Enough". That was ABC's first single.'

'Yeah,' he says excitedly. 'Teeeeeaaaaaaars are not enough. tears are not enough. Ah, great single that. There's this bar in town where they do karaoke and I love to go along and do all the New Romantic hits.'

'Have you ever been in a band?' I ask.

'Ah that's me one regret on life,' he says. 'Oi wish oi wish I had been in a band. Ah, I've got it (sings) Blue print that says that the boy meets girl. Whispers girl meets boy. Yeah.'

We are nearly there. I give him a few directions, pay him and open the door.

'Dere ya go! Hey, your shoelace is undone!'

'What?' I say, looking down.

'Ha ha ha ha ha ha ONLY JOKING MATE! By the way, I think you should stick with the Australian thing. Goes down better here. See yer.' And with a roar of the motor, the funniest man on the planet is gone from my life forever.

7.30 pm

Back in Dundrum, me, Deidre Mac and Seamus the Lodger watch a nondescript football match on TV. I chat to Seamus the Lodger about, er, football. We get on quite well in a classic blokeish dysfunctional better-not-say-too-much sort of way, although it does seem our relationship has been freeze dried, so we can only talk about, er, football. Seamus's room is a shrine to Roy Keane, one of the major gods in the Celtic sporting pantheon. Strangely (or should I say worryingly), Seamus is probably my best male friend in Dublin. And we only grunt at each other about twice a year.

9.45 pm

Irish women on the other hand are amazing and beautiful and lovely and sexy and sensitive and intelligent and talented and successful and funny and strong. Slightly over the top maybe but it has to be said, as many of them will be reading this at some point to check I say nice things. I go out with a crowd of them – Sarah, Rachel, Deirdre Mac, another Deirdre – to a local pub, The Willows. More friends appear and the talk is of house prices (in Dublin, as in London, house prices are the new rock 'n' roll), and various people say they can't afford to live in Dublin any more. In Dublin now house prices have not just gone through the roof in the last couple of years, they've gone into orbit with a monkey at the controls like that old Russian satellite of the 1950s. Or was it a dog? You have to have the dosh of a past-it musician or populist politician to pick up a decent house these days.

11 pm
I am in O'Donahue's in Merrion Row with Sarah and we name the first pint after David O'Leary, the man who scored the winning penalty for Ireland in the 1990 World Cup second-round match against Romania.

12 pm
We end up meeting the others again at the Bridge Club Bar, somewhere in the centre of town (but *where* is a secret. If I tell you I'll have to kill myself before the Bridge Club gets me first). All I can say is it's in a deep underground cave, a bit like Batman's lair, underneath a normal Georgian terraced house. There's a bloke on the door who asks for the secret password. 'Er, we've . . . come to meet my Mum and her friend Mamie and . . . to get drunk in the Bridge Club Bar,' says Sarah, concentrating hard. He lets us through. Brilliant. Inside are lots of big booths with bench seats. And a Big Beautiful Lock-in. A crowd of foxy looking middle-aged women sit at the table opposite us. It's the Secret World of Bridge.

We're all gabbing about house prices – again. They all seem to really believe there is some sort of house price spirit at large in the country. It's really all the Celtic Tiger's fault. Where did the money come from? Lots of trade with Britain. Computer companies in from Japan and the USA. Tax breaks or something? U2's crappy singles? I totter back to the bar for more pints.

'Is it all going to end, this Celtic Tiger thing?' I ask the barman, who smiles at me and serves someone else. The irony is that the term was coined after the phenomenal economies in the Far East, the 'Asian' Tigers. And we all know what happened to them. Most people seem to think it will hit the skids eventually, but they didn't say it with that much regret in their voice (though it's good that people don't have to go abroad to find work any more). As though all good things must come to an end. And they seem to think that some of the old ways weren't so bad. Perhaps shiny new Heritage Ireland and the old Ireland can live side by side without one taking over completely? A country of community spirit and condoms.

It's been another long day, and the lights are starting to go out all over my brain. Once again my short-term memory tank is full. What the hell have I been doing? It occurs to me that I am now some pissed-up wannabe-Boswell and all these assertive women, and everyone else in Ireland, are Samuel Johnson. Someone gets up to order a taxi. They have a card. Please God it isn't ABC cabs.

A Brief History of the Leprechaun

Unleash the leprechaun within

1   Is it because people didn't understand the laws of perspective in the old days so that they'd see someone in the distance and presume they were tiny people? It's possible, they'd see rainbows in the distance as well, so the tiny people and the end of the rainbow might, in the eye of the viewer, converge.

2   When rabbits run past you quickly, they might be mistaken for small people.

3   Why do they always have that strange Afrikaaner-style facial hair?

4   I once asked the singing leprechaun what he thought. He sang 'When Irish Eyes are Smiling'.

Who were the leprechauns? Some say they were one of the races who were defeated in the myth sagas – the Fir Bolgs, say, who got duffed up by the Tuatha De Danann. We have fairies in England but they were always a bit poncey, they were . . . fairies, really. All they ever did was twitty around the bottom of overgrown gardens belonging to nice middle-class families with over-sensitive daughters.

Leprechauns were different. None of that New Age shite – it was pots of gold they were interested in.

My theory is that they are a race of jockeys who couldn't get work so went to live underground, learning to live off nuts and berries or in some cases rabbits and tigers that had escaped from zoos. Tiger meat is very high in calories so they would cure it and cut it into very thin slices, like salami. Jockeys have to watch their weight. If they get fat, they're not jockeys any more, apparently. When St Patrick came to Ireland the jockeys were pagan, but he soon converted them and the Jockeys for Jesus sect of leprechauns was born. But were they good jockeys or bad jockeys? How can you tell the difference? Old people used to say that if you threw some ground ginger in the face of a jockey, then held up a mirror to his face, the bad jockey would start to smell of cheese. If a jockey comes to your door you have a choice – to either take him out with a punch and a kick to his little jockey genitalia, or be nice and say hello, after which he may lead you to his pot of gold.

How do you find out more about leprechauns? The easiest way is to sit in an Internet café and type 'leprechaun' into a search engine.

The Leprechauns are merry, industrious, tricksy little sprites, who do all the shoemaker's work and the tailor's and the cobbler's for the fairy gentry, and are often seen at sunset under the hedge singing and stitching. They know all the secrets of hidden treasure, and, if they take a fancy to a person, will guide him to the spot in the fairy rath where the pot of gold lies buried.

from Enchanted Forest
(http://www.geocities.com/EnchantedForest/2512/leprechauns3.html)

He looks like a small, old man (about two feet tall), often dressed like a shoemaker, with a cocked hat and a leather apron. According to legend, leprechauns are aloof and un-friendly, live alone, and pass the time making shoes . . . they also possess a hidden pot of gold. Treasure hunters often track down a leprechaun by the sound of his shoemaker's hammer. If caught, he can be forced (with the threat of bodily violence) to reveal the whereabouts of his treasure, but the captors must keep their eyes on him every second. If the captor's eyes leave the leprechaun (and he often tricks them into looking away), he vanishes and all hopes of finding the treasure are lost.
(http://www.ssncf.org/IrishLegends.htm)

The Leprechaun: the one shoemaker seen mending shoes. Catch him and get crocks of gold. A thrifty professional. Take your eyes off of him and he vanishes. Red Coat seven buttons in each row and he spins sometimes on the point of a cocked hat.
(http://members.tripod.com/foxylana/lep.html)

Lucky Leprechauns, Inc. offers its unique and collectible good luck Leprechaun charms for players of bingo, poker, lotto, dice, slot machines and many other games of chance.

Players of Bingo say our five Lucky Bingo Leprechauns spell the difference between winning and losing. Each Lucky Bingo Leprechaun has his own name and can be visited by clicking on the appropriate shamrock or name.

(click on your favourite pastime)
(http://www.luckyleprechauns.com)

(I kid you not!)

ORANGE COUNTY

Midlands

TRIM · NEWGRANGE

PORTARLINGTON

LIMERICK · THURLES KILDARE

ADARE

ORANGE
COUNTY

Hungover Adventures with the Sea-Urchin-Moustachioed Guard

The Curragh, Co. Kildare

Driving out of Dublin the car seemed to mirror my mood, stuttering, whining, cold. The N7 main artery southeast out of the city was pockmarked with roadworks, picked scabs in the tarmac ringed with cones. It was stop-start-stop-start driving where the subconscious takes over the clutch control and I just observed the other motorists with a red disinterested eye. Sitting in the passenger seat, without his seatbelt on, was that lazy little fucker the singing leprechaun. I couldn't bear to look at him – his stupid grin was annoying me. As Gram Parsons whinnied and wailed out of the speakers about 'The Streets of Baltimore', I thought to myself how crap and unromantic the Emerald Isle appeared on this shittiest of frostdrizzled mornings.

Before leaving I'd tried, pathetically, to get enthusiastic about looking for a good price for the car. There were a few garages in south Dublin that dealt with Opels but it seemed that I hadn't done my homework properly (Not a first for me, admittedly) – plus most of the salesmen seemed to know they were talking to a crap negotiator. The Corsa 1.4LRi, ah sure I know that car, it's a grand motor, they'd say, and this model is pretty rare in Ireland, but really it's already been superseded, value-wise, by more feature-heavy Opel models over here. Ah shite, I thought, superseded value-wise. There's a thing. And then there was the Registration Tax for cars being brought in and sold from abroad. The what? The Registration Tax. The cost of this varied depending on the size and age of the car, but in my case it would cost about a thousand pounds, which the dealer would have to work into any price he . . . might be . . . able to give me . . . as it were.

The traffic started to thin out a little and I was able to speed up but still, I had to admit it, this was crap. I don't mind driving but it's boring on your own (cue sad eyes and 'When Irish Eyes Are Smiling') and I felt like seven bags of shit. The landscape was flattish farmland with little villages in the distance and the occasional tree. At a roundabout, in automatic pilot mode, I saw a brown tourist sign for the Curragh of Kildare and turned off towards it. I stopped for a quarter of an hour in the Curragh, a vast expanse of open land that is covered in the turf of Irish stereotypes – springy, moist, gently rolling here and there and so very, very green that it dazzles. Somehow it suggested wealth and prosperity to me. I wanted to lie down and stare at the sky. All I knew of the Curragh was from the Christy Moore song:

> 'The winter it has passed
> And the summer's come at last
> The small birds are singing in the trees
> And their little hearts are glad
> Ah, but mine is very sad
> Since my true love is far away from me
>
> And straight I will repair (car reference – good)
> to the Curragh of Kildare,
> For it's there I'll find tidings of my dear.'

It's nearly always a mistake, writing down the lyrics of songs you like. They never seem to quite work on the page. Plus that's another hundred quid down the drain in royalties. Anyway, I didn't see any trees. There was no-one around. Eventually a lone horseman galloped past, glancing at me. Then silence again. In the distance a jogger, wearing a white helmet, trotted towards me. Then about fifty yards away he stopped and just stared. Then he started up again and ran past me, still staring. And I knew what he was thinking. That bloke has nicked that car from a woman.

Back on the road, about ten minutes later, I was slowing down as I came up to a roundabout and saw a guard standing in the middle of the road. The hotheaded singing leprechaun started to twitch (a bit like Dennis Hopper does when he's being interviewed about who wrote the script for *Easy Rider*). I hoped he wasn't packing a little leprechaun weapon (.09mm I think they use these days). All I know about guards is they are all six foot five, descended from some ancient race like the Fomorians and ride bicycles. This guard was a skinny bloke with bird-like face and a way-too-big-for-his-bone-structure ginger moustache. His body movements were like Alex 'Hurricane' Higgins – sort of twitchy, nervous and ever so slightly camp. The guard put his hand up, obviously desirous that I stop, with this other hand firmly on his hip. He looked like the 'cop' in the Village People, about to slink his hips and start boogying across the tarmac. As I stopped, he walked over to the car and did the international signal for winding down your windows, which when you think about it is also a bit of a 1970s funkster movement. What if I'd had electric windows? What then? He perhaps should have done a Marcel Marceau mime-like movement – a button press, followed by palms outstretched and slowly coming down.

I wound down the window, to the rhythm in my head of 'Car Wash' by Rose Royce.

'How's it going?' I asked, Peter Fonda-like.

'Can you turn the engine off, please.'

'Sorry?'

'Turn off the engine.'

He was edgy and seemed to be moving from foot to foot, as though dying for a slash.

'What's your name?'

'Excuse me?'

'What is your name?'

'Bradford.'

'Is this your car?'

What should I say? My name wasn't on the registration papers, which were in an envelope on the passenger seat. If we had a fight and he shot me or whacked me on the head with his truncheon ('Hit me with your rhythm stick, hit me, hit me . . .') he would soon find them. And even if the car had been in my name, no-one would believe me. It didn't have enough blokey paraphernalia, like souped-up speakers or alloy wheels.

'I am now going to ask you to step out of the car,' he said sternly, his moustache bristling like the tentacles of one of those multicoloured sea urchins in a David Attenborough *Life on Earth* special.

(David Attenborough voice-over: 'And so the sea urchin moves off from the coral, its tentacles bristling like the hairs on the ginger moustache of a jumpy Irish policeman who has confronted a perfectly innocent motorist on the road from Dublin to Cork.')

I waited to see how he would ask me to get out of the car. Perhaps he'd start doing the Harlem Shuffle. Suddenly I heard a revving engine behind me and looking in the mirror saw a police car coming up fast.

It skidded to a halt about ten yards behind me and a burly copper jumped out. 'It's not him!' he shouted, then jumped back in the car and did what can only be described as a Sweeney-style wheel skid before racing across the round-about in the direction of Cork. Not to be outdone, Sea Urchin

Boogie Policeman leapt into his car (without so much of a word of 'sorry to have troubled you'), which was parked in the left-hand lane of the roundabout, and did what can only be described as a Starsky and Hutch meets Dukes of Hazzard wheelspin swerve skid with triple salco, before racing off in pursuit of his mate.

An hour or so later my Guinness residue was now only just seeping into the part of my brain responsible for keeping the steering wheel in the right direction. I looked for a place to park and found a little road which led into another little road off which, as I was climbing a hill, was the official Worst Road in Ireland. Massive potholes that had turned into bottomless lakes peppered the road like a diseased lung, more hole than highway. Not the ideal road surface if you're trying to keep a car in tip-top saleable condition. The Corsa was going up and down like a yacht in a storm – I managed carefully to either go over most of them or avoid them until another would suddenly loom up and the car would lurch downwards as I cursed my ill-fortune. I had to get off this somehow and when a small left turn appeared I took it. I soon realised that what I'd been on was actually the Second Worst Road in Ireland. This was the real thing, with thin flaky little ledges of tarmac – the rest was simply hole under which could have been anything – Mineshafts? Bogs? The gateway to another world? After ten minutes I eventually found a little lay-by surrounded by pine trees and scrub and parked the car. Thanks to the highly effective police roadblock, my hangover which had been in swift pursuit of me for several hours, like some vengeful spirit, had finally arrived. It was starting to rain again. I wound the chair back and fell into a fitful sleep for an hour or so, then wound my way gingerly (the only way to do it in Ireland) back down the hill and headed west.

Cupán Tae, Cáca Milis, Mo Ghrá Tú (A Cup of Tea, a Slice of Cake, I Love You)

Adare, Co Limerick

Adare is a thatch-roof, blue-green, neatly trimmed, tightly tweaked, sweet-flower-smelling village in the twee English style, with a rich and wrecked abbey and placid medieval river flowing through lush watermeadows at one end of the town and a little Irish music shop at the other. Walk around in a place like this for a while and take a deep breath. You can smell the sweat of giftshop fatigue. In the centre of the little town is a museum on the history of Adare which is basically about the Fitzgerald family, a crowd of evil-eyed baldies with goatee beards – at least that's how they're portrayed in the pictures. In fact they all bore a remarkable resemblance to Robin Cook, the Labour MP. They got too big for their boots and the English came along and beat them up. I walked from one end of the town to the other. And then walked back again. I sat in the park for a while reading the *Limerick Leader*. The weather kept changing very rapidly – sun rain wind sun wind rain fog snow. I hummed the Crowded House song 'Four Seasons in One Day' (though I'm not going to be tricked into writing it here as that'd be another fifty quid or so down the drain). Then I got up and walked back to the tourist centre. I had a pot of tea in the café there which reminded me of holidays in Yorkshire with grandparents in the mid-seventies – coach parties of old people in zip-up anoraks, the women all with the same curly blondish hairstyle, fried food, fat dads and side-parted hair tucking into fish and chips, harassed mums, bored children. I think I said all this aloud.

The thing was it felt more like England than the Ireland I always carried around in my head. Perhaps this was a good thing, showing me the common ground. But I was disappointed. There was a names survey centre there, which comprised a computer and a kind middle-aged woman with specs and a patient smile. Huddles of curious North Americans shuffled about, then the bravest would say their name. She'd obviously made many people very happy already that day.

'Hot dangit Mary-Beth, we're related to James Joyce!'

'Wah, thyers wonnerful Heyank!'

I wanted to have a go. Me me. English surnames are usually prosaic, said the kind lady. I didn't think my name was prosaic, bottom lip sticking out. We don't usually bother putting English surnames on the computer because traditionally they either denote a job or a place. I did my upset face.

Kind Lady with Computer: OK, what's your name?

Me: (with triumphant smile) Bradford.

Kind Lady with Computer: See what I mean?

Me: (upset face) What?

Kind Lady with Computer: Well, your family are from Bradford.

Me: (with triumphant smile) Yes but it's not the Bradford you think it is.

Kind Lady with Computer: It's in the north of England, Yorkshire.

Me: (with triumphant smile) Aha! No, we're from Bradford on Avon. (Half smile.) Possibly.

Kind Lady with Computer: How do you know?

Me: (no smile) Hmm. Isn't there a Bradford in Ireland?

Kind Lady with Computer: I'm afraid not – but there's a Broadford.

Me: (with triumphant smile) Ah well – I'm nearly Irish then.

I have to come to terms with the fact that my surname is just sort of solid and uninspiring – Bradford is from Anglo Saxon and means 'crossing in the river'. It's also derived from the Norman *Bras de Fer* – 'Iron Arm'. It could be more interesting with a little bit of fine tuning. On one trip over with Ryanair I received not only a ticket in my name to my address in Parfrey Street but also one for Mr T. Bravesford of Parsley Street as well. I phoned up Ryanair to sort it out. They said I had also paid for Mr Bravesford. But there is no Mr Bravesford. Well why did you buy a ticket for him? I didn't. Well you did because it's down on the computer. I would have to write to them and send the ticket to head office in Dublin, or else go in and see them personally. I then got it into my head for some reason that in a parallel universe I was called Tab Bravesford. This Tab Bravesford was a slightly more dashing and adventurous version of myself and had somehow punctured this world so that the two realities were coexisting somehow, and was travelling in Ireland simultaneously with me.

If ever you (and your similarly-named alter ego) fly Ryanair, check out the inflight magazine. Tucked away at the back is an advert for the world registry of surnames, which supposedly tells you everything you need to know about your family name – ridiculous products like this are cashing in on people's rootless existence, people who want to know the past, what they are from and who they are. Yet I suppose in a way they don't go far enough – how about a potato with your name engraved on it in gold leaf? A singing leprechaun with your family crest that sings your name to the tune of 'When Irish Eyes are Smiling'?

I have also often wondered if there is an Irish version of 'Tim'. I know a few Irish blokes called Tim but everyone seems to call them Timmy. An Irish guy called Barney the

Cocktail Maker used to call me Taigh. The trouble with the name Tim is it's not very impressive, coming as it does from a Greek name meaning 'follower of God' – it's also too similar to the Latin 'timorous'. That kind of reputation sticks – how many ferocious characters in history have been called Timothy? King Tim? Tim Hitler? Genghis Tim? Tim the Impaler. Tim the Lionheart. Tim the Terrible (mmm, not bad). Timorous. Timid. Tim the Conqueror. Tim the Great. Tim Bonaparte. I have never been interested in reading articles about tennis but once saw a Martin Amis piece about Tim Henman and he basically said what I already knew – Tims don't put the fear of God into anybody. Your name is like a shop front and people make assumptions about you because of it – Tab Bravesford could be a tough and exciting travel writer, Tim Bradford – which, literally means 'follower of God at the crossing of the river' – sounds like a respectable lawyer in a small country town.[1]

I had to come to terms with the fact that there was nothing remotely Celtic about me. Or in the way I sounded – Irish speech always gave me hellish problems too. To me Irish has always sounded not just like a language from another country but a language from another planet. I was once in a little pub in Spiddal, outside Galway, which is in the Irish-speaking area (Gaeltacht), and found myself listening to the locals who were speaking about a recent Man United game. They were all middle-aged blokes – one was huge, bull-necked, red-faced, close-cropped white hair, the other the same age but with a wild mop of black curly hair; the third older, about seventy-five, long nose, cap, leather skin. After buying a pint I slowly sidled up the bar until I could listen in on the conversation.

Bull Neck: fnah snah a gorraa sna blah aa snah Ryan Giggs snah fnoor a snah blah blah mnar Manchester United.
Curly: fnah snoor mnoor a snoo a mnaa a gn Roy Keane snaa.
Big Nose: Bnaa ffoo munoora blah fnaa Roy Keane?
Curly: Roy Keane nadir smir fir.
Bull Neck: Ha ha . . . Roy Keane i Ryan Giggs snaa foloor moor a snoo fmaa.
Big Nose and Curly: Ha ha ha ha.

Gaelic Irish is an early Indo-European language, one of the Celtic tongues related to Cornish, Breton and Welsh and from which sprung Manx and Scottish. I've picked up two or three little phrases which come in mighty handy when I'm travelling round one of the Gaeltachts: *cupán tae* – cup of tea,

---

[1] My uncle's name is also Tim Bradford and he is a respectable lawyer in a small country town – he obviously has an understanding of the ways of the universe which I lack.

cáca milis – slice of cake, *mo ghrá tú* – I love you.[2] Though they weren't really much help with the lads in Spiddal – I didn't really fancy getting personal with Bull Neck.

The thing is, I'm a totally lazy linguist.[3] I won't do drills if I can learn something quick. I once tried a book called *Learn Spanish With Paul Daniels*. Obviously, I think Paul Daniels is not a talented person but if he could let me in on the secrets of language I'd go with it. But of course, he couldn't. I bought a CD rom for my computer called *Learn Irish*. You press on a picture and a voice says the word in Irish then you have to say it as well through a microphone. It's pre-school stuff but very challenging for me. A few years ago I bought a twelve-tape language course called something like *Hippy Meditation Higher Consciousness Zen Learn French in a Week Without Doing any Work You Lazy Bastard* which came in a big box with a big thick book. The idea was based on a concept called Accelerated Learning. With classical music playing in the background the student is expected to take in and understand the new language subliminally. I can just imagine a French oral exam using this stuff – OK, now, Marie-Claude wants to reach a higher state of mind but doesn't know the way. Can you direct her? Turn right at the charcuterie and left at the boulangerie and it's at the end of the street.

I found out from experience that there's no substitute

[2]Very recently Irish has become an official curriculum language in English schools. Which is some kind of victory when you think about it.

[3]At school I learned that Henry VIII could speak five languages – English for sensible things, French when trying to get off with a member of the opposite sex, Italian for explaining to the police that it was the other guy's fault, officer, he jumped a red light, German for not understanding jokes and Spanish for exclaiming with joy as you chuck a donkey or goat off a church tower. The attitude to languages in England is such that many people are lucky to come out of high school with the ability to ask for a couple of beers and the way to the football ground. No wonder back in the eighties English football fans spent years rampaging around Europe. They only wanted to go to the toilet, but didn't know how to ask.

for being thrown in at the deep end. A couple of weeks hanging around with gruff French farmer types, tractor-driving weightlifters with purple noses and flat caps in Normandy pastis bars soon put hairs on my chest and verbs in my head. I could say the words, but whereas they made them sound like love poetry, my East Midlands voice box simply mangled them.

The Celtic peoples simply have more attractive voices. Kind of sing-songy. What's attractive in England? Cockney certainly isn't. Manchester isn't. Norfolk can be OK and sing-songy but Norwich is harsh. Geordie is OK, Brummie is terrible. East Midlands nondescript. Yorkshire blunt. West Country sounds thick. A lot of English people can mimic accents from other parts of the country and thus think that Irish accents are easy to copy. They've heard Mícheál O'Hehir doing the Irish Grand National, Johnny Giles' staccato Dublin and Eamon Dunphy's camp drawl when watching Irish games in pubs; they've seen the Hollywood films with Americans attempting a country Irish brogue. As for me, I'd always presumed I was brilliant at Irish accents, but I've only ever managed to remotely copy three people – Frank Carson, my uncle Cyril (although he's not my real uncle), and the former footballer David O'Leary (currently manager of Leeds United but by the time this book comes out, who knows where he'll be, maybe a fisherman diving for Dublin Bay prawns out near Howth, perhaps with my uncle Cyril captaining the boat – actually David O'Leary has a good physique for prawn diving – long and slender with an elongated neck for peering round giant clams or shipwrecks). My Dublin sounded like a melange of Scouse and Manchester, my Cork sounded Pakistani, my Ian Paisley sounded like Geoff Boycott. This is what I've been told, of course. By other people. As far as I'm concerned my accents are totally great.

Perhaps I just don't have the vowel sounds to do Celtic

voices. All I can do is say 'boy' in a Cork accent and 'nothing' in a Dublin accent. My own accent is too flat. In Lincoln-shirese you can talk while drinking a pint because it's mostly through the nose. Lincolnshire is mostly just flat fields and small, 50cc Yamaha motorbikes (the yammy fizz) – and the accent has developed sounding like the engines of these bikes, a nasal whine – particularly amongst bikers them-selves. (Though I could never be sure whether the bikers talked like their bikes, or the bikes sounded like the bikers.) A similar thing happened in rural Norfolk, where people's voices sound like the sheep that they tend. In London, the accent sounds like their indigenous species, the evening newspaper seller. Upper-class English people sound like horses and that's mostly what they do all day – in feudal times the posh lads would have been the only ones with horses, after all. In Northern Ireland they made ships so their voices sound like foghorns. Dubliners sound like Scousers because of the popularity of the Beatles in the 1960s.

Apparently in London now you have more chance of get-ting a job with an Irish accent than if you are a local.[4] This is partly to do with the fact that the Irish education system is thought to be better than the English. Like France it doesn't focus too narrowly on either the sciences or the arts and thus perhaps produces more well-rounded students, but this is not the main reason. It's simply the way they talk. Irish people sound intelligent and enthusiastic and sharp. Or maybe it's just the mad eyes which intimidate potential employers at the interview stage.

[4]*Irish Post* 26.9.98, 'An Irish accent is good for business', by Paul Gribben.

In Adare my favourite reading matter was a guidebook to hotels in Ireland. I had become fascinated by the various hoteliers' faces. I almost wanted to go to these establishments solely to gaze at their impressively idiosyncratic physiognomies. Big noses, broken noses, big jaws, little eyes, big eyes, no necks, five necks – I ended up phoning a fantastic-looking couple at Hanratty's Hotel in Limerick to ask if I could come and stare at them. No, they said, so I asked for a room instead.

I looked down the street and saw a red-faced bearded man in a jobo jacket staring at me from about thirty yards away. He then walked towards me and muttered 'beautiful day' as he passed. He stopped about three or four yards away, bobbing his head like a duck. I looked up and he was just staring at me. Then he coughed and started up a conversation.

'Smoke? Smoke? Smoke?'

I looked up and smiled, forcedly, then looked down.

'Smoke? Smoke? Smoke?' he said again.

'No thanks,' I said, still smiling weakly and wishing I was somewhere else. He shook his head. 'Smoke? Smoke? Smoke?'

'Ah no,' I said, 'I don't smoke. I haven't got any.' My smile was now stuck. I think he thinks I like him, I thought. Or, I then thought, he thinks I thinks he thinks I like him.

'Ah!' he said, and nodded. My smile was hurting now. He shuffled over to me, his medieval-looking rags flowing in the gentle breeze.

Red-faced Beardy: 'Is that a watch? I've got a watch.'
Me: (smiling like a mad skull) It's a compass.
Red-faced Beardy: What's a compass?
Me: It shows directions. It stops me getting lost.

Red-faced Beardy: Eh?

Me: Well, if I'm lost it shows me where to go.

Red-faced Beardy: Eh?

Me: Well, say I'm up a mountain and it's foggy I could find my way back to a village.

Red-faced Beardy: Which village?

Me: That's not the point.

Red-faced Beardy: Eh? Does it tell people where you are?

Me: No.

Red-faced Beardy: Mmm.

He was clearly unimpressed. He bobbed his head like a duck, staring down at the compass. I paused for a while then he started to tell me about the Limerick bus that we were waiting for. Well, I understood the words 'bus' and 'Limerick' – the rest was wasted on me.

He pointed at his wrist and smiled.

'North!' I said, pointing at my compass and looking up the street.

'Eh?' he said.

'That way is north.' I was jabbing my finger now.

It's a top technique. Out-mad the mad person – it usually works, and Red-faced Beardy looked at me as if I had just escaped from some secure institution, then shuffled away back to his corner. A couple of minutes later a tall guy who looked like an ex-surfer New-Agey type ambled up and said 'All right' in a strong Antipodean accent (My disguise – it worked!).

'Smoke? Smoke? Smoke?' said Red-faced Beardy, ambling up to the newcomer as if trying to kiss him. The fellow immediately walked straight off back down the street without looking back or uttering a word. Red-faced Beady looked puzzled, looked at me, then muttered a sheepish 'Eh?'

'South!' I grinned, pointing at my wrist, then at the rapidly retreating Australian.

Looking for an All-encompassing Theory of the Universe in a Hurling Match

Limerick to Thurles

I have always loved the Victorian parts of towns near railway stations. Parts which have nearly always seen better days. Large red brick hotels, oversized pubs, once-genteel boarding houses now flaking and peeling, the smell of strong cider in the air. There's always a Railway Hotel where once upon a time you would have been guaranteed a good basic room with a wash basin, but now you get wall-to-wall satellite sports programming, garish coloured chalk menus on blackboards, a thousand kinds of heavily chemicalled draught lager and a fight, if you are so inclined.

Limerick railway station was an interesting mixture of big-nosed farmers, evil alcoholic villains and full-lipped long-haired Eurobabe backpackers. One interesting thing I noticed in Limerick is that backpacks are getting smaller. Maybe the Eurotraveller, particularly the Eurobabe backpacker, doesn't use as much stuff, or maybe their clothes are getting skimpier. Anyway, the backpacks are now tiny. Personally I think it's connected to the dumbing-down of our culture, people just don't read as much anymore. In the old days a traveller would take a variety of reading matter to keep himself occupied. A small library, containing some classics, poetry, local travel writing, guidebook, *Ulysses* by Joyce (if in Ireland), *À la recherche du temps perdu* by Proust (if in France), *Not A Penny More, Not A Penny Less* by Archer (if in England), a bible, a foreign language dictionary, a nineteenth-century novel, some Shakespeare, a post-modern writer and a history book. Now your average backpacker just goes down to the local Internet café, downloads whatever information they'll need for that day, then sits in a coffee bar and talks gibberish about pop stars at 100 mph.

This railway district has undercurrents and overtones – or undertones and overcurrents – of violence purely because of its inner-city feel, its grimy shabbiness. It probably comes from reading too many Dickens novels, though in fairness I've only read three. Old-fashioned violence as well, a Victorian blade between your ribs. There's something intensely frightening about knives, something ancient and magical that sends a shiver up your spine. You can understand Queensberry Rules, a kick in the guts or even a headbutt now and then as the acceptable risks of bumping into people at nightclubs or, say, taking the piss out of a sixteen-stone skinhead's Lambretta[1] in a dodgy part of Birmingham, but there's something darkly, secretly evil about knives, something silent and deadly.

And so I had that in mind when I got to the wide streets of Limerick City. For years, whenever I mentioned Limerick,[2] people would suck in their breath – *Psssewwwweh!* – as

[1] That was a stupid thing to do. He cracked my nose, which now goes blue in cold weather.

[2] There's something that I'd like to tell
I stayed in Hanratty's Hotel
I watched too much TV
And ate Chinese nightly
(The chow mein had an awful smell).

though they were taking in the last remnants of a runty little spliff at a party, desperate for a last-minute hit before they head off home in a smelly late-night minicab. Evidently this attitude is something to do with the city being famous for fighting; fisticuffs and, of course, knife-related violence. People made Limerick seem like some Godforsaken gang-warring mixture of the worst of Los Angeles, New York and the Marseilles docks area. Wander round the streets at night and you'll wake up in hospital, if you wake up at all.

Limerick was founded by the Vikings in the tenth century. Perhaps the city's violent reputation goes back this far, though to be fair to the Vikings they weren't really into stabbing so much as slashing, burning, beheading, chopping into little bits, pillaging and, of course, raping.[3]

A powerful family called the Robin-Cook-Lookalike-Fitzgeralds, Earls of Desmond, ruled the area in the 16th century. Others called them after a girl's name – the Geraldines. They had come over with the Normans (good boy's name) in the eleventh and twelfth centuries and in time, like most of the families that settled in Ireland, became completely Gaelicised and ruled like independent princes. Back in England that greatest of all centralising monarchs and all-round philandering fatlad, Henry VIII, decided to cut down on their power and thus set about attempting to make Englishmen of them. The Geraldines, stung by the suggestion that having a girl's name meant they'd be no good at fighting and with a gung-ho leader in James Fitzmaurice Robincook Fitzgerald, revolted against English rule. A vicious war started up in Munster which ended with the defeat of the

[3]The Vikings have been getting some better press recently and it's even been suggested that the raping and pillaging bunch of marauding Scandinavian baby-eating devil-worshipping sadists was all a myth and in actual fact they were all gentle, peace-loving eccentric uncle-type figures with leather elbow patches, who were kind to animals and adored anything to do with monks. The truth, as ever, possibly lies somewhere between the two.

Fitzgeralds and the confiscation of their estates and their goatee beards.

They're still obviously a bit mardy. Richard Harris is from Limerick – and used to get into fights after his all-day-and-night benders. That girl from the Cranberries is too and she's dead stroppy; you wouldn't want to get in a scrap with her. So is Peter Clohessy, a talented nutcase hardman rugby prop forward who played for Young Munster and who had a terrible disciplinary record.

Walking through Limerick you certainly get a bit of a buzz, particularly if you've just spent a few days in the peaceful tourist areas of Cork and Kerry. For a start the people look very different. Big families walk the streets, the men with button-down shirts, short hair, weather-beaten, pinched, scarred faces, mad eyes; fat women, dirty-faced kids. They're probably in their twenties but look ten or more years older. There are people selling cheap rubbish – toys, teacloths, batteries – at the side of the small streets running off the main road. Traffic, fumes, a rush of energy. Less tourists than anywhere I've been so far in Ireland. Near the station big old buildings, hotels, pubs, sad old fellahs shuffling about from pub to pub, battered-looking Chinese takeaways (Ireland has the lowest number of Chinese people working in Chinese takeaways in the whole world). Recent improvements in the city have seen those evil symptoms of economic success, fun theme pubs, appear where once would have been honest, dirty, seedy old men's boozers with piss on the carpet where you might get stabbed for breathing too quickly (but where men were men and not consumers in a brand-marketing concept).

I'd been told about the Munster Hurling Final between Waterford and Clare a week before, but only decided to go on the morning of the game, leaving the hotel and heading off to the station around lunchtime (I'd checked in my timetable that a train would be leaving for Thurles at 1.30 pm). For some reason I expected the station to be full of bouncy and enthusiastic hurling fans waving flags and shouting raaaay raaay raaaay raaaay as all sports fans do when they are herded together in one place, but it was virtually empty. In front of me in the queue was a short speccy guy with big teeth and spiky hair,[4] who was arguing with the man in the ticket office (a dead ringer for an ex-U-Boat captain: steely-eyed middle aged with close-cropped blond hair) about when the trains were supposed to be coming in. I imagined he must be a local trainspotter and was prepared to embark on a citizen's arrest procedure (it's the only way, readers, to get these people off the streets). The ticket man was shaking his head vigorously, as though one of his crew had asked for extended shore leave, then he went away for a while (to check the periscope, or something) and Speccy turned to me and said something very quickly, like, 'theeoo na dra torless befaa ga'. By this stage I had already learned how to filter a sentence – place it in my mind, then rake over it, searching for words or phrases that I understood – all the while putting on a sort of grimaced smile. (This process only

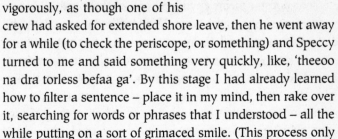

---

[4]In truth he looked like the Austin Powers character, played by Mike Myers, in the film of the same name. Though Powers is more a Waterford name.

took a couple of seconds.) However, I had to ask him to say it again.

'It appears, old chap, that there are no trains to Thurles that will get us there before the hurling match begins,' he said, my in-built translation mechanism now functioning properly.

That can't be right, I thought. Behind me a couple of young Clare girls with long wild curly hair and little excited smiles fingered their scarves and cursed under their breath. Well, they said to each other out loud, oh fucking shit. I took a timetable out of my pocket and found the relevant page.

'That can't be right,' I said in that way that only Englishmen do when they are indignant about some kind of public transport foul-up, 'it says here in the timetable that there is a train at half-past one.' I jabbed my finger at the page in question, to emphasise how clever and organised I was. The two girls laughed in that tinkly Sharon Shannon squeezebox sort of way.

'That doesn't mean anything,' one of them said. 'No-one reads those.' She had a point. Why the hell was I taking the timetable as gospel? I already knew not to trust anything written down – better to ask locals, usually an old man or young street urchin hanging around a bus stop or station platform, who would tell me that on this particular day the transport in question always came fifteen minutes early for reasons which no-one seemed to understand and which probably went back to the Megalithic era. I brandished my timetable for a few more seconds, then relaxed my frown. Then rolled it up and did that trick where you can see a hole in your hand,[5] as if to distract attention away from the fact that I was so obviously a thick tourist. Meanwhile Speccy and the Captain continued their debate about trains. An older man joined us, hoping to get to Thurles.

Old Man: Have they run out of tickets?
Dark-haired Girl: Ah no, they haven't run out of tickets, holy God!

Speccy was getting impatient. His line of argument was that he had spoken to a station master at Ennis in Clare and had been told that there would be a train. And then he said something along the lines of 'and anyway, you know who I am, sure enough'. What *did* he mean? But no-one would sell us a ticket. We stood around, the five of us, as Toothy chatted away in a singsong accent about the semi-final and how the Waterford defence might stand up to Clare. And then he disappeared. I didn't even see him go. Perhaps he was never there. Like a faery.

Red-haired Girl: They say it happens. Faeries come disguised as sports fans and ingratiate themselves with us. Then they just disappear, after offering to sell you a cheap ticket or merchandise item.

Suddenly the barrel-chested stationmaster (a big-smiled Mr Nice compared to the Nazi U-Boat captain in the ticket office) told us that a train from Ennis was coming to the station especially to pick us up. We all went back to the ticket window, where the guy begrudgingly sold us tickets before barking some orders in German to the pretty little colleen next to him and the ticket office

[5]You must know this one. Roll it up and stick it next to your outstretched palm, keeping both eyes open.

disappeared beneath the waves of an imaginary North Sea ('Schnell schnell! Man ze torpedo tubes!'), to the sound of a siren going off, with just its Iarnród-Eireann-emblazoned periscope showing above the platform. Then it headed off in the direction of the newsagents.

The train was crowded with families, groups of young men, pockets of late-teenage girls, all with wristbands, scarves and shirts in the Clare colours. Speccy suddenly reappeared in front of me. I bought him a beer and he told me about the girl who was usually on this train, who he really liked and who he thought quite liked him actually. Are you sure? I said. Oh yeah, he replied. You wait and see. Is Finoola around? he said to the barman, looking back at me and winking. Ah now, said the middle-aged guy behind the bar. She recently got engaged and she's gone away on holiday with her fiancé. Speccy's face drooped sadly and I suggested we go to find a seat. Obviously this part of his day was not going exactly to plan.

And so the train clattered along. You don't get old trains like this in England any more. They're either 125s, Network South East (modern or old) or the little two carriage ones. It was all wood inside the carriage, with a nice little cubbyhole type of room that was the bar and which must have got very snug on Saturday nights. We sat down at a tiny table near the bar and Michael – Speccy – started to tell me a bit about himself and hurling. I had never been entirely sure about the rules but the way he explained it all seemed quite simple.[6] One point if you knock the ball over the posts. Three points if you can get it in the goal. Different teams have different

[6]Basic rules of the game: Hurling is played by two fifteen-member teams. The hurley (the stick used by the players) is a narrow-shafted stick about a metre long, ending in a curved blade. The *sliotar* (the ball) has a cork centre and a leather cover. At each end of the field are goals, formed by two posts with a crossbar, like a rugby goal. A net hangs back behind the goal. The object of the game is to catch the sliotar on the blade of the hurley, carry it, and then hurl it into the goal.

styles, he said, and the fortunes of a team will ebb and flow over the years. Take for example his team, Clare – they had not won an All-Ireland final for eighty years until 1995 and now they had won two in three years and were undoubtedly favourites this year. Wow, I said, just like my old home team in football, Lincoln City – they're really shit and never win anything either. No, he said, Clare aren't shit. They play a fast vigorous game. Some teams would make shorter passes and lots of hand passing. Others would just whack it upfield in big shots and get it up as quickly as possible. This was, in his mind, he said, the true spirit of hurling. Though many people, old fellahs particularly, didn't think the players were as skilful as in the old days, there were still some great guys out there. Jamesie O'Connor of Clare and Tony Brown of Waterford. This guy should be on television, I thought as he rattled away, like the train. Then I looked at him again and decided radio might be more his thing.

I have a ticket to pick up from some friends he said. You

Players can only pick the sliotar off the ground with the hurley – although they can then take it off the hurley using their hand, as long as they don't throw it or run with it.

The team gets three points when the sliotar is hurled into the net, and one point when it is hurled over the crossbar between the goalposts. Even though hurling, one of the fastest team sports around, is a pretty rough and dangerous game, serious injuries don't happen very often.

The game became scarce during and after the famine years, with the mass emigrations to America. Then in 1884 the Gaelic Athletic Association (or in its Irish translation – Cumann Luthcleas Gaeilge) set down a standardised set of rules of the game and a league competition was first put together. The first All-Ireland Hurling final was played in 1888 on 1 April in Birr, Co. Offaly, when Thurles from Tipperary defeated Meelick from Galway in a 21-a-side contest. The GAA was founded in order to promote and organise Ireland's traditional outdoor games and set out the future of Irish team sports for the twentieth Century, emphasising Celtic culture at the expense of the Anglicised forms of sport available. They go back to more ancient ways and are more in tune with the times of Yeats and Lady Gregory and the Celtic Twilight. Some say the GAA has too much power and is too political, strait-laced and old-fashioned. Other praise the fact that it has stuck to its roots and not totally caved in to the power of sponsorship and bland late twentieth-century entertainment values.

can come with me if you like and I'm sure you will get a ticket. I thanked him for the offer but said I wanted to just wander around and get a flavour of the event. Ah, fair enough, sure, he said. They shouldn't have messed with me, they know who I am, he said. Who are you? I asked. My uncle is a well-known politician, so they know they shouldn't mess with me. He didn't look like the sort of bloke you wouldn't mess with. But then I'd always thought that Martin McGuinness looked like a cuddly old English teacher, the sort who would take you for a pint after school and tease you about girls you fancied and your lack of knowledge of Ovid, so I'm no great judge.

As Michael started to tell me about the intricacies of the Clare political scene I drifted in and out of consciousness, staring out of the window at the farmland colours, the faint wash of hills daubed into the background. A mass of crows took off from a ploughed field as the train went past, reminding me of the scene in *Out of Africa* where Robert Redford and Meryl Streep are in a plane buzzing the wildlife out in some national park. I suppose I was Robert Redford and Michael was Meryl Streep.[7] Two round hills loomed up in the distance and I thought of Maria Guevara's Breasts, a mountain range in South America with two prominent peaks, apparently reminiscent of a celebrated sixteenth-century Spanish beauty – perhaps a modern equivalent would be Salma Hayek's baps. As the train rocked from side to side – I could hear the blah blah of loud voices at the bar kids asking their Dad who Manchester United were playing that day – Michael telling me that 'the people at Limerick realised

---

[7]Actually it would have been a massive improvement if *Out of Africa* (the only film I have ever fallen asleep in at the cinema) had been about the Munster hurling final rather than a couple of upper-class types in Africa. They would obviously have had to change a few of the main scenes and set the film in Tipperary rather than Africa. *Out of Tipperary*, they could have called it. Redford a hurling coach, Streep the wife of a hurler who's gone off the rails.

they had to pull that train in when they knew who they were dealing with, even though it wasn't supposed to stop there'. I felt as though I was travelling back in time. I played the 'what olden days costumes would they wear?' game – the bar lads would be eighteenth century, the kids Victorian era, Michael I saw as a mad druid type.

As soon as I got off the train I could tell by the smell and the way the wind blew that Thurles was a small market town. I just know these things, having been brought up in a small market town myself. It's a mixture of wood polish, sausages and two-stroke engine oil. The difference being that this is Ireland so the smell is sweetened by the aroma of burning peat (typical for late July), breaking the dryness like an old man on a busy city street with a well-stuffed pipe. It all seemed very suburban and I looked for signs for a town centre, then we turned a corner over the railway bridge and the whole scene opened up before us. Plump crowds spilled out onto the street from every available pub orifice, attracted by elemental forces to chip vans and hot dog stalls. Michael said he was off to find his friends and asked me for one last time if I'd like to accompany him. I suppose if I had I'd have been able to write a whole book about hurling, but my natural inclination to drift in and out of things got the better of me so I said thanks, but I'm off exploring. Good luck, he said, and remember you'd better be supporting Clare after my sporting lesson. I laughed and he disappeared into the crowd, in the instantaneous way he had done back at Limerick Station. I thought of going for a quick one at The Hayes Hotel, where the Gaelic Athletic Association was formed in 1898, but the gridlock of red-faced suppers crammed into the doorways, exalting in their Mecca, tempted me to try a less fundamentalist establishment. I found a small pub nearby. It had different levels of noise, quiet talkers, whisperers, loudies, shouters, singers. In or outside? – I weighed it up. I was getting sticky on such a moist, close day but I hate Guinness in a plastic glass and would rather stand amongst the bodies and sweat. Someone shouts something in my ear and I just say 'yeah' because I haven't understood a word he's said. All around the classic sports fans high-decibel 'murmur murmur' was drowning out everything.

I supped up then headed back out onto the street. Moving into town from the station were Clare fans, having got the train from Ennis and Limerick, and I became caught up in the blue and gold tide, while the Waterford contingent walked in from the opposite direction, most having come by bus or car on the main road and parked at the other side of town. It was like a dance, opposing forces coming together and touching but only slightly then merging or going off into separate directions, the different colours – the blue and yellow of Clare and the white of Waterford – making patterns in the grey light. They all merged in the town square and headed off in different directions, into alleyways and pub lobbies. I walked into a long bar and reached the back, where they had only two pumps. Harp and Guinness. Old men stood around and it felt like a good place to be. I got a proper glass too. I stood out in a little courtyard where it was drizzling slightly. A huddle of middle-aged men watched a swallow diving above an old medieval tower. I'd never seen that before, but I'd watched Elvis swallow-diving in the movie *Acapulco*. I positioned myself next to a family group. The oldest, a man with noble, battered face and flat cap, was holding court, talking about past finals and great players, and techniques. Next to him, two middle-aged guys in their fifties. Then a thirtysomething and a late teen. The two youngest didn't say anything, just clutched their pints and took it in. Even the old guy's two sons waited for a suitable opening before speaking. The old guy was the channel, the playmaker. In the parlance of sports tactics, he pushed the play.

I didn't see much sign of sponsorship. The hurling championships are sponsored by Guinness but there didn't seem to be the plethora of branded merchandise you get at, say, a British sporting occasion, never mind an American one. Who knows how long this will last? There must already be forces pushing the players and counties in the direction of at least semi-professionalism. I don't mean to sound like an old uncle with a pipe.[8] The players are all amateurs. Noble men. Train hard. Don't drink.

Apart from warfare and group dating, hurling must be the oldest team sport in the world. It's there in the Celtic myths[9] – it's what the legendary warriors did in their spare time between stealing bulls and each other's wives. Setanta, on his way to meet his father and the fated meeting with Cullan's hound, whiled away the journey over mountains by hitting a sliotar around with a hurley. You can see elements of the game in more modern concoctions such as football and rugby (as well as the slightly more effete pastimes of hockey and lacrosse[10]). The first hurling I'd ever seen was the All-Ireland clash between Clare and Offaly in 1995, from a pub in Waterford. I had been impressed by the frenetic pace and skill of the game, but TV never gives you

[8] I've thought about the times I feel like moaning on about things and have come up with a solution. In pubs, say, you could have an old pipe dangling from the ceiling so that every time someone wanted to give out about pop music, politicians, fashion, sexual mores, whatever, they could go and hold the pipe and come across as a bit of a crusty old cove. For the traveller, like me, a smaller pipe attached to an item of headgear with some wire might do equally well.

[9] Legend has it that the first hurling match took place in 1272 BC when the Fir Bolgs defeated the Tuatha Dé Dannaan in a twenty-seven-a-side game.

[10] Please don't write in if you're a lacrosse or hockey player and think you're hard. It's merely a comment about the presentation and culture of the game rather than a dismissal of the individual players' physical prowess (though I bet you're all a load of public school jessies).

the real picture of any team sport[11] – plus in hurling the ball is too small to see when you're watching a smallish TV from the back of a crowded bar. They should make it bigger.[12]

There's a stillness at the start of the Munster hurling final, an emptiness which the fans try to fill by bellowing the names of their heroes and sounding off air klaxons so that the noise level brings to mind a huge medieval battle, though without the blood (that will surely come soon enough). There's the odd drum, too, which adds to the ancient aura. Old faces and wild eyes all around me, red cheeks and long-nosed profiles wait eagerly for the start. I imagine that the start of battles in the old times was like this – the pageant before the blood. Then the referee's whistle blows and there's an explosion of energy on the pitch, like the psychic spark that flamed in the nothingness before creation and an inquisitive ball of fire and light rushed outwards into every-thing, as the two sides smack each other's hurlies into the ground and the legs of their opponents as they rush for the sliotar. I'm enthralled by the energy, as a Waterford forward gets strealed across the back of the legs by his Clare counter-part. I'd always imagined the game as a load of big-legged farmers chasing around hitting each other with sticks. Now I know for certain that's exactly what it is. Then a few seconds later it's mayhem, barely controlled violence as everyone chases the ball like a swarm of small boys do a football in a playground kickabout, hurleys clashing as if in an elaborate and dangerous dance.[13] The crowd are now suddenly so excited that the back of my neck begins to tingle. I've never

---

[11] For instance, people who've only ever seen football on TV completely miss out on the angles of attack, running off the ball, dummies, niggles, physical tussles, acceleration and all-round general skill of the players.

[12] Someone should do something about it.

[13] Hurling is, apparently, the fastest field sport in the world. Who measures these things? And why?

experienced an atmosphere like this before. I'm at the Clare end, but a few Waterford lads are in front of me, screaming at the referee. A middle-aged Clare man with a red face and small, blue, watery eyes makes some comment about them 'fecking off to the other end'. They laugh at him when a Clare defender makes a mistake. Then pandemonium as two players are sent off. Klaxons are off again, banners swirl in the wind. Then it starts to piss it down and the crowd huddles closer together, becoming even more a single organism. I'm in sporting heaven.

Sometimes at a match, of whatever sport, I love to just watch one person, see how he copes with the pressure of the game. By doing this you try and get inside his head. It's best not to choose the stars of the team, who often do things instinctively and are not like you or me, but the lesser players, the ones who are operating at the peak of their ability all the time just to survive, the ones who really make an effort. The ones where you can almost see in their eyes the fear of making a mistake and the real desire to do well. These are the sports stars I've always respected, the ones who put their psyches on the line. The ones for whom it's a battle. The ones who are no different from the people in the crowd. I choose to watch Mark Sullivan, the left-back for Waterford. He looks athletic but slightly frail and is marking a big powerful ginger lad who is obviously a bit of a star. Sullivan, I find out afterwards, wasn't first choice for this game but came in at the last minute after the original player was injured. Even more reason to watch him. He's new. It's going to be strange for him. He does OK, but makes a couple of mistakes which lead to Clare goals. Can't criticise him for effort, though, and he looks to be giving away about thirty pounds to his opposite number.

Another player I start to watch is Jamesie O'Connor. I remember him from the game I saw on TV – he's skilful and small. A teacher, in the various photos I've seen of him he has always got a different hairstyle from the others. They either have a crew cut or simple short back and sides. Jamesie must have been a punk or soul boy when he was younger or maybe even a goth – has shaved sides with a floppy fringe. You can tell he's never quite happy with his look.

There's a part of the human brain which is specially designed for watching sports. After about twenty minutes warming up suddenly it kicks in and you get this mad rictus-like expression on your face and start shouting 'raaay raaaay raaay rayyyy' along with the thousands of people alongside you in the stands. It doesn't matter if you don't support either of the teams. 'Aiieeeeeeeee. Raaaaay raaaay raaaay raaaay.' Years ago I went along to watch a Manchester United game in the press box at Old Trafford for an article on what the press do and I just got caught up in the atmosphere. 'Raaaaay raaaay raaay raaaay,' I went, as the guy in the sheepskin frantically tried to get me to tell him who had just gone off. Back in the bar after the game I was still whispering 'raaaay raaay raaay raaay' to myself. No-one would talk to me because I wasn't a proper journalist.

It occurs to me that hurling is a bit like quantum physics. Then it occurs to me that I don't know anything about quantum physics. So where did that thought come from? Spooky, huh? But it's all those things bouncing around at high speed or something. I'm losing you here, aren't I?

Later that night I phone up my brother, Snake, who has a PhD in laser physics and a very large brain and say to him, after the usual how's it going?, 'It occurred to me that hurling is a bit like quantum physics. Then it occurred to me that I don't know anything about quantum physics. Snake, tell me about quantum physics.' Ten minutes later I realise why he is the one in a white lab coat polishing his cerebral cortex every night and I am the one travelling around being a layabout and scribbling things down on beer mats. So here's my all-encompassing theory of the universe in a hurling match: the universe is all pingy with things flying all over the place and has a start and a finish and so does hurling.

I have a quick pint at O'Connor's bar and get chatting to the landlord's daughter, who seems dead impressed when I know the names of some of the players.[14] As the blue and yellow draped figures wave their flags and blend together in the streets I wander off into the night back to my drab world of public transport and Europackers.

[14]If chatting up Irish women is your thing, memorising the names and stats of hurlers and Gaelic footballers is a handy way of getting in with them.

Why is there Orange in the Irish Flag?

East to west, Portarlington, Co. Laois

It's a question I have asked a few of my Irish friends. Why *is* there orange in the Irish flag? Is it something to do with orangemen and Protestantism?

'It's not orange, it's gold,' they say. 'The green white and gold.'

That's not gold. Gold is shiny. That's . . . orange. And anyway, where would gold come from?

'Er.'

Exactly.

'Er, how about the Wexford gold rush of seventeen-something or other?'

Hmmm.

'Or 1820 when workmen found a hoard of torques and bracelets and melted them down.'

OK, so they have a point. But is it enough on which to base one of the colours of the national flag? That's like England having black and grey in the flag because of coal and tin. It's highly implausible.

There's something about the Midlands. Quiet. Slow-paced. Big sky. Some of it is like the Midwest of the US, or counties like Lincolnshire or Norfolk. You don't get too many American tourists in Portarlington either. (I'd come to the old Huguenot town of Portarlington in Co. Laois because it is where Annie's family originally came to from the continent, along with other Protestants escaping persecution in the late seventeenth century.) Areas like this were called plantations. Protestants came over and were given the best land to farm, and the Catholics were driven off (as in most other parts of Ireland). Ownership of land has been one of the big issues in Ireland for centuries. What happens if Ireland is ever united? Will they give land back to people who had it seized, like in German unification? Portarlington was founded in 1666 and it became a wealthy town, centre of education, silversmiths and banking. The town has notable Georgian, Huguenot and Victorian architecture, and it hosts an annual French Festival.

I just wanted to see if anyone remembered them and wandered around feeling like one of those TV historians, searching for clues and showing my best side to the camera. Unlike the more touristy parts of the country, where I could blend in easily with the Australian backpackers and German beer drinkers, here I soon began to be noticed by local people, who looked curiously at me and wondered what this dishevelled tinker figure was doing in their respectable little town.

I went to the library and talked to the librarian, Marie McCraith, who got out some documents about the family and a couple of books with references. One had a photo of Annie's grandfather, who had been a local magistrate, land-owner, cycling champion, dog owner, shooting champion and Golf Club founder. A quiet lad who kept himself to himself, obviously. Marie told me that the family once had a house at the far end of the town, where the borders of Laois, Offaly and Westmeath meet by the river. I fancied a bit of a session but there wasn't music on anywhere – Portarlington isn't really a music town. Back at the hotel I flicked through the channels on the TV trying to block out my thoughts for a while.

I phoned Annie's dad. He told me to check out Roche's pub, where some of his old cronies might still be hanging out. I went from one end of the town to the other. There were quite a few pubs, but no Roche's. I asked a few people. No-one seemed to have heard of it. One lad suggested I investigate Paddy Finlay's bar. 'That's where all the old fellahs drink nowadays,' he said.

The average age in Paddy Finlay's bar was about sixty-seven, but went down to sixty-three when I entered. I asked the barman about Roche's and he checked with the landlord, a big shuffling man in his seventies. 'Ah it's not been there for fourteen years. There's an electrical shop there now.' A few of them laughed. 'Your guidebook must be a bit out of date there.' I got a Guinness and sat down in a corner, slightly away from the action.

A drunken greyhair was holding court in a rich west-of-Ireland accent, talking about his 'ranch' and his beloved animals.

'It's Southfork, sure it is. I'm a half a millionaire you know.'

'Better get back to your animals then, John, watch your investment,' said the barman.

'Ah, no, I think I'll have another brandy.'

'I think you won't there.'

'Ah, now.'

'Now yourself, John.'

'What is this when a man can't get a drink?'

'You've had a drink all right there, John. More than one in fact.'

Old John slumped back in his chair and went quiet for a while. A couple of blokes in their thirties at the bar (now you see why the average age is so young) were talking about hurling and discussing which was the best team.

'Up the banner. Come on the banner. Clare forever!' shouted John.

'Now tell me, are they both on the same day, these games?' asked one of the thirtysomethings, a flat-nosed fellow.

'No they're not, there's one on each Sunday.'

'No,' said John, 'they are both on the same Sunday. And Clare will be the best. The banner county,' he shouted, 'bann ner coun teeeee! We were the first to fly the tricolour, in 1914. It was Eamon De Valera, the Clare man. Clare, the rebel county. The first county.' He then sang a song in a rich baritone, 'The Rose of Clare'.

The others smiled and enjoyed the song. 'What's the history of the Irish flag, then, John?' asked the barman.

Silence. They all looked at each other with quizzical expressions.

'I think the white is supposed to represent peace,' said the flat-nosed guy at the bar. 'And the green must be Ireland.'

'Why is there orange in the flag then?'

Silence again. I presumed it was because of Protestantism, United Irishmen and all that, but didn't say anything, just let them go on about Jaffa Cakes, vitamin C tablets, red lemonade, carrots and that mobile phone company.

Old Paddy the landlord shuffled over and sat next to me for a couple of minutes asking how I was. He was obviously a little bit curious as to why a 'youngster' like me, and an Australian to boot, had come into his pub. I told him I was English. Then John piped up again. 'The banner county. Home of poets, musicians and freedom fighters. 1914 it was. Did ye ever hear the banner roar?'

They tried to calm him down. He asked one more time for a brandy then headed off into the night.

The next morning I went down to Matthews' coffee shop. Annie's dad had mentioned the Matthews brothers on the phone the night before. Ronnie Matthews, an energetic guy in his sixties, was the local historian (there were a few books in the window). He got out a pile of old stuff, photocopies of newspapers and public records. He scanned through them, but there was nothing on the family. He sent his regards and gave me a local book to pass on.

'Go to Sean McCabe, the barber,' he said as I was leaving. 'He's the real local historian around here.'

A hundred yards or so back up the main street was Sean McCabe's little shop, with a tri-colour in the window. Inside Sean was cutting a little boy's hair and an old bloke was sitting on a stool waiting.

'Hi,' I said, 'I don't want a haircut, but . . .'

'Well you're no good to me then, are ye?' smiled Sean and the old man laughed wheezily. 'Aye, ye two've got off on the wrong footing already.'

'I'm allergic to barbers usually,' I said.

'I can see that,' said Sean, looking at my tangled mop.

'I just wanted to ask you some questions.' I told him about what I was up to. Sean put down his scissors and comb and took me out into the street, leaving the boy there staring at himself in the mirror.

Out in the street Sean, a striking looking man with a promi-nent brown moustache, sniffed the air. 'I think,' he said, 'you may need to go out of town to find what you're looking for.' As we stood there two old men walked into his shop then walked out again. Sean grabbed my arm and led me back down the street. He saw someone in a car and said hello how's it goin'? Had they heard of this family? Wasn't there still one around here somewhere? The hardware store, said the man. I felt like a fifteen-year-old doing my local history project again. After making enquiries in the shop I walked through to the back and there was a fellow called George, standing behind a counter, a quiet-looking man in his early sixties with dark slicked-back hair. I chatted to him for a while. He knew some of the family but was from a slightly different branch. He drew me a map of how to get to the old family home, a big house out in the country which had been sold while Annie's dad was away flying bombers for the RAF during World War Two. In the street again there was a buzz. People were looking at me as though they had heard something was going on and it must be exciting. Ronnie Matthews appeared in front of me from nowhere and pointed back up the street. He told me to go to a house where the widow of the author of a book on the golf club lived, who had a photo of some of the family. He thrust another paperback local history book into my hand. We shook hands and smiled. 'Cut!' said the director, and that was the end of the show. Standing there in the grey and unmagical main street, with its practical shops and mums pushing prams, shoppers bustling about, friendly people waving at me, already *knowing* who I was, for God's sake, after me having been there only twenty-four hours, I felt that Portarlington was a little bit too much like my old intimate home town for my liking. Within an hour and a half I was on the move again.

The Search for the Celts

Trim, Tara and Newgrange, County Meath

The Celts are back. No longer content to be the put-upon people of Europe, they have started to push back into their traditional habitats of mainland Britain and the Continent, brandishing their *diddly-aye* music and their Gaia Appreciation workshops.

What is it about them? Why are the Celts and their myths so enduring? This thought occurred to me in the bookshop at the foot of the Hill of Tara in County Meath. Tara is nearly five thousand years old and was at one time the most important archaeological site in the country – the seat of the High Kings of Ireland[1] who for a hundred years ruled over all the tribes in the country. In this bookshop (which is about 4,980 years less old than the mounds of Tara) I saw a fellow with long blond hair and a droopy moustache with Celtic-style tattoos all over his arms, walking proudly but slowly through the shop, looking like a 3-D Asterix burned out on drugs and alcohol and about to enrol himself in the Betty Ford clinic. He had a girlfriend waiting outside who looked exactly the

[1]As opposed to the Small Kings who probably lived squeezed in next to the musicians in O'Donahue's on Baggot Street in Dublin and made extra cash as jockeys in their spare time when they weren't 'Kinging'. (Note – Jockeys are hard workers, most of them merely low-paid serfs in a big money business. They are to be applauded for their dedication to the sport, their fitness, their grace and good manners, their judicious use of the whip and their high-pitched voices.)

same except for the droopy moustache – hers wasn't quite as big. I heard him ask the girl behind the counter for something – a cup of tea, possibly, a plastic 'I Love Ireland' fish (or perhaps W. B. Yeats's *Golden Dawn Potato Cookbook*). He sounded as though he was from Holland or Belgium and it occurred to me that you never see people – especially people from Antwerp or Utrecht – styling themselves on other cultures from two thousand years ago such as Roman warriors, Greek philosophers or Carthaginian fish sellers.

The Celtic look isn't hard to put together. It's partly early-period Freddy Mercury, part Teutonic biker chic, with a bit of ZZ Top and a soupçon of Julian Cope. The problem is having the balls to be seen in public. At music festivals in England, however, the Celts are now everywhere. And they're called Jeremy, Polly, Elizabeth and Miles rather than Caractacus, Boadicea or Setanta. They wear swirly-patterned tattoos around their upper arms, perhaps only for the weekend, with little waistcoats over bare torsos. The really original and stylish ones (usually the Jeremys) sport those hilarious multicoloured tricorn jester hats. They keep their magic hounds close by their side, attached to bits of Celtic string. The healing field at places like Glastonbury is a breeding ground for the new Celticity, with natural remedies and mild psychotherapies based on pagan religions and Druidic beliefs (though with the human sacrifice taken out).

What is it about the Celts that is so bloody attractive? Why are we all so fascinated with this bunch of brawlers and pissheads? Perhaps it is to do with the fact that, unlike the Romans, Greeks or Egyptians, they rather cleverly left no written record of their existence. What we do know is that they liked pretty swirly patterns, had long hair, made beautiful jewellery, were good at fighting each other but crap at fighting Romans and liked a drink and a sing-song. They left behind weapons, pots, countless forts and burial mounds and, of course, enough jewellery to stock every stall in Camden Lock market for the next twenty years.[2]

The Celts, who once inhabited most of northern and central Europe, were gradually pushed west, first by the Romans, Angles and Saxons, into Wales and Cornwall, then into Ireland by the Normans and English and finally the Scandinavian backpackers. Celtic genes live on in various parts of Ireland – jovial dark-haired men with long lashes and grand and impressive beer guts and beautiful otherworldly women, with cascading red or black hair and slightly slanty eyes occasionally show their faces and everybody is spellbound and wants to have their babies. Strangely, no-one fancies the preening idiots with blond quiffs and vaselined chests who do long stints at the Hammersmith Apollo in musicals like *Fiddledance* and *Lord of the Blarney*. There's just no accounting for taste.

You'd think that in Ireland searching for the Celts would be easy. But like the Celtic general in Britain who, on looking at the invading Roman army, declared, 'Wahay lads, what a piece of piss,' you'd be wrong. One place to look is the cosy, rolling farmland of Meath. It certainly didn't seem very mystic or Celticky. In fact it reminded me of nothing else than my home county of Lincolnshire. (A huge area of flatlands, with the odd hill – full of farmers, village halls, Trade organisations, Tory voters and a large and popular selection of football-playing lotharios.) Meath seemed to be full of prosperous little towns that all had a couple of hardware shops, old-fashioned men's outfitters, a Berni-style steak restaurant, and a well-fed, content-looking populace.

Anyone who's read the Irish Myths and Legends properly will know that you can't look for Celts in a car. Celts don't

---

[2]This changes constantly, like the amount of fossil fuels that mankind has left to burn. In ten years time, when proposed increases in the number of Celtic style artists and jewellers are taken into account, we could be looking at a European Celtic artefacts surplus leading well into the twenty-second century.

like cars and will try to avoid them. So I found a B&B at the edge of a little town called Trim, the site of one of the biggest Norman castles in the country, and set out on foot. Trim is aptly named, with a couple of hardware shops, an old-fashioned men's' outfitters, a Berni-style steak restaurant, and a well-fed, content-looking populace. It didn't feel like the heartland of Celtic lore. On the search for bands of low-lying Celts, I felt that I was more likely to run into a Young Farmers' tractor-pulling display team.

I eventually found some interesting Celtic artefacts, on the wall of a little backstreet pub where I'd stopped to have a pint of Guinness. They were mostly photos of famous Celtic warriors. One of them looked particularly like Mel Gibson in the film *Braveheart*. Coincidentally, many of the battle scenes from *Braveheart* were filmed at Trim Castle, giving employment to crowds of locals. A talk with the landlord confirmed my suspicions that there were Celts everywhere. Unlike other, more commercial parts of the country, where Celts might wear their hair long and wear swirly jewellery and sell 'mystic' art in their cute little craft shops, just so you know where they're coming from, man, the Eastern Celts in Meath sport crew cuts and the football shirts of English Premier

League clubs. Manchester United and Liverpool mostly, with the odd Arsenal and Aston Villa thrown in. Their myths were many and powerful, with much talk of Ryan Giggs and Paul McGrath. Rather than asking you to get in touch with your inner being they ask you to get in touch with someone you might know who can get World Cup tickets. The younger inhabitants wear the green and yellow of the Gaelic football team. It was the barman who suggested a bike ride out to Tara.

The search continued by bike, first along the main road past ruined abbeys and castles, then off onto smaller lanes with high hedgerows, circling birds, neat houses and huge stud farms. I saw none of the little brown tourist trail signs that I'd become used to in other parts of the country. I didn't even know if it was the right direction. Then I received a sign. A mad dog bolted out from a driveway – as they do in many parts of Ireland – and proceeded to attack my wheels. I gave it a couple of kicks, then was forced to take a sharp right turn, away from the little group of houses. A couple of miles further down this road I came to a village with a little building in front of a green. The Tara and District Credit Union Ltd. I was getting closer. I could literally feel the ancient aura.

And then suddenly there was another sign. A brown tourist one with 'Tara' written on it. A further two miles and Tara suddenly loomed up to the left. I parked the bike outside the gift shop and walked up to the deconsecrated church, where I was treated to a nice low-tech audio-visual show with Celtic, swirly, Clannad-type music and slides with quaint illustrated reconstructions of the era, and a voice-over that sounded like the big-chinned guy who does the Barrett Homes adverts (you know, where he steps off a helicopter and takes off his helmet). The only other people there were a couple from the North of Ireland with their bored son and three Japanese tourists.

Outside on the hill I got more of an idea of Tara's power –

you could see for miles in every direction. It then started to piss it down with rain. Out of the downpour I saw a group of mysterious-looking figures coming towards me from one of the mounds. It was the Japanese tourists, trying to get their camera to work in the rain.

Next day I went to Newgrange. It was a totally different experience, completely and professionally organised with little buses to take tourists to the three main sites of New-grange, Knowth and Dowth. I ended up only being able to get into the latter. Inside was a museum with all kinds of recre-ations of the past. It reminded me somewhat of Celtworld, the failed entertainments complex (with lots of technology, holograms and virtual reality mysticism) which was erected in another part of Ireland, the tacky amusement park of Tramore, County Waterford, in the very un-Celtic sunny south-east.

If I was a mad un-eco-friendly entrepreneur with no sense of decorum, I'd have built Celtworld on the hills around Tara, amidst the gleaming detached bungalows. I'd have nicked standing stones from various circles and dolmens, Christy Moore would be piped through every room, there'd be electronically controlled moving Our Lady figurines buzzing about the place, perhaps a moving statue rifle range, a tacky jewellery shop, a 'fight the warrior and win a tenner' booth and, of course, the biggest bar in Europe. It would be run by that blond lad from *Diddleydance* and a couple of public-school hippies from Glasto. If only the Celts had had some kind of instantly recognisable foodstuff that could be re-created as a fast-food product. If they went for people's stomachs, rather than their sentimentality, or love of swirly jewellery, or their insistence on having wild orange hair, then they'd really be back in business.

THE CELTS WERE TOUGH

Dunphy v. Charlton: the Celtic/Anglo-Saxon Dichotomy as Played Out by Me and My Friend, Kev

Football

At Cork Airport there's a statue of Big Jack Charlton in the arrival lounge. But he's not holding a football or shouting at some Cockney bloke with an Irish grandmother. He's fishing. It's a very pastoral, overly romantic view of such an arch pragmatist. Can you imagine Bill Shankley having a hobby and it being turned into a statue? Then again, I can't imagine a statue of Alf Ramsey beckoning travellers at Gatwick airport. Charlton created something permanent in Irish culture and increased national self-esteem. Grown men and their kids were walking up to the sculpture and touching it as if it was a holy statue. So did I.

George Best, Johnny Giles, Derek Dougan, Danny Blanchflower. When I was a child I knew they were all Irish and that was that. I wasn't quite aware that some of them played for Northern Ireland so were actually UK citizens and not real Irishmen. They sounded Irish to me. They looked Irish, too – particularly the exotic Best. They were mostly little niggly dark-haired blokes who'd nutmeg you (Best) or nut you (Giles) given the opportunity.

In the mid to late seventies I became aware that 'Eire' was actually a different country. This was confusing because in rugby Ireland played as one team. It seemed stupid to me that the likes of Best and Dougan couldn't play in the same side as Giles or Don Givens. 'Eire' or ear-ruh sounded slightly mysterious and very non Anglo, which I didn't understand, as of course Irish people just spoke English with a funny accent.

Next in line in my Irish (and footballing) education was Tom Coleman. He had the look of a slightly smaller version of the actor Harry Dean Stanton. Tom was the manager of Rasen Wanderers under-15 team. His son Kev – one of my best mates – was the left back and I made it to the right back slot. Some of the other dads were involved, in a coaching, bus driving, shouting, nagging or general hanging-on capacity. My dad wasn't involved. Being a rugby man, he couldn't quite get out of his system the feeling, although he knew it wasn't true, that football was for girls. But Tom was the driving force behind the team. He was good-humoured and enthusiastic and – this was why I liked him so much – he *did* suffer fools gladly, so as well as me there were a few other bits of driftwood and old rubbish lying about in various positions in the team.

And Tom didn't burden our grasshopper minds with anything as sophisticated as tactics. I remember one cup final, when we were by far the inferior team but thanks to our dogged spirit we went in at half time only 1–0 down, Tom said to us in the changing room – and these were his very words, spoken in his soft Galway accent – 'Knock it up field and run after it, lads.' It was a great speech and we went out there and, of course, got thrashed. But this team talk struck a chord with me.

Whereas Kev – with his mercurial Celtic genes working overtime (his mum was Scottish), would dribble and pass and shout at team mates, ref and opposition, I would diligently run alongside the opposing winger and attempt to trip him up before he got to the byeline. A contrast of styles. I didn't mess about with fancy stuff like Kev. Kev might weave his way past two or three of the opposition before getting rid of the ball; for me – if I made the tackle – it was either a hoof into touch or a hoof up to one of our forwards, in the true English style. So Tom's battle cry to knock it upfield and run after it was, in a sense, down to his complete understanding that he had to make the best of the very raw materials at his disposal.

A few years later, the dichotomy between weave-dribble-pass and 'knock it upfield and run after it' became a big issue in Irish football when Jack Charlton was given the job of managing the national team. Charlton's philosophy of management was like his playing style – tough, simple and uncompromising. It soon became clear that he was creating a team that would block out space for the opposition with the forwards pressing the opposing defenders then knocking long balls into space behind them; getting the ball into the danger zone as quickly as possible. It was football the way I had always played it. Jack was a 'Tim' through and through. This didn't go down well in some quarters, being seen as a betrayal of the Celtic virtues of skill and wizardry. The writer and broadcaster (and former Irish international footballer) Eamon Dunphy was the champion of the 'Kev' faction. He believed Charlton's style was evil. Players like Liam Brady and Ronnie Whelan were not going to be used to their full potential because of Jack's obsession with long balls.

I always liked the conflict between Charlton and Dunphy, which, simply put, seemed to be based on the difference between Celtic wizardry (Kev-ism) and Anglo-Saxon pragmatism (Tim-ism). It was ever thus in sports involving teams from the British Isles. The two men were both strong-willed and incredibly sensitive.

Jack took over a team that had always underachieved and made it overachieve. I think they were at their peak at the 1988 European Championships – most Irish fans would admit that in Tim mode they were lucky to beat England but as Kevs they should have drawn against Holland (they lost 1–0) and beaten the USSR (1–1 draw). But the finest matches were both against Italy in the World Cup. In 1990, after some pretty turgid Tim-ist displays that saw them draw their group games and beat Romania on penalties (the winner scored by David O'Leary – a Kev who looked like he should be a Tim) they played a great Kev passing game in the quarter finals against the Italians and were unfortunate not to get a break. Four years later they met Italy again in the first round and a goal from Ray Houghton separated the teams (both Tims by that stage).

I watched the 1988 game in the flat I shared with my old friends Plendy and Ruey and when Ray Houghton's goal went in they started to dance around doing jigs of joy. They both had Scottish parents, and although born and brought up in England, it was as if it had only just occurred to them they weren't actually English. I became highly sniffy and indignant at this slight. I can understand you supporting Scotland, you bastards, I said, but why Ireland?

Their response was simple and intellectually rigorous. 'Ha ha ha haaaaaa. Ha ha haaaa. Haaaaaaaaaaa!' they sang and jumped up again to dance around the room, while pointing at me. I started getting all pseudo-logical on them. Why should Scots do this? I had always supported the Plucky Nations – Ireland and Scotland – if England weren't playing.

But of course, nationality can be defined sometimes by what it is not, in this case Englishness.

In the 1990 World Cup the 'olé olé' brigade of Irish support (it became a sort of moronic chant whenever Ireland played) had reached its zenith. I went to follow Scotland that tournament with my Anglo-Scottish flatmates and felt jealous that the Irish and Scots could celebrate their national pride without guilt. Again I was on the outside looking in.

In '94 Ireland did quite well in the World Cup again but it was the end of the road. People were so used to great success that they became bored when there wasn't a hysterical aspect to the games. The 'olé olé' bandwagon was largely becoming discredited by then – even some of the players were keen to distance themselves from it. It wasn't so much about football as about national pride. It was the same for Michelle Smith in swimming (though she was dropped like a hot potato after the doping scandal) or Sonia O'Sullivan in athletics.

One rather cuddly aspect of sport in Ireland is that Irish people call their sports stars by their first names, Michelle, Sonia, Mick (McCarthy), Jack, Paul (McGrath), Dennis (Irwin), Roy (Keane). It's like a village football team. Everyone knows everyone, or so the myth goes.

Ireland didn't qualify for Euro '96, the 1998 World Cup or Euro 2000. I'd been at the Castle Bar in St Stephen's Green as Ireland were on the verge of going out to Belgium in a play-off match. Even though there was still time for them to save the game, the people in the pub seemed to sense that luck had run out for the team. Where once punters would have screamed at the TV and shouted 'olé olé' mindlessly in Dalek-like voices for all they were worth, now they idly chatted. Perhaps they were bored with football now. When the final whistle went and Ireland were out, the atmosphere didn't seem to change remarkably. If this was England there would be the possibility of a riot. Maybe my sneaking

suspicion was correct – that the Irish weren't really into football so much as wanting an excuse to be patriotic and have
a laugh. All along perhaps they just wanted to see how far the
joke would go.

But then the success of their under-16 and under-18
teams, in the European and World Championships respec-
tively, led to another upsurge of football fever. I pointed out
to quite a few people that in England no-one would give a
toss if we won those tournaments but they all told me to shut
up and fuck off back to Australia.

Some Ancient Sagas of Magical Creatures

Finbarr, the Lobster of Moral Outrage

And Finn Mac Cool did look on his new bride Ethel and verily his testosterone levels shot through the roof of his ring fort. 'I shall leave thee standing here naked guarded only by my faithful servant Diarmuid while I do go play *gulf.*' For *gulf* was the entertainment of the lords and they did do their business thereof therein, thereof.

And Ethel, off with Diarmuid did run, so Finn did consult his magician who brought in Finbarr the lobster of moral outrage.

'It's outrageous – they should be banned!' said Finbarr. And so they did cook Finbarr and eat him and afterward they were full with the pleasures of moral outrage. 'Something should be done about it!' they all shouted.

Sean, the Dublin Bay Prawn of Neutrality

And so it came to pass that Queen Maeve was called in to settle a dispute between two farmers. One had stolen the other's chickens so he had stolen the first's pigs, so *he* had stolen the second's sheep so he had stolen the first's horse so he had stolen the first's bull so he had stolen the second's wife so he had stolen the first's eldest son so he had stolen the first's house so he had stolen the second's house so he had stolen the rest of the first's stuff so he had stolen the rest of the second's stuff and by the time they had come to Queen Maeve the first had the life and house and family of the second and the second had the life and house and family of the first.

Queen Maeve wanted to be impartial and so she did barbecue Sean the magic Dublin Bay prawn of neutrality. The gift that Sean gave was for the eater to be totally impartial in any matter. And of course after eating Sean, Maeve could not decide who was right and who was wrong.

'I can see it from both sides,' said she, 'and I really don't want to make a decision. Um er um errr.' She did deliberate for days but it was no use. Sean's powers had gripped her in a state of total neutrality.

As it was, the dispute settled itself. The two farmers carried on stealing from each other until they had stolen their old lives and stuff back.

Kevin, the Carp of Storytelling

And long before the legend of the Blarney stone did exist there was in the kingdom of Erin a magic carp called Kevin who had magical powers of storytelling. And the legend was that whosoever should eat this Kevin would for ever be a magical storyteller. And so it came to pass that Finn Mac

Cool did fish the mighty Shannon river one morn and did catch Kevin.

'Hey, did I tell you about that time I was in Rathmines with the girl from Aer Lingus?' said Kevin. And Finn did stand back and say, 'No, I haven't heard that story.'

'Yeah, well, her fellah was this guy from the Northside up off near the station, the main one, yeah and blah blahblah etc. etc.,' so Finn Mac Cool did kill Kevin and eat him and after that he was never the same man.

For the next day he did lead his troops into battle and he was talking non-stop. 'Hey, did I tell you about that time I was in a battle with the Fir Bolgs and I got off with that Fir Bolg chick?' and his warriors got mighty bored and did feck off and Finn was left alone talking to himself.

SHANEWORLD

West

SHANEWORLD

Lost Highway – A Clever Use of the Film Title to Describe the Little Roads around Cork City

County Cork

Cork has long been my favourite Irish city. It's got the bustle, noise and pollution of Dublin without the shiny suits, mobile phones, rowdy vomit-caked English tourists and crazy house prices. There's something of the grand old European metropolis about it, the 'seen-better-days' feel of Georgian houses with peeling paint on winding lanes, particularly looking up at Richmond Hill and the church at Shandon, then at the split river which brings to mind the nickname 'Venice of the N25'. There are little streets with craft shops and rickety old men's boozers, two breweries (Murphy's and Beamish have their headquarters here), some fine little restaurants tucked away and a small but lovely art gallery. There's a film festival, a folk festival and a jazz festival every year. Sometimes I wonder why I don't live in Cork.

It is a bugger to drive in, though. I had already checked where the garages were, so drove around to them, but no-one seemed to be interested. I couldn't even get a price out of some of them – one bloke had a good look at the Singing Leprechaun sitting there in the front grinning, as if to say, 'What's he got to smile about?' Then he said he wasn't interested. I got tired of this so I parked the car by the river. I had arranged to meet some friends, Theresa and Molly, on the corner of Brian Boru Street about half an hour later so made some phone calls to more garages. It was the same old story. 'Yeah aid bay interested shar but ye'd have te bring it in now an ay caerrn't say ai'd gev ye mare dan tree grand.' Another said no outright and I gave up, and sat down and did a sketch of the river. Theresa and Molly arrived and we chatted about this and that, then I drove them back to their house in a little village out past Blarney, to the north-west of the city.

At the house we had some food, Molly went to bed, then Theresa and I sat up until about four in the morning going through several bottles of red wine, me blathering about the car – 'Yeah, well, it looks like a girl's car, I'll grant you that, but it's got a bit of a kick, yer know . . .'. It was very irresponsible of me because she had her driving test the next day (although she hadn't managed to get hold of a car that was suitably insured for her to drive). I offered her mine but it would have been too complicated to sort out in time. After some more wine and some impassioned poetry reading we hit the sack. Next morning, while I had my second successive hangover, Theresa was in a bad state. There was no way she was going to be able to even pick up car keys, never mind drive. She glumly told me that she wouldn't get a test through now for several months. I felt terrible. They waved me off and I headed into a labyrinth of little roads. Theresa had given me directions – something like left, left, right, right, straight on at a tree, left, right at the faery ring, left at the old man on the cart, straight on for two miles, right, left, third turn on your right and you're on the Mallow Road. It didn't take me long to get lost. I'd got a gift from Molly before I left, a little painting she'd done recently. I looked at the mixture of coloured lines and blobs and realised that I had more chance of getting onto a main road by using this as a map.

I've always enjoyed driving in Ireland, getting lost on little country roads like this. I like the feeling of taking it easy. There is a lot of road and still, in comparison with most countries in Europe, not that many cars. It's still a healthy country, the arteries of travel still clear and pumping effectively.[1]

Even some of the main roads have a slow lane, if you just want to check out the scenery (or if you're driving an articulated lorry and there are about two hundred vehicles behind you). Drivers in Ireland can be divided into four different categories: local drivers, old ladies, English tourists and farmers. Farmers[2] on tractors are like pheasants. They'll wait

The tractor/pheasant connection

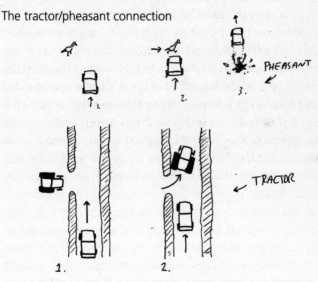

PHEASANT

TRACTOR

1.   2.

---

[1]The amount of cars on the roads has started to increase dramatically in recent years due to the prosperity of 'Celtic stripy big cat' years.

[2]I haven't got a thing against farmers. I'd like to say that some of my best friends are farmers but it wouldn't be true. I know some farmers back in Lincolnshire who are great lads. But there was this posh little prick at school who used to boast that his dad had got a subsidy from the EU to build a gate that they didn't need. He thought this was hilarious. Also, as a kid I was in love with a girl whose dad was a pig farmer.

and wait for a car – sometimes for as much as three or four days. Then when one does come they will shoot out and hog the centre of the road.

If the farmer is just going back to his farm from a field but has been made to wait a long time because there was no car for him to annoy, he will become agitated. When a car does eventually come, he will deliberately drive on to the next major town or tourist destination, calculating that this is where the car will be heading. This won't bother the local driver unduly. He'll simply overtake at 100 mph when he gets to the next dangerous bit of road. He'll do this, moreover, while reading the sports page of the *Irish Independent* and swigging from a can of Harp.

The old lady driver will not be too upset either. After all, the tractor, which will be travelling at its cruising speed of about 15 mph, will be going twice as fast as her own top speed. It is the English tourist who has most to fear from the farmer. For a while he will stay back, chugging along and saying to himself (or any passenger that might be unfortunate enough to be travelling with this driver – unless it's a midget green fabric-based musical toy, in which case it won't care), 'Ha ha! Isn't life grand? The rural vibe! Gives you time to take in the surroundings when you're going slowly. I love driving like this.'

He will want to bond with the farmer, in fact, pointing out to his passengers that he understands country ways and he feels bad about eight hundred years of British persecution, etc. He'll do this sticking his thumb up and grinning a lot in the hope of catching the farmer's eye.

The farmer will look in the wing mirror and think, 'Who is this stupid fecker gurning away behind me? I'd better go even slower and move out into the centre of the road, just in case.'

The English tourist will be able to handle this for a while – for a few hundred miles or so of winding country lanes. Then he'll decide it's time to get tough and decisive – it's time to overtake. He'll weave into the centre of the road but he won't be able to see anything. Then back again. This will go on for ages, with the farmer moving out into the centre of the road, as if in a dance, following the English tourist's movements. Eventually the road will widen and become straight at last, the English tourist will see a massive gap and the road ahead for three or four miles. With a surge of testosterone he'll rev the engine in triumph. Then the farmer will suddenly turn into the nearest field and the English tourist will spend the rest of his life a bitter and twisted alcoholic.

The roads aren't always quite so lovely. One early autumn evening a year or so earlier Theresa had been driving us in her little late-seventies' Ford Escort, on the main road from Cork to her house in driving rain when the car simply gave out. We were stuck in the slow lane with no lights, no warning triangle, no torch, nothing, as large lorries lumbered along the slow lane toward us. We were sitting ducks, so I ended up standing out in the storm about thirty yards along the road using an empty Chinese curry sauce box as a reflector for about forty-five minutes. Each time a lorry came towards me, I started to jump about – eventually they would all veer off at the last moment, like lumbering dinosaurs. Eventually the Mallow AA recovery vehicle – an old guy and his wife in a pick-up truck – arrived and took us back through the pitch black night to Theresa's house. The car has now been put out to grass at a local garage, though apparently there are a few people interested in purchasing her as a runabout, the crazy bastards. According to official figures road deaths per head in Ireland are twice that of Britain. It used to be because of all the rust buckets being driven, though by the time of our breakdown the Irish Government were operating a buy-back policy on old cars – if you bought a new car they'd give you a grand for the old one. Now it's because up to a quarter of all Irish drivers have not passed their tests. As soon as you get a provisional licence you are allowed to drive on your own and, as Theresa found out after our session, it can take an age to actually get a test – there just aren't the resources to get everyone tested quickly. Perhaps some of the money from EU grants that's been pumped into road building and improvement (especially prior to the Tour de France in 1998 – though, obviously, only the roads on the actual route got done up) could be channelled into getting people passed and educated properly for road use. Another theory is that increased prosperity is the main cause behind the high death rate – people are buying bigger and faster cars as life has started to speed up.[3]

But not everywhere. A couple of miles before the Mallow road an old car with a lady driver suddenly appeared in front of me in an example of flagrant plagiarism of the official tractor/pheasant principle. Being an English tourist, I simply put my feet up and said to myself, 'Ha ha! Isn't life grand? The rural vibe! Gives you time to take in the surroundings when you're going slowly. I love driving like this.' Driving alone, you have to get used to talking to yourself sometimes.

[3]'Deaths on Irish Roads' (Snappy title, hey?) – Ronan McGreevy, *Irish Post*, Sept. '98.

Fungie the Dolphin, the Johnsons of Enniskillen, the Talking Dogs and the American Poet

Dingle, Co. Kerry

Like thousands of sentimental saddos before me, I was going to Dingle to see Fungie the dolphin.

I'd stayed the night before in Tralee where, after booking into a hotel, I did three things. I bought a figurine of a pretty lady in blue robes and some nice beads attached to a little cross at an Our Lady Figurine superstore near the main street. I sat in a Chinese restaurant staffed by big, loud, beautiful country girls and ate until I could hardly move – spring rolls, pan fried squid with ginger; broccoli in chilli; a big plate of moist noodles; chicken and black beans; too much rice. And I went to bed early. For the first time since 1977.

In Dingle I decided to do it properly this time. At the little office on the quay, I booked a boat out to see Fungie, but when I turned up a few hours later, alone, with my eagerly desperate 'Dolphin Loving' expression, the weather had turned. Four years earlier my Dad and I had gone in search of the little creature and stood at the quayside for about ten minutes looking out into the bay. He didn't show, so we gave up (we're an impatient family – for instance, we celebrated the Millennium in 1998) and decided to continue our

Seagoing Mammal Search in some of the many pubs in the town. Nobody had seen him, they said, but we did find amazing little bars that looked like someone's front room with only one other person drinking, always a square-headed lad with heavy black eyebrows. My dad impressed everyone with his knowledge of Guinness, before we both fell over.

'It's too choppy,' said the thin Chet Baker lookalike fisherman. 'It'll be much too difficult out there.' I thought of saying, 'Let's do it the hard way,' but suspected it was probably an old joke round these parts. I got my money back anyway and decided to celebrate in Dick Mac's famous pub, on a little side street opposite the church. It's an old-fashioned hardware shop on one side, the other a great little bar with old-fashioned snug. I fought my way into the snug just as a crowd of wealthy and well-fed Eurotourists were vacating it, and sat in there on my own, like an extra from *Ryan's Daughter*. About ten minutes later a good-looking dark-haired family came in and said mind if we join you. Not at all, I said, as they squeezed in on either side of me. I sat quietly as they jabbered away – strangely all the kids, who looked quite alike, had different accents. The lad, in his thirties, sounded as though he came from the north, as did the short-haired girl with him (his wife or girlfriend); the very pretty young one with a mass of black curls sounded like a Dub, and the other daughter, an attractive New-Ageish lass, had a strange Anglo-Dublin-Ulster hybrid. The two parents, him beardedly benign, her strong-boned and handsome, both sounded northern English. Eventually curiosity and impatience got the better of me and I had to ask about their entire family history. They were the Johnsons from Enniskillen. Mum and Dad were from York and had moved over in the sixties for a better standard of living. They saw my raised eyebrows. The North, they said, was a wonderful place to live. The kids had lived all over since, hence the accents. We all chattered and talked shite for a while. They'd seen me doodling and making notes when they came in and the father now mentioned it and asked if I was writing a book or something. I lied and said no, not wanting to ruin the funny and spontaneous nature of our conversations. He told me they knew of a writer, Carlo Gebler, who'd done a book on the North called *The Glass Curtain*. I'd never heard of it but agreed to check it out.[1]

The Johnsons of Enniskillen had come to Dingle for the same reason as me, to see the dolphin. The difference was that they had organised it properly and were going swimming with all the gear, to give it hugs and ask it questions about world peace and the meaning of life, that kind of thing. Why don't you come out with us, they said? It'll be great. I don't think so, I said. Ah, go on. They told me where they would be meeting, very early the next morning. Then it was time to be kicked out of the pub.

The next day I woke up and thought of hooking up with the Johnsons of Enniskillen. The idea of frolicking with the dolphin (as well as the pretty youngest Johnson from Enniskillen in a skintight diving suit) was certainly attractive and would no doubt be extremely therapeutic. But not as attractive and therapeutic as going back to sleep again for a few hours. It was raining anyway.

Later on in the day I got talking in the kitchen to a skinny Scandinavian woman called Carem (or something like that) who was also staying in the hostel. I told her I was going out for a walk and she asked would I mind if she came along, because her friends were drinking in a pub and she didn't know Dingle that well. We went out of town past the craft

[1] I found it a few months later in the Travel Bookshop off Portobello Road, but haven't got round to reading it yet.

village then got down off the road and followed the shore-line. As we went around a little headland, two dogs suddenly appeared and ran alongside us. One was a proud, sleek, black labrador, the other a stumbling, hairy, dirty little mutt. They had decided to adopt us so we gave them names and personalities. I thought the labrador was called Rex, a Trinity college graduate and antiques dealer. Carem said that the other dog was Shaggy, a part-time poet. Perhaps, I said, he was thrown out of University College Dublin in his second year. Probably, she said. The rain started to come in from Dingle Bay, blurring away the hills in the background. Rex and Shaggy bounced along over the pebbles in front of us and we talked away to them, waiting occasionally while they jumped up the grassy dunes to the back of the thin beach, to check out and bark at the slow feeding cattle.

Rex & Shaggy

Rex: Woof woof.
Shaggy: Rufff. Rufff.
Rex: *Aha, gentle reader, ahah. Travels in Irishry. That sounds promising – it suggests that nationhood could be a state of mind. But the phrase seems to me typical of much that is in this book. It sounds good but it's shallow and meaningless. Basically he could've just sat on his arse and made it all up.*

Shaggy: *Ah, give him a break. He's really a cartoonist, you know. There's loads of nice little drawings in the text.*

Rex: *You see, he admits he's not really a writer. It would be absurd for people to buy this book. But I understand the publisher's theory behind it. And it's quite audacious. Basically his name is Bradford so it's quite likely that he's going to find his stuff right next to Bill Bryson . . .*

Shaggy: *Who's Bill Bryson?*

Rex: *Shut up. Poor unsuspecting grannies, maiden aunts and kindly pipe-smoking uncles who don't understand rap music or the Internet will enter the shop hoping to buy the latest gagfest by the corpulent and successful American writer and by mistake will end up purchasing this bizarre tome.*

Shaggy: *Ha ha, look, though, it's got a cartoon of us in it.*

Rex: *Has it? Oh yes, ha ha.*

Carem and I walked in virtual silence, apart from the odd aside when we'd comment on the action in a 'dog voice' and have the dogs making up names for us. We got a bit soaked. Carem said she had to get back because she and her friends were heading off later that day.

Rex: *This formal messing – I hate it when people try and do that Joyce thing and be stylistically wacky.*

Shaggy: *Have you ever read Joyce? It seems to me that a lot of people bang on about him but as soon as you ask them what they've read they go all quiet.*

Rex: *Er, um, I saw the film of* Ulysses *starring George Peppard.*

Shaggy: *That was Jack Kerouac's* The Subterraneans. *Funnily enough although a lot of Kerouac's stuff is about travel, did you know that he never actually drove a car himself?*

Rex: *Look – some more cows to bother!*

Shaggy: *Rufff. Rufff.*

Rex: *Woof woof.*

We headed back, as the rain battered down harder. As we got to a little row of houses on the headland a woman's voice called out 'Sheba! Jenny!' The dogs started barking again.

Rex: Woof woof woof.
Shaggy: Ruff. Rufff.

They ran towards a house and across the lawn. Then stopped and looked back at us.

Sheba: Woof.
Jenny: Ruff. Ruff.

It felt a bit sad. The end of the little afternoon world we had created. How about, I said, if Sheba is a belly dancer from North London and Jenny teaches post-feminist linguistics at the University of East Anglia in Norwich? Carem was too cold and wet to join in. Back in Dingle, I intended to check out the Internet café and pick up some e-mail, so we said our goodbyes outside the hostel. I noticed a little red mark above her eye. On closer inspection, the mark was moving. I realised Shaggy/Jenny had given Carem a present. A blood-sucking little tic had lodged itself on her eyelid. An interesting fashion accessory, I thought. She didn't agree.

At the 'net café I searched on a Dingle-based site to see if there was anything of interest going on. There was a crystal workshop coming up, and a Check Your Allergies session at one of the health food shops, or a poetry workshop with the Irish-American poet Michael Donaghy. Unfortunately it wasn't on for another few weeks.

Back in London in 1994 I had actually taken a poetry class with Michael Donaghy, somewhere around squawky, acquisitive Sloane Square. The class was the expected mixture of sensitive young men, fragile middle-class housewives, people just out of therapy, people just in therapy, a dour Scottish person and an African lad. I had never really studied much poetry, either at school or university. If you do a yoga or fitness or painting or sculpture class you'll be taught by someone who knows the ropes, all right, but that's about it. But Donaghy was a real poet, having won the esteemed Whitbread poetry prize and the Geoffrey Faber memorial prize for *Shibboleth*, his first volume of poems. What was he doing teaching a bunch of deadheads and no-hopers like us? He mixed a certain punky gravitas with Irish-boyish enthusiasm and soon I was dipping in and out of poetry anthologies and finding poets that I actually liked – Patrick Kavanagh, Tom Paulin, Don Paterson. I finally managed to track down one of Donaghy's books, *Errata*, his second collection, a mixture of anecdote, Irish music and the classics set in New York and Chicago.

At that time – as ever – I had *too much* time on my hands and one of my ongoing 'projects' was an imaginary Pogues-like punk-folk band of which I was the Shane MacGowan-like figurehead – leader, songwriter, singer, charismatic front man. It's good fun when there's no-one else there to burst your bubble. I named this fictional combo Malignant Flanagan, after a line from one of Donaghy's poems, 'The Classics'.

I have still to get my head around Irish Americana. In 1990 I stayed in Boston for four days and didn't meet one person who claimed to be an American. This might have had something to do with the fact that I stayed in a house with four Irishwomen. I'd worked with one of them for a few months at the *Financial Times* and we left at the same time. She to take a job as a nurse in Boston and me to just piss away all my savings in a three-month-long round-Europe trip. I took her number, as I often do when I leave somewhere and expect that, as I often do, I will never see someone again.

But I made the effort, thanks in part to a bloke called Charlie, a friend of a friend who gave me a free first class ticket on Air India to Kennedy Airport. Admittedly I wasn't his first choice of travelling companion but all the sensible people he knew were in gainful employment. I was, like an actor, resting between jobs (in fact I was still recovering from the three-month European booze fest). In Brookline it was trams, Irish pubs, spritzer and Guinness, darts, more Guinness. I met a bloke whose grandfather had come over in the 1930s and he had an outrageous Irish accent, seemed to be saying all the begorrahs and bejaysus stuff like a Hollywood version of Irishness. On the last night, at a St Patrick's day concert it was like Kilburn, tears and singsongs. Is it in the genes, this deep nationality, I thought?

'You've had an hour,' said the speccy Internet Bloke. 'Do you want more time? It's just that there's other people waiting.'

I picked up various bits of mail then headed out into the real world of rain and hangovers again. I had a quietish time that night at a little session, then walked slowly back to the hostel, past the harbour where *Ryan's Daughter* had been filmed. The clouds had cleared and the spray of stars made the sky seem more white than black. I recalled one of Donaghy's poems, 'O'Ryan's Belt', and also picked out what I thought was Mars. Tomorrow would be real night skies, real music, real Irish Americans searching for their roots. Tomorrow was Doolin.

Is Irish Music Any Good?

Doolin, Co. Clare

Scattered across the bleak hills of west Clare, Doolin is not your picturebook west-coast Irish village (unless the book in question is *Places Which, From a Distance, Look Like Someone Has Kicked a Pile of Empty Milk Cartons Across the Scenery*). Modern bungalows, with isolated sections of ranch-style fencing attached to unfinished Mediterranean porticoes, are constantly bursting out of the natural landscape, eager to join with other equally disastrous results of easy planning laws on the other side of the valley. Where do the people get their inspiration from? If Texas Homecare moved to Doolin and really lived up to their name – i.e. served up DIY kits of ranches – they would clean up.

Built on a series of small hills around a little valley (the River Aille runs through the village), Doolin has a round tower at one end and the ruined keep of a Norman castle at the other. You could sling a rope between the two and do tightrope walks for charity ('Hey, Sean, I can see your house from here,' etc.). If you can get out of the idea that an attractive village should be based on the twee English model – church, thatched cottages, village green, androgynous vicar on bicycle – you'll enjoy Doolin. And even if, a few hundred years ago, the people in this area had actually had the money to build decent houses, we – that's the British, us, the bad guys – would probably have burned them down anyway just for the hell of it.

But apart from what it actually looks like, it's quite an attractive place. Doolin itself, or Fisherstreet as part of it is sometimes referred to by pedantic locals with red ears and long sideburns (you know who you are), is basically just a main street, with a pub at each end and a pub in the middle. It's the scene of one of the world's greatest pub walks. Start at O'Connor's at the south of the village near the harbour. Turn left and walk past the tourist shops and over the little bridge, then follow the road as it straightens out towards the north. Walk for a mile. Stop at McGann's. Have a pint. Then exit the pub and carry on walking north for about fifty yards until you reach McDermott's. Buy another pint and sit down. Wonderful.

There isn't enough space here to detail the pub politics amongst the locals, but if I briefly mention that so-and-so fell out with whatsisname so they can't go in that pub because the sister had been dumped by the son of the landlord whose brother went out with the cousin of my sister's friend's great grandmother in 1883, you'll get the idea. But the result is that most of them only frequent one boozer at any one time. And this will change over the years as some imagined slight forces them into the arms (and pints) of their former enemies. There's also a post office/general store, a chip shop (which does excellent curry sauce for the discerning post-beer palate), a couple of restaurants, a few B&Bs and a hostel. On the outskirts of the village is the ubiquitous art and craft shop ('Experience the west of Ireland by buying one of our chunky woollen sweaters which will make you look like an over-weight university lecturer. Guaranteed.').

Although Doolin is rather unprepossessing at first, it *is* in the west. And the west is where they all head: middle-aged Italians with impeccably casual clothes, expensive sun-glasses and beautiful children. Pony-tailed German youths in assertive glasses and Bob Marley T-shirts. Scandinavians in dungarees who sit in the musicians' seats and make a shared glass of Guinness last about four hours. English crusties searching for the Mother Goddess and cheaper beer and a new lead for their dog ('SIT, Uther Pendragon!'). They are all looking for something. *We* are all looking for something. What?

It's because the west of Ireland is a mystical, mythical place. Since ancient times, people have looked in that direction for magic sanctuaries. Think of Tír na nÓg, Camelot, Swansea. But unlike many quasi-spiritual, isolated ancient sites, Doolin has no surface mystery. It's not covered in stone circles. No legendary battle took place here. No hero came here to die. Even statues of Our Lady refrain from crying blood or going walkabout in Doolin's main street. But there's the possibility that here the landscape and the people might still be connected in some way to the strange spirituality of the old Celtic legends – such as the hamster of Nachal and Shami Slammer, the Goldfish of Clever Things. At least that's what some of the more hopeful New Age tourists have been led to believe. And if you were a local and clever you'd nod sagely and keep on selling them the nice swirly pendants, pots and pictures.

Doolin apparently lies on a convergence of ley lines, which may explain the energy and frisson in the atmosphere. This seems to be the explanation for many old places in Britain and Ireland where there's any sort of life and activity and creativity. It may sound boringly rational, but my rather simple theory is that the remarkable fizz in the air of Doolin is more a result of a surfeit of Poitín (the illegally distilled demon drink), the lack of quality accommodation for discerning ABC1 tourists and, most importantly, the competitive atmosphere in the music scene. Because that's what you'll go to Doolin for – the sessions.

One of the things I love about Ireland, apart from fantastic-looking, passionate, wild-haired women who can drink and arm-wrestle all night then fix your car in the morning, is the poetic, ale-fuelled music. It says to me 'mystic-joy-in-the-utter-melancholy-of life'. It also says 'whack fol de daddio' too, but only when I put on the wrong track. The epiphany of Irish music is that moment when 'A Pair of Brown Eyes' by the Pogues comes on the jukebox at ten to eleven in a smoky North London pub and people stare down at their pints in wistful contemplation (though, to be fair, they're often staring at their pints just so that no-one can accuse them of staring at *their* pint, and thus demand satisfaction 'outside'). And when you're staggering through the subway, past people begging for loose change, expecting to be confronted by the usual Eurobusker singing, 'Lert me tek yoo bah thee 'and an' led yu thro ze strets ov lerndun', and you suddenly hear this beautiful bazouki playing and for some reason you can never understand, you just want to dance like that preening idiot in *Riverdance* (you know, the one with the blond quiff and the vaselined chest who went off in a huff because his name was only fifteen feet high on the posters and he'd categorically stated they had to be fifteen feet and four inches). But it's especially about those times when you are sitting in a pub in Doolin and a little old bloke with a red leathery face gets up and, in a high-pitched, wheezy voice, sings some ancient ballad about sea, existential angst and death (and he looks so rough it seems as though it's the last thing he'll *ever* sing). And you stare into nothingness – that bit just to the left of the bar – and wonder if your life is, perhaps, just a little bit shallow.

I first stayed in Doolin in 1992 (and have been back several times since) and the first place I was directed to was the pub in the centre of the village – McGann's – where I was amazed to have a free run at the bar. This was because everyone else was simply mesmerised by the wonderful solo turns popping up around the small back room. It was all

great music, apart, that is, from the nightmarish Kate-Bush-like trilling of a German goth, which went on for about fifteen verses. She was probably making it up as she went along because she knew that after this disaster she'd never get another chance and the people were too polite to terminate her 'turn'. Still, she seemed happy enough. She was pissed off her face, mind.[1]

As well as our group, half Irish, half cynical English, there were, as usual, a couple of Scandinavians sitting in the musicians' places in the corner of the pub, smiling goofily out at the rest of the clientèle, oblivious to the fact that we were all glaring at them. They were soon ushered out of the way and the sessions began. Guitar, banjo, bodhrán and whistle. We sat silently sipping and listened intently as it wound itself

[1] Although at the time of writing I do not frequent it as much as I used to because of some obscure subclause in the Pub Politics Charter (i.e. some friends of mine have fallen out with the landlord), I still like to start my Doolin stopover in McGann's. It's the quietest of the three pubs, partly due to the fact that the clientèle (German and Scandinavian backpackers) have read their Celtic literature in which it is stated that people must go 'Shhhhhh' like tight-arsed librarians before every piece of music. Ah, those lovable daft blond bastards.

into an energetic (swirly Celtic?) circle of melodies and motifs. Next to me was a strange unshaven fellow drinking mineral water, tapping his foot maniacally. Rumour has it he 'killed his father with a hammer', and had been banned from drinking in the pub after getting too rowdy one night. Rather than go somewhere else and neck ale to his heart's content, he regularly turned up at McGann's and bought only soft drinks. I took the advice of the resting banjo player and ignored him. Though I'm sure it was all bollocks and that he'd had had an affair with the workmate of the sister of the barman's Swedish friend's babysitter . . .

Eventually the pipes, played by a long-haired gypsy-looking guy in dungarees did a solo spot. I thought he looked like a slightly less runty version of 'Come-on-Eileen'-era Kevin Rowland, but the women were mesmerised. He wasn't *that* good looking, really. Meanwhile the fiddle player smiled down at their table full of brimming pints of Guinness. Then all the other musicians came back and the session went into foot-stomping overdrive – purists might call it a reel, I suppose. Or a jig. Sort of thing. Listen to these reels and it all seems so simple. Sixteen-bar motif, repeated, then another sixteen-bar motif, repeated. And it just goes on and on.

I get jealous in these moments. It's then that I wish I could play an instrument properly. But thanks to an accident with a door and a next-door neighbour when I was two, during which I lost the top off my little finger, left hand, I have struggled with the virtuoso passages and scales needed for session work. Many people have pointed out that the great jazz guitarist Django Reinhardt managed with only two fingers on his left hand, and went on to reinvent the genre. This somewhat undermines my position. Funnily enough, my mother's main concern was that I'd never be able to play rugby. She was dead right on that score, to be fair to her.[2]

The thing is, though, is Irish music any good? It's a pleasant enough soundtrack to getting pissed in a whitewashed country pub, but it can sound trite and contrived to the untrained ear. Until my first trip to Ireland in the mid eighties, my experience of this musical form was reduced to two or three key moments. Firstly the Spinners on BBC2 – a crowd of bearded Liverpudlian teachers with woolly jumpers (Hey – the Doolin art and craft shop!) who came on after *Pot Black* on a Sunday evening. We watched the snooker round at my Gran's because she had a colour TV – snooker is crap in black and white ('and so he goes for the grey then the grey, the grey and the grey'), and we'd sit through a couple of Spinners numbers before falling into a deep, deep sleep. Then a folk club above a pub in Louth, Lincolnshire, where I was mesmerised by the sight of bearded teachers in woolly jumpers (spooky or what?) sticking their fingers in their ears and singing 'gentle ladeeeeeeee' over and over again in Spike Milligan voices. Well, so I exaggerate a bit. Sometimes they did Harry Secombe voices too. Finally *Playaway* with Brian Cant (strangely enough, also on BBC2) in which he would burst into song at the slightest provocation.

Cant (now there's a good old Celtic name – from the *Cantii* tribe of Kent) was a sixties–seventies phenomenon, as influential in his way to kids as Dylan, the Beatles and the Velvet Underground were to teenagers and twentysomethings at the

---

[2]Learning the guitar was harder than I expected. It wasn't until I got hold of the Clash songbook that I learned to play anything remotely similar to a real song. I bought it one Saturday afternoon at Langford's record shop in Market Rasen and took it along to the Ropewalk, the local football ground. I was half-way through 'London's Burning' (mostly E major) when Mr Brumpton, a geography teacher at our school, got the ball on the half-way line and dribbled around three or four defenders before burying the ball in the net from twenty yards out. We (the crowd) all got up and cheered. Mr Brumpton waved, slightly embarrassed but dead pleased with himself. We (there were five of us) exchanged commentaries on the goal then I got back to reading. A minor and a minor 7th – pretty basic chords but you still got a good facsimile of the song. Later that day I perfected the chords to 'Police and Thieves', Lee Perry's classic covered by the Clash on their first album.

time. If only his name had begun with a K he would have been assured a place in the post-modern stars' lexicon. Cant did all the voices for the rural puppet animation trilogy, *Trumpton*, *Camberwick Green* and *Chigley*. Of the three, it's *Camberwick Green* which has stood the test of time. The series can be read as a playing out of anachronistic class structures in modern Britain. *Trumpton*, the urban scrawl, entrepreneurs, go-getters, civic administrators, *Camberwick Green*, the fast-disappearing rural idyll, *Chigley* the even older feudal system, the Lord Belborough character, juxtaposed with the Communitarian philosophy of the workers who all dance the same steps at the six o'clock whistle.

Cant's rendition of 'PC McGarry' (n. 452) remains the highlight of consensus-era children's TV folk music.[3] 'PC McGarry' was the link between Jack Dixon 'PC 49' period of neighbourhood coppers, and the more aggressive *The*

---

[3]I've also been told there's a bar called McGarry's (note A) somewhere on one of the main streets of Ennis (about twenty miles from Doolin – a grand looking town, not to be confused with Enistymon, slightly nearer and with a name that reminds you of the long elegant parts of a flower), but that it's number 238. I'm probably being wound up. A bit like the music box at the start of *Camberwick Green*, hey kids? But if McGarry's does exist, I'll have a pint there then go out and find the nearest bookshop, where I'll head for the philosophy section and pick up a book of Kant (note B). The first passage my eyes alight on will become my theme for a day of music and beer.

Note A
I've subsequently discovered that I was given false information and what they were referring to was McGariggle's on O'Connell Street in Sligo. Which kind of ruins this story, really. Fuck it anyway, as PC McGarry might have said.

Note B
I did go to Sligo and went to McGarrigle's. The next morning in the bookshop there was no philosophy but I did pick up a copy of *Shanks*, the biography of former Liverpool manager Bill Shankley by Dave Bowler. And the first passage I turned to was about Shankley's captain, the indomitable Ron Yeats. Coincidentally, the Yeats museum is about thirty yards down the road from the bookshop. Crap coincidence, perhaps, but enough to keep me going in this heroic project.

Sweeney. One string guitar intro, then the jaunty riff, then the chorus, culminating in the self-revelatory, 'PC McGarry number 4 . . . 5 . . . 2 . . .' . . . *der der der dum, de dum, de der der der der de dum de dum de der der der der de dum de dum de dahhh . . .*

It's fear that makes people dislike Irish music. Fear that you might have to sing yourself. We all do crazy things when we're drunk, but you'll know if you've sung a ballad on your own in a session – who can forget the sweaty palms, the increased heartbeat, the trembling? Even some Irish people are scared. They call it *diddly-idee* (from the Gaelic *díghle ad* – meaning 'music of the woolly-jumpered one'). It's the sort of thing that your boring uncle with a beard would be into. And before any irate folkies write in, *I* am often a boring uncle with a beard. And yet I've been to many parties during which my Irish friends who are scared of Irish music get very drunk and proceed to do an impersonation of their boring uncle with a beard. As I walked down. Her eyes so blue. Fair autumn wind. Bonnie lassie. Heartfelt, no doubt about it. But up there in the cringe stakes with 'Streets of London' and 'Yesterday'. And what's worse is that you know you're next up.

Although he's not everyone's cup of tea, one of my favourite Irish musicians has always been Christy Moore, a man who's done his fair share of gigs and sessions in and around Clare. Opinion seems to be divided over this great Irish troubadour. Some say he's pretentious. Some that he's too political. Even fellow singers I've talked to don't, for some reason, really approve. But I think that's all crap. To me, Christy is a genius, punk, hippy, mystic, politico, lover, comic all rolled into one. OK, so he's no oil painting – or at least he's an oil painting by Lucien Freud (he looks like a prop forward or light-heavyweight boxer). His best songs describe the characters he has heard of or encountered on his musical travels. A wandering bard. But I see him as a recorder of our times in the best oral tradition, the epitome of unpretentiousness.

Irish music has become big business in recent years, with Boyzone, The Corrs and B*witched following in the footsteps of U2 and Sinéad O'Connor. There's also been a new brand of Celticky music doing the rounds. Some of it, however, especially the ethereal high production 'mood' albums that seem to emanate from the States (*Celtic Swirls*, *Swirly Celticness*, etc.), is merely a slightly more ethnic version of the Mantovani *Strings* albums. A more interesting angle had been taken by musicians like the Afro-Celt Sound System and Jah Wobble, with their world music infusions. Arabic pipes, Spanish guitar, dub bass, added to the yearning sound of Celtic fiddles and whistles.

I determined to buy Jah Wobble's 1997 album *The Celtic Poets* because it fused urban London and Blake with the Celtic, with titles such as 'London Rain', 'The Great Hunger', etc. etc. Except for track no. 3, which was called 'Market Rasen'. My home town, in Lincolnshire. What could he have been thinking? Friends told me not to be so daft, like some sad, anal teenager thinking that a star has written a song specially for them. (For a couple of years I was also convinced that 'Armagideon Time' by The Clash contained a reference to me. 'Tim Bradford, arh eauug oorrgh euuurggh oooohhhh Armagideon Time', sang old Joe Strummer. Take a listen if you don't believe me – it's on the twelve-inch version.) Of course, I knew that there was nothing in the Jah Wobble connection but it was just another sign to me of the things I should have been doing. Like writing to Jah Wobble and asking him why. I wrote to Jah Wobble, like a sad anal teenager. Like the mystic and mature musician that he is, Jah didn't write back.

A musician friend of mine who also used to review world music for Q magazine, once played me a CD of Islamic pipe music. I listened to the whole album under the illusion that it was uilleann pipes. There is a connection between the Eastern, Middle Eastern and Celtic traditions, but it goes back further than the Irish Celtic era, perhaps back to the root culture of Indo-European warriors, the forefathers of most of the peoples of Europe. The thought of incredible charioted beings charging into battle playing bohdráns and singing, 'When She was Sweet Sixteeeeeeeeeeeen', is absolutely terrifying, and makes you glad you live in the twenty-first century.

A place like Doolin[4] is seething with amazing people, mad characters, poets, artists and entrepreneurs who in another setting would be mould breakers, movers, shakers and horse thieves. They come here because they have been hurt by the real world, or need more ancient rhythms in which to fulfil their life ambitions. Or they fancy getting off with Scandinavian backpackers. One such madman, er, I mean lovely eccentric rogue, is Ted McCormac. Ted, a Dubliner (though not actually a Dubliner as in Dubliners, Chieftains, Spinners

---

[4]**Quick guide to Doolin**

Places to stay in Doolin:
Cuckoo's Nest
Doolin Hostel
Self-catering houses

Pubs:
O'Connor's (most touristy)
McGann's (quiet. The session pub)
McDermott's (used to be for locals – now packed out)

Music:
Rough Guide to Irish Music – Various
The Time has Come – Christy Moore
Sharon Shannon – Sharon Shannon
Anything by Mico Russell
Rough and Ready – Ted McCormac
'Camberwick Green', Brian Cant and BBC folkies
The Celtic Poets – Jah Wobble
The Best of the Pogues
The Black Crow – Altan
The Spinners Greatest Hits (fine stuff)

or whatever – he's from Dublin. Though like the Spinners he *does* wear woolly jumpers) is a bear of a man with a mass of grey blond curly hair who not only sports the folk musician's *de rigeur* impressive beard but also an equally impressive missing leg. Unlike many (all other?) great Celtic bards, he's a teetotaller. He is also a raconteur who loves to surround himself with people, which he manages to do by playing bass and singing in various sessions in the area.

He knows the stars too – at night he'll point up to a little red dot in the sky and shout 'Mars!' to anyone who's listening.[5]

MARS!

Ted knows everything there is to know about the district of Doolin, and what he doesn't know I'm convinced he makes up. He'll tell you that the best way to see the Burren, the ancient limestone area a few miles out of Doolin, a world conservation site, is through a small local tour company called Doolin Tours. This is run by . . . Ted himself. Doolin Tours is a little blue bus that operates from the converted barn he lives in next door to his daughter's cottage. Pop in to visit him and he'll tell you how Brian Boru fought some big battle there or thereabouts and mad Marie-Rua married an English soldier to keep control of Lemanagh Castle, then threw her English husband off the battlements, etc., etc. At the time of writing, Ted is packing out McDermott's[6] with his regular sessions, miked up to his new £1,000 amp (partly for sound, partly, no doubt, to piss off the purists), with his bass guitar tutor sometimes sitting in to give him moral support.

At the risk of sounding like an advertisement for Doolin Tours, it probably *is* the best way to see the Burren for the first time (book early to avoid disappointment). Unless

[5] I am now related to Ted. That's Doolin for you . . .

[6] It's now McGann's again – See note on Pub Politics chapter.

you go out on a golden summer day (very rare) the Burren usually looks magnificently bleak. A terrible beauty, as some have described it. Stone everywhere. Grey stone. White stone. You try to imagine families scratching a living from this land over the centuries, as they were gradually pushed west by the British. You take all this in while Ted will chatter away at the front, explaining about how Brian Boru fought some big battle there or thereabouts and mad Marie-Rua married an English soldier to keep control of Lemanagh Castle, then threw her husband off the battlements, etc., etc.

Doolin is now becoming well known as a mad music place, with the odd travel piece in the English broadsheets giving testimony to its *craic* and its food. Then there's the celebrity visitors like Paul Hill and his wife who can be glimpsed occasionally in McGann's. Several people have told me that it's time to move on, that everybody will be in Miltown Malbay or Lahinch next year or the year after. But they never do move on. Doolin will always be packed and slightly chaotic. Lying beside the shore at the harbour near O'Connor's pub, staring at the big sky, feeling at ease with the world, when there is not a sound and no-one around, my only advice is to live in the present – learn an instrument, kiss a colleen, fall in love, fill your belly with existential Irish stew, find 'Mars!', sink a pint, stare at someone else's pint, have an argument, change pubs, build a Spanish archway, try to sing a song without dying of embarrassment. Basically, don't *plan* anything. No-one else does, or ever has done. Apart, that is, from mad Marie-Rua.

The Day the Earth Stood Still

Limerick to Galway

I decided to take a bus to Galway and found myself, as is usual in these public transport moments, next to a thirty-ish Europacker who seemed more interested in the Italian-language version of *Hello!* that she was reading than the scenery outside the window. Just look out there dammit, I wanted to say, see the soil become thinner, the walls more numerous, feel the history, the hardship, the conflicts, the mystery, the ancient sites. Suddenly I saw a sign that said we were ten miles away from Gort and I got all excited, as I always do when I recognise a placename that appears in a well-known film. Paris, Texas (*Paris, Texas*), Walsingham in north Norfolk (*Elizabeth*), St Michael's Mount in Cornwall (Michael, the Al Pacino character, in *The Godfather* – OK, so I'm struggling here).

In the fillum *The Day the Earth Stood Still*, Gort is the giant robot who accompanies some skinny alien guy in a baggy spacesuit whose name I can't remember to Earth and who famously stands majestically proud and tall at the top of the little ramp of the spaceship that the skinny alien guy in a baggy spacesuit whose name I can't remember uses to get himself from the flying saucer to the ground of New York City. Gort was a proper robot, like the cybermen in Dr Who. The Daleks were not proper robots – they had little fondue forks for hands (though some of the higher-ranking Daleks had to make do with plungers). I can't remember whether I said all this stuff aloud to the woman next to me, but as I pressed my face against the window and started singing 'Oobee doobe doo dap dang a doh doo' – like the black-clad female jazz singer in the cool subterranean club while the skinny alien guy in a baggy spacesuit whose name I can't remember goes native in a suit and tie and sips a martini – she buried her head even further into the magazine. The skinny alien guy in a baggy spacesuit whose name I can't remember eventually gets beaten up, or shot, and Gort goes out to find him. I had always wondered what Gort means.[1]

I saw that film a couple of times when I was a kid and it always frustrated me that the human race – specifically those loudmouth New Yorkers – just couldn't get their acts together and be nice to people who were slightly different.[2] I had walked around Gort one Tuesday lunchtime a year before, with this in mind – why they had been so cruel to Gort and his master. I had long hair and was unshaven, with a baggy, dishevelled jacket and an open-necked shirt. I looked like death. My face was white, my eyes were gone and each step felt as though it was taking up all my energy – I looked like a tinker-school drop-out ('no graduation day for youuu-uuu . . .'). I went into a shop to buy a paper and the look the woman gave me said, 'No we don't have any scrap metal here for you.' She seemed surprised when I only asked for an *Irish Times*. I had wanted to immerse myself in the local culture but really couldn't be arsed, so went and had scampi and chips in a local café. Gort's stony greyness reminded me of riverside towns in Yorkshire or the Derbyshire Peak

[1]Gort is Gaelic for field.

[2]Of course, the same thing would have happened if the skinny alien guy in a baggy spacesuit whose name I can't remember had turned up with his metal pal in my old home town in the early eighties. He'd have got duffed up by a crowd of denim-clad bikers after the pubs had shut and that would be that – all-out intergalactic war.

District. They are outwardly pretty but the preponderance of grey stone suggests hidden angst, melancholy, repression, stern fathers with top hats and fuzzy side whiskers saying thou shalt stay and learn thoust Latin and not have Christmas dinner with the rest of the family, and kids being whacked before bedtime with the family bible. Though I could be over-reacting.

Anyway, in the film the skinny alien guy in a baggy space-suit whose name I can't remember is not your typical Hollywood leading man – I may or may not have said that to my temporary travelling companion, but she certainly wasn't listening. For a start he's too skinny. He looks ill. He's got lean, rugged, dark-haired regular looks, but haunted eyes and very pale skin. He is anti-hero, a proto-Shane Mac-Gowan, except he's clean shaven. A similar look to Robert Walker, that spooky skinny guy who was in *Strangers on a Train* with Farley Granger. Or Monty Clift with TB.

That Tuesday afternoon in Gort it had been raining. It was raining now, too, as we passed through north Clare. I saw another sign and started singing the Christy Moore song, 'Lisdoonvarna'). I always get excited when I recognise a placename that appears in a well-known song. I remember being at the Lisdoonvarna Matchmaking Festival once – not for me, oh God no, no no no, just there with friends, oh yes, ha ha, checking out the scene and all that. A few of us stood at the bar of the Ritz Hotel in the market square and ordered pints. The place was full of eager old lads, mostly farmers probably, of weird shape and mien. One of our crowd, a pretty young guard called Carmel, had had her fortune told and it has said she'd meet three older men who'd change her life, so was on the lookout. Every time a group of three men were spotted, she and her friend (who always carried a pair of knickers and toothbrush in her handbag 'just in case') would grab each others' arms and go 'wwooooooorrrr'. I didn't think they were treating the Festival with the respect it deserved. They scanned the talent voraciously – being a guard, Carmel was hoping that the promise of handcuffs and uniform would be a winner. 'Gets the blokes going, you know.' Er, no, I said. After a few more pints she'd said, 'I'm looking for a beast, a big bad man.' I asked her why and she wasn't quite sure how to explain it. She said she'd written to the organiser, Willie Daly, and told him she was rich with a good career and 'wanted a beast, simple as that'. The last I remember of that night was the bizarre sight of some farmers with heads the size of small cars getting in nicely with a group of satin-dressed young lovelies, while I tried to do 'beast' impressions to the unimpressed police-woman.

The Italian tourist had finished her magazine and was staring straight ahead. We were nearly there. I saw a sign for Galway and thought of humming the entire James Galway back catalogue to myself. Then I realised the only thing I knew was 'Annie's Song'. I suddenly felt lonely and was already getting tired of trying to be Irish. But I looked forward to seeing *The Lonesome West*, a play by Martin MacDonagh, tomorrow as part of the Arts Festival with some theatrical non-alehead, civilised people, followed by a quiet stroll around the beautiful little city.

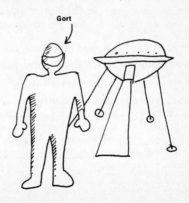

Conversations with the Future Foreign Correspondent of the *Irish Times*

The Galway Arts Festival

Galway[1] is a mad city of torque brooches and armbands and fourteen-year-old Italian and French students in identical garish waterproof jackets eating sandwiches in Kennedy Park and waiting for something to happen, but it never will, unless by 'something' they mean being accosted and then weed on by a bearded drunkard who smells of cumin powdery BO, devilled kidneys and Special Brew.[2] It's a city of didgeridoo

[1]Guidebook stuff . . . Galway is known as the city of the tribes. It used to be very English. Loyal to the crown. No Os or Macs were allowed inside the city unless specifically invited. The Claddagh was the little fishing community on the other side of the river. It lasted up until the 1950s when, in its wisdom and for reasons of health, the council knocked down the village and built council houses in their place. That's where the rings come from. You wear the heart pointing towards you if you're in love, and out if you're looking for love. Got to get it right.

[2]Though even the drunkards seem to have their pecking order. Some aren't even bearded and stand in pairs in scruffy old suits leaning against the rusty modern art sculptures, looking like civil servants who got sacked back in the early sixties after one liquid lunch too many. They stare off into nothingness and occasionally mutter the odd word to each other. Others are more true to the genre and sit around in groups on the benches, with hair all over the place and cider, shouting 'argh!' and 'egh' at each other and hold Who's Got The Reddest Face competitions.

buskers, hair wrappers with mousy beards and little round specs from nice families in England (most likely from towns like Salisbury or Norwich, gentle souls who did an Arts degree, got a nice job, went a bit 'crazy' then decided to find themselves in their mid thirties – got a young European girlfriend and just took off, man). A city of long-nosed pensioners with red speckled cheeks, of wild-haired arts undergraduates, baggy-eared Gaelic footballers and craft shop workers with nervous eyes and unpublished poetry in their coat pockets. It's a city of great creativity, with all the detritus that entails, but also a party town of beer and music and fishing boats and estate agents.

I'm there smack bang in the middle of the Arts Festival. And Galway is a town full of people who love the arts. The Arts are lovely, that's what people in Galway would say. I had arrived to see *The Lonesome West*, playing for just one more night at the famous Druid Theatre just off Quay Street.

What is an 'Arts' festival?

Perhaps first of all one should ask the question 'What is Art?' After that question has been asked it should probably be answered. But not by me. I haven't a clue. I only got an E in my Art A-Level so am probably not qualified. I had actually put the question to the ever-knowledgeable Terry one night earlier that year. He is a handy walking dictionary as well as being a useful moral philosopher and a grade C A-Level artist to boot, the bastard.

'Art is the physical creation of a mental concept,' he declared with a-hundred-per-cent confidence. I asked him to say it again, so I could write it down.

'Art,' he said, in his drunken attempt at gravitas, 'is the physical creation of a mental concept.' So, Terry, if I developed the concept of hitting someone then carried it out physically, would that be Art? Terry looked perturbed then said 'yes' because he had to look after his new theory. This was his baby now. No matter, it was a definition and I wasn't about to split hairs.

What is a festival?

Is this for the German market? Whatever – a festival, er, it's a sort of party I suppose, where like-minded people get together, sometimes in a field (as in rock festival) or a grimy fifties' classroom in North Wales (literary festival). Or a damp wooden church hall on the outskirts of a small village in the East Midlands (harvest festival). The common denominator is a central concept ('Art!' – quiet, Terry) that everyone is into, plus unadulterated fun and laughter (particularly in the case of harvest festivals).

Review – *The Lonesome West* by Martin McDonagh

Martin McDonagh is the new Brendan Behan (without the drink problem), the new John B. Keane (without the pub), and the new Sean O'Casey (without having W. B. Yeats as a pal). I'd never seen one of his plays and I don't know what

he looks like[3] but I know he's younger than me and very
talented so naturally I'm really jealous.[4] McDonagh became
hot in London around 1996 with his *Leenane Trilogy*, of

[3]Although recently I was out drinking at the Anchor Bankside in London with a
group of blokes and telling them about my visit to Galway and a friend of a friend
told me that Martin McDonagh was a mate of his and a really nice bloke. Why
don't you meet up with him? And I said I like the idea of him but what would I
say to him? That I'm writing a chapter in a book about the fact that I've never
seen his plays? My mate Tom played football with him in Regent's Park now and
again and for some reason I stopped hating him then because, well, when did
Oscar Wilde ever play football in Regent's Park with his pals? But I forgot to ask
what position he played, because that would have been important, tells you a lot
about a man, if not a playwright. Wilde would have been either an old-fashioned
centre forward or a goalkeeper, John B. Keane on the wing, Behan mid-field
genius, O'Casey Nobby Stiles hardman. I imagine Martin McDonagh and his
brother as sort of literary equivalents of Jack and Bobby Charlton. But which is
Jack and which is Bobby?

[4]This has been going on for years. When people are older than me there's always
the chance that I'll one day equal or even overtake their achievements, be it in
writing, politics or number of famous actresses they've been out with. It's highly
delusional of course. But if they're younger, then they've already bettered me, so
to speak, not that they've done it on purpose or anything.

It's mainly happened with football. For years I would note the age of an up-
and-coming player and, if he was older than me, think, 'There's still time for me
to make it. There's still something to look forward to. Thank you, Footy God.' I
felt that some players had grown up with me, the ones who were the same age
and who hit the big time at around the same period that I should have done if I
hadn't gone off to college to watch films for three years and drink too many pints
of Tolly 4X.

One star in whom I had a particular interest was Mark Smalley, a central
defender who started his career at Notts Forest and has done the business in a
small business sort of way at a variety of other clubs. In the late seventies,
Smalley was a dashing left-winger for a crack East Midlands under-fifteen club
side, and during one particularly fraught North Kesteven Cup Final I had the
onerous task of being skinned by him. He was a class above the rest of the honest, pimply fourteen-year-old virgins (Sorry Bon – never believed you, mate) on
the pitch that day, and we all knew he was going to 'make it'.

The last time I saw him play was in the late '80s at Brisbane Road, when he
came on as substitute for a half decent Leyton Orient side. After that he moved
on to Mansfield Town and Maidstone United, then I lost touch, with only his
grinning features in my 1989–90 Rothman's Yearbook to remind me that he ever
existed. I had observed his descent through the divisions with genuine sadness,
and it felt all the more real because he was born only a day later than me. OK, I
admit it, he represented all my hopes and fantasies about football success.

contd overleaf

which *The Lonesome West* was a part. This is reckoned to be his best play so far, about two brothers squabbling over possessions and territory in a small house in the West of Ireland, after their father has died. There's an alcoholic priest and a tease of a girl in there too. McDonagh is reasonably famous but in the tabloid world of the UK it's not so much for his plays as for getting into a barney with Sean Connery[5]

But does it work both ways? During half time in that cup final back in 1979 he may have had his ear to the changing room wall as I was explaining to our manager (after he'd asked what I planned to do at the end of my football career – in about 45 minutes) that I had dreams of becoming a writer and after my O-Levels was set on emigrating to Paris and moving in with one of the dancers from the Crazy Horse Club, whose picture I had seen in a Sunday supplement a few weeks earlier (she had already moved upstairs with me to my bedside table).

Perhaps after that incident I became Mark's representative in the world of literature, and in vain he would scour the *TLS* and bookshops throughout the East Midlands looking for my name in lists of Young British Writers, or a reference to my completion of the Great Lincolnshire Novel.

Something eventually has to give. In the last couple of years I have realised that as players become ten or more years younger than me and Mark Smalley, that I am going to have to do something miraculous to make it in top class football. Reading old football books is becoming a bit of an emotional nightmare. I used to flick through old copies of the *Topical Times* Annual when I was in need of reassurance, such as after the break-up of a long-term relationship, but now I look older and more lived-in than the pictures of all my old favourites like Frannie Lee, Allan Clark and George Graham. Imagine what I'll look like in twenty years time.

Looking back over the distant dreams of childhood, I recognise that I have one advantage over Mark. If you check out the recent copy of *The Topical Times Book of Young British Travel Writers*, you'll notice that most of them are aged between fifty and sixty.

[5]Apparently what happened was that Martin and his brother John, who also plays football – and is also a writer (though of Country and Western film scripts rather than plays, which sounds like an even better job) – were at an *Evening Standard* awards night and taking the piss a bit when presentations were being given. So Sean Connery who's at a nearby table comes over and does his Sean Connery voice saying something like, 'Dohn't be show rood.' And Martin goes er yeah sorry. Then John pipes up no Martin he can't say that no-one tells my brother to fuck off. So Martin goes right fuck off Sean Connery and Sean Connery fucks off. It's a great little story though probably not true, alas. It's maybe not so interesting until you consider the sycophantic press Connery has had in Britain for most of his career. Though whatever you think about him personally I've only ever met a couple of people who didn't think he was the best of the Bond actors (a gay guy I knew at college believed Roger Moore was 'the one' for some reason).

about something or other. Maybe he called the actor a bald rich supercilious old git or something. Or perhaps he was simply rude.

Anyway, every goatee-bearded culturally copped-on arts tourist in town was hatching plans to see his play at the Druid Theatre, clucking in their gregarious coteries in O'Neachtain's, Galway's bohemian, 'flamboyant' old-style pub on Quay Street, about new Irish Theatre and The Arts. Being fatally drawn to large groups of clucking art pseuds (it goes back to a crush I had on a denim clad left-wing drama teacher when I was thirteen), I couldn't stop myself legging it down to the Festival box office to book a seat.

The Festival box office was just off Quay Street, the cob-bled medievelesque main shopping thoroughfare in the city. I stopped briefly at the windows outside where there was an exhibition of drawings by Tom Matthews,[6] whose style I recognised. They were all reasonably funny, particularly one, which made me roar with laughter: a bloke is talking to someone on a mobile phone while having sex with a goose, with sheaves of paper between him and the squawking bird. The caption reads, 'I'm just having a gander through your CV as we speak.' OK, so it's not exactly sophisticated, but it had a certain charm. Well, not even charm so much as a really corny play on words. I've never been into the idea of buying original art, except from charity shops, or from friends who are eager but skint, but I decided I had to have the 'I'm Having A Gander Through Your CV . . .' no matter what the cost, dammit (actually £50 unframed).

[6]Tom Matthews works for the *Irish Times* – I hope he doesn't mind me saying it, but Martyn Turner is undoubtedly the most famous cartoonist in the country. Turner does grotesque caricatures in political illustrations – Matthews is more of a gag man. He also does cartoons in Gaelic for the Irish language section of the paper.

I walked in feeling like Charles Saatchi, about to add to my collection.

(Scene – arts festival box office in a West of Ireland city)
Arts Tourist: (Staring at the intelligent-looking short-haired woman behind the counter and smiling in an enigmatic artsy sort of way) I'd like to buy the cartoon of the bloke having sex with a goose.
Clever-looking Short-haired Box-office Woman: Ha ha ha – is that right?
Arts Tourist: (Puffing out chest in Arts Patron fashion) No, really. (Clever-looking short-haired box-office woman goes off for a minute or two. There is laughter off stage then she returns, smiling.)
Clever-looking Short-haired Box-office Woman: Right you are, OK, I see what you mean. It *is* about sex with a goose, isn't it. I think you'd need to talk to Tom Matthews himself. He's due to pop in in about half an hour – you could meet him.
Arts Tourist: (Arching eyebrows) I'd like that.

(Scene – a coffee bar in a West of Ireland city. A dishevelled traveller sits at an outside table staring at a cup of tea. Occasionally he sips from the tea then takes a watch out of his pocket, then continues staring at the tea. This goes on for half an hour. The figure then places some money on the table and gets up and leaves.)

(Scene – arts festival box office in a West of Ireland city)

Arts Tourist: (Staring at the intelligent-looking short-haired woman behind the counter) I've come to meet Tom Matthews the cartoonist. I want to buy one of his drawings. The cartoon of the bloke having sex with a goose.
Clever-looking Short-haired Box-office Woman: Ha ha ha – that's the cartoon of a man having sex with a goose, yeah?

Arts Tourist: Hmmm.

Clever-looking Short-haired Box-office Woman: Well he was in here just now but he's just gone down the pub – you might catch him.

Arts Tourist: Which way did he go?

Clever-looking Short-haired Box-office Woman: That way.

(And so the chase begins. Arts Tourist leaves and walks down the street then stops and winces, looks down at the pavement then walks back quickly to the arts festival box office.)

(Scene – arts festival box office in a West of Ireland city)

Arts Tourist: (Staring at the intelligent-looking short-haired woman behind the counter) Erm, this Tom Matthews . . . what does he, er, look like?

Clever-looking Short-haired Box-office Woman: He's got white hair and a moustache and has a red scarf. Ha – ye can't miss him!

(Scene – the first pub down from the box office. A bloke with a moustache is drinking alone. Arts Tourist goes up to him and looks around for his scarf. There is no scarf.)

Arts Tourist: Awww.

(Scene – out in the street two guys standing, one, flamboyant and with a red scarf but no moustache)

Arts Tourist: Are you a cartoonist?

'Flamboyant' Red Scarf Man: No, I am from the Netherlands.[7]

---

[7]Cue seventies-style British sitcom laughter track.

Ah, Eurohumour – sure, you couldn't make it up. After several more fruitless searches in the pubs around Quay Street I decided to call it a day and went back to the box office. The intelligent woman behind the counter told me they'd get in touch with Tom Matthews and find out what to do and I could pick up the cartoon the next morning. I saw this as a success of sorts. (Yess, ha ha, victory to the intrepid arts festival goer! Arts Tourists 1 – Box Office 0! To O'Neachtain's we will repair, for ales and jigs!)

I then wandered back out onto the main drag and saw a couple of bedraggled figures sitting at the side of the street selling henna tattoos. They were sort of gooey brown and apparently would last a week or so.[8] I made up the design myself, a sort of squiggly Celtic sun in the style of a five-year-old with delirium tremens.[9] Was it 'art'? I had had the mental concept and she had physically created it. The couple was from Mexico City and were travelling around Europe painting squiggly shitty lines onto people's arms – for cash! Clever, marketing-savvy bastards. I've been to Mexico City, I said. Very busy. Lots of Volkswagen Beetles driven by maniacs. Ah, but Mexico City is beautiful, said the grave, pale-faced young man: the sun and sky, the mountains, the people are happy, it is paradise, it is lovely. The Mexicans said they were here for the festival and might watch some theatre later because that was what they loved. Theatre in Mexico City was beautiful, poetic, it was lovely, it was butterflies floating around your head, it was . . . but my mind had wandered off – Theatre! Greasepaint! Curtains! Er, remembering lines! Intervals with drinks! Air kisses at the aftershow party! Iconoclastic young playwrights! *The Lonesome West*! I legged it back to the Arts Centre to get a ticket. On

---

[8] Some of my friends have roses and rock 'n' roll hearts. However, tattoos are usually done in the High Celtic style.

[9] If you are five and an alcoholic and can draw great Celtic swirls, I apologise.

the way I passed a tacky-looking boozer with a red flyer in the window, on which was written details of the Miss Galway competition way over on the other side of town in Salthill. I laughed the hearty laugh of a seasoned theatregoer. It seemed a bit pathetic and ridiculous that they'd have something like that on in 'Arts' week.

Of course, I hadn't booked. That would be far too unspontaneous, or should I say 'intelligent, organised and mature' for someone whose great-great-grandfather was a horseperson.

Clever-looking Short-haired Box-office Woman: Hello again. What can I do for you this time?

I explained everything. There were no tickets left, she said, with pity yet also some surprise that a fan of graphic representations of goose-buggering would also have an interest in the theatre. What a Renaissance man, she was probably thinking. If only I wasn't stuck here behind this counter that guy might *show me the world*!

Clever-looking Short-haired Box-office Woman: You could go to the Druid theatre to check if there's any cancellations.

At the theatre the woman in front of me asked if there were any tickets for *The Lonesome West*.

'No we've sold out.'

'Oh how embarrassing.'

It was my go. Like a deaf lemming, I too asked if there were any tickets for *The Lonesome West*.

'No,' she said patiently, as if speaking to somebody very stupid, 'as I said to the lady just now, we've sold out.'

I had to try to find Tom Matthews the cartoonist now. After all, it was really all his fault that I'd missed out on *The Lonesome West*. If I didn't get him then my whole visit would have been wasted. This is an arts festival. Cartoons are art. I wandered around various pubs and cafés, thinking that a guy with white hair and flamboyant red scarf can't just go and hide in a little place like this. But he did. So I decided to go and see something else and wrote on my hand to remind myself to turn up tomorrow.

(Scene – the Box Office again. A clever-looking long-haired woman is now behind the desk)

Arts Tourist: Look, I need to see a play or some art or something – are there any other plays on tonight?

Clever-looking Long-haired Woman: Well, there's *Dancing at Lughnasa*.

Arts Tourist: (Stroking chin and nodding slowly) Ahmmm ahmmmm. Where's that on?

Clever-looking Long-haired Woman: Some church hall at the edge of the city.

Arts Tourist: Right, I'll have a ticket then.

Clever-looking Long-haired Woman: None left, you'll have to go down there.

Dancing at Lughnasa

This is a play set in 1930s rural Ireland about a summer festival, pagan dancing, repression and all that jolly stuff. I trudged down to some hall on the outskirts of town, passing joggers and dog walkers and leaving behind the tie-dye mystical ponytailedness of the town centre, into the suburbs. A woman with a kid stopped her car and asked where she could find the venue for *Dancing at Lughnasa*. We wandered up and down the respectable street until we found a padlocked church hall. She sort of cursed in a very well-brought-up way, then got in her car and drove off. I hung around for a while for no particular reason, thinking about what to do next. A film had just been made of the play, starring Meryl Streep. It's funny, I hadn't thought about Meryl Streep for years and now she turned up twice in the space of about sixty pages. You just can't write her off. I walked slowly back into town.

On my way back in I passed one of the town's music pubs, near a place where the river sort of splits in two, guarded by a lonely-looking telephone box. Mike Peters was playing that night. Mike Peters from The Alarm. What was their song? '68 Guns'? '22-Gun Salute'? 'The Guns of Brixton'? (Actually, I know that that was by the Clash.) The Alarm didn't really look like pop stars if my memory is correct. Ugly lads with positive punk hairdos. No, it was bigger than that, it was eighties Pop Big Hair. Why was hair so big back then? The eighties was full of these sorts of enthusiastic but limited bands, lots of passion but somehow the attitude was all wrong. In another era, say the mid to late nineties, they'd have been allowed to get away with being dressed like brickies. But in the mid eighties they had to look like outrageous hairdressers or no-one would buy their records. What a crazy time. Whatever I might have thought of Mike Peters I decided this was the arts event for me. I would return.

The Spanish Conceptual Art Pieces

Further into town I popped into the Arts Centre, wondering if they might have any tickets for anything. This turned out to be very different from the Arts Festival box office, like some old council offices that have been turned into gallery space. Upstairs was a fine exhibition of photographs by Martin Parr taken on a day at the Galway races – lots of outdoor fill-in flash character studies. Downstairs was a selection of Spanish conceptual pieces. There was only me in there until a scruffy little family walked in. The dad stood proudly in his vest and tracksuit trousers as the kids and his missus wandered around the works looking bewildered. He was not sure what was going on (like me) but knew it was good that they were there – he'd done his bit in the culture wars. I had an uplifting feeling as this little patriarch made his bid for family self-improvement. They traipsed out reasonably

quickly with raised eyebrows as if to say, 'What was that lump of shite all about?' Ah but what do I know about people, patronising git that I am – he was probably an installation artist himself come to check out the opposition.

An afternoon with a future foreign correspondent of the *Irish Times*

Being mid-afternoon by now, I decided it was time for a bit of a break, so went and sat at a long bench in the back room of the ancient wooden interior of O'Neachtain's with a not-too-cold pint of Guinness. At the far end, a blond ponytailed Eurotourist with little round specs who I decided was called Wolfgang started barking orders at the slumped and lived-in Irish couple to my right.[10]

'Excuse me, ve are a big group could you move up please.' A not unreasonable request – it was just the tone that

[10]The Angles and Saxons may not have invaded Ireland in the Dark Ages but they're certainly making up for it now, as are the Romans.

rankled. The woman, with a sharp face and a mass of curls in a short cut, looked up and winced. Her man – like a slightly pudgier Gabriel Byrne – simply sat still with his head on his chest and eyes closed, as if someone had just shot him in the forehead. Wolfgang repeated his order.

'Zere is more room up zere for you. Zere are more off uss zan you!' The woman punched her man on the shoulder – 'Dermot, get up!' and they picked up their drinks and staggered six feet closer towards me, her grumbling, him smiling with his eyes still closed. They sat down, her next to me.

'Bloody tourists. Bloody Germans and bloody English. They're all over the place. A load of poofs,' she spat in inner-city Dublinese to no-one in particular, as her man settled down into the Just Killed position and closed his eyes again.

'Yeah, fucking English,' I said in my best RP accent.

'You an Australian?'

'Er, I'm English,' I said, staring down at my pint.

'Oh. But you don't mind us sitting next to you, do you?'

'Not at all.'

'You're all right then.'

She asked me what I was doing in Ireland and I said travelling around trying to pick up Irish women while writing a book. She punched her man.

'Dermot, Dermot,' she said, 'he's writing a book. Dermot's writing a book too, aren't you Dermot.'

'Nnggg,' said Dermot.

'Dermot wants to be Foreign Correspondent on the *Irish Times* but he doesn't know how to go about it. I think he'd be brilliant. I said he should get in touch with them, but he refuses to.'

Dermot shook his head, eyes still closed. 'Ngg, ngggg.'

I asked her what she thought about the Arts Festival and she started ranting about how unfair arts funding was and that normal local people didn't get a look in and that it was all just geared for the tourists.

'What is art?' I asked.

'How do you mean?'

'Well, if I asked you to write down in my notebook what you think is the definition of art, would you do it?'

She thought for a couple of minutes then started scribbling.

'Art is stuff that's done in such a way that normal people understand it.'

She took a swig of drink. 'This place is full of poofs. Look at them all poncing about.'

'Eh? How can you tell?'

'You can just . . . *tell*.'

Then Dermot stirred. 'Nnnng,' he said. I went to the bar and bought them a drink. When I got back they had swapped places. While the woman, Maggie flirted with the young blond German guy she had previously been slagging off, me and Dermot made pleasant conversation for a while. I can't remember what I said to him, but he suddenly draped his arm around my shoulder and said, 'That's it,' finally opening his eyes slightly, 'That's the thing. The thing.' He jabbed the air with his finger. Then he smiled and nodded and shut his eyes again with a 'Nnnnngg'.

'What thing?' I asked, stupidly.

Dermot's eyes prised themselves open. 'It's the thing. You, you. It's YOU. You understand. You. You're the man.'

'What?' I said.

'You know. You know. The thing.'

Dermot had plainly fallen in love with me. He wouldn't let go. Maggie introduced me to a German guy with a Cork accent. He was a party piece. He looked like an orthodox German until he opened his mouth. He combined the robotic teamwork and luck with refereeing decisions of a German with the charm and wit and sparkle of the Irish. He seemed incredulously happy at this good fortune. 'It's terrible,' said Maggie. 'He doesn't know what he is. He should make his mind up.' I rather admired the Cork German. He seemed to have the best of both worlds. Dermot started to bum cigarettes off him while Maggie went off at a tangent into a rant about the English and Oliver Cromwell.

'The most evil bastard ever! And he was a bloody poofter.'

I then went into a long-drawn-out spiel about what's great for one country may be disastrous for another and how at school we were taught by earnest left-wing teachers who were themselves products of the radicalism of the sixties and seventies that Cromwell was essentially good because he challenged and defeated for ever the absolutism of the crown. It laid the foundations for the world's most democratic parliament. It wasn't a proletarian revolution like the French one – there were various groups agitating for further reform like the Diggers and the Levellers but they never got anywhere near real power – in reality it was one set of nobles against another, one gang with floppy hats against the other with soup pans on their heads. Irish people of course have a very different view of Cromwell. He came over to break the back of the Irish Catholics partly because they had supported Charles (though some rich families hedged their bets and supported both sides). But basically he was a hero to the English, he freed us from the yoke of absolute monarchy.

'Absolute shite more like,' said Maggie. 'That's a load of bollocks.'

'Nnnnnggg,' said Dermot.

She then slagged off arts funding (again), flamboyant arts tourists, gays (again) and the English (again).

We loped out to a little Chinese café round the corner, Dermot with his fist full of cigarettes he'd bummed off the Cork German, Maggie still banging on about poofs and Oliver Cromwell. We ate some chips and as she ranted Dermot started to become more and more vociferous. 'Fuck them. Let 'em try. Let 'em try!' He went to the toilet and on his way back got in an argument with one of the beefy waiters. 'Fucking Japanese. Are you the man? Are you?' We were asked to leave. Dermot held my hand and wouldn't let go. They invited me back to their tent where, they said, there was a full bottle of vodka. I said no thanks. He looked at me sadly. They walked off towards the square, arm in arm, Dermot perhaps dreaming of filing stories from the far-flung corners of the world, Maggie still furious at the misdeeds of seventeenth-century English closet homosexuals.

I got out my notepad and jotted down some thoughts. I had to write it down, all this oral history, these myths and false legends, for it to become my memory. Then I'd walk around tomorrow with my pack on my back stuffed full of bits of paper with similar scribble on, like a Memory Snail.

Review of Mike Peters in pub

After having a quick wash then a snack in Abrakebabra ('It's magic – wolf it down and it comes right back up!') I headed down to the music pub to catch the ex-anthemiser from the Alarm. As I was strolling down Quay Street I passed a little pub – called simply 'Murphy', I think – that I hadn't noticed before. And so went in.

It seemed to be the perfect combination of old lads in their seventies and young women in little strappy dresses. At my table was an old Scots guy, being 'tucked in' by his daughter and son-in-law. She was nagging him, telling him what time they would be back for him – I could tell he couldn't wait for them to go. He had two hours to get wellied before they returned.

He sat there with a stony face for about half an hour. He was so quiet he made me seem gregarious. I could tell I'd only get one chance to try and talk to him. Then I got self-conscious and felt like a parasite, sucking people's stories out of them. Like Dermot, the *Irish Times* 'correspondent' . . . what do I give them back? I decided, though, that this was what I wanted to be like when I was an old man. Telling my relations to fuck off so I can drink in a quiet pub in peace. What else is there? I tried to get inside his head. What would I want if I were him?

I said, I'm buying a whiskey, did he want one? Ah that'd be grand lad he said, please, with a bit of water. We started to talk about football. He'd played for a junior team in Scotland in the 1930s, worked down a mine – left early every Saturday to play football. He supported Celtic. What did he think of Dr Vengloss, the Celtic manager from Prague? His eyes twinkled. 'He writes the cheques eh heh heh heh heh.' He used to play 'back kick' (which I suppose must be a fouling 'special teams' position) in a 2-3-5 formation. Players could look after themselves in those days. But he didn't begrudge money going to young players now. A lot of the Republic's players were going to England, he said. He just wanted to be part of the craic. Another old man appeared, even older than Old Back-kick. I was in 'his' corner, so had to move. With him was an Irish Frasier lookalike in a Bavarian jacket, a local doctor or poet. The two old blokes talked to each other around me. I left. Good luck to ye lad, he smiled. As I left he moved round to become the junior partner.

'Where are you off to then lad?' he shouted. I'd missed the gig by now.

'Er, I, um, was thinking of going to see the Miss Galway beauty contest. Fancy going?'

'Ah no, that's young man's business. Good luck lad.'

Miss Galway Competition

Leaving behind the old guidebook Galway with its hair twizzlers and didgeridoos I made my way north to Salthill, a more prosaic working suburb of the city. Miss Galway was taking place in Bogart's night club. A classic night club name. Big pub nightclub down the back in a hall with a smaller bar.

People were already earnestly looking at their programmes to check the form, like a horse race, lots of serious expressions. The programme was a sheet of heavy A4 paper folded in half with photocopied photos of each contestant grinning gormlessly, their age and occupation, the judges and a few inches of space for the sponsors – Budweiser, Connacht Mineral Water, Sienza Clothing Ltd and 'Flowers by Kay'.

Lorcan Murray, the compère, was a patronising git of the old smooth school, smart grey hair and a sucked-in belly like a gym instructor, with the girls doing their mat work at the other end of the sports hall. One was a little girl-next-door bird, her head darting around with nervous energy. She twittered away about her neighbours in some out-of-the-way village and I could just see her in, say, forty years time, chatting away in a village shop about the comings and goings of people. She was gorgeous. The next contestant, trying to get in with the compère, pulled her tummy in so that her tits stuck out at right angles. One a curly haired country girl with a thick accent whose father fished and who loved children. 'I *love* children,' she said. Applause. Then came an anorexic English-looking blonde air hostess with prominent pubic bone showing through a clingfilm[12] thin dress. She hadn't got a man at the moment. Even more applause and laddish cheering. Then a Russian student who didn't like Irish men because they expected women to do all the ironing and washing (she was very pretty but only got sporadic applause for this subversive attitude). She said she spoke six languages. Name them, said the compère. Then came a shy sales assistant from Spiddal, and finally a student with wild red hair. She'd got a man so the lads didn't like her at all. As they pranced about on stage I looked around me – I felt so out of place, so scruffy, long-haired and unshaven after travelling around. All the lads were well ponced-up, eighties-style, thick gel, shiny little loafers, pressed trousers, nice shiny shirts with a crappy little smear of a moustache to set off the look. Maybe they would be the lucky one who'd get off with Miss Galway. That's what we were all thinking. I hit on my chat-up line if, for some reason, I got within speaking distance of the little village shop girl: 'My great grandmother's family were horsepeople.'

The blokes next to me, thin little whippet and his big-arsed mate, both in suits and clean looking, were clutching pints to their chests and discussing the scene:

[12]Strangely, Irish people go to the cinema to watch a *fillum* yet cover their leftover food with cling *film*.

Bigarse: I wouldn't fancy my bird prancing about on stage in front of all these idiots.

Whippet: (Ogling someone's arse) Aye.

Pause

Bigarse: I liked the air hostess. You could see her nipples through that dress.

Whippet: Aye.

Air hostess was the winner (Shopgirl came nowhere), to riotous applause from the snappy dressers, who stuck their chests out, jumped about and roared like eager-to-please lion cubs. Air hostess would go on to the Miss Ireland final, to be held in some airbrushed nightclub in a prestigious Dublin suburb (though I consoled myself with the fact that Shopgirl would have memories which would never leave her and she'd probably become a bit of a local celebrity in a small way). At the end of the night there was a tacky disco so I got up there, scruffy smelly and hairy, and proceeded to shuffle my butt to crap disco, like a tramp with his can of superbrew who's walked in on an under-thirteens youth club party and staggers straight onto the dancefloor trying to snog the teacher. Miraculously, I started to get what's known in the nightclub scene as Dancefloor Attention from Young People. It's a while since I've been hit on by nineteen-year-olds – not since I was nineteen, in fact – and I can only put this down to the fact that all the other blokes looked like Adolf Hitler (if he'd shopped at Mr Byrite).

On the way back into Galway I went to a phone box and rang Annie up in Texas then ranted on to her about 'beauty contests and how the-nicest-one-should-have-won-but-didn't-it's-not-fair-and-jeez-you-could-see-the-winner's-pubes-through-her-dress'. I then staggered off. That's the last I remember. I woke up in the morning in my B&B with the contents of my rucksack everywhere, all my memories spilled out on the floor. I could feel a headache rushing like a banshee wind down the corridor towards my room. Then something started moving in my guts – the very physical creation of a totally mental concept.

Alone on Yeats's Mountain with Only a Compass and an Egg Mayonnaise Sandwich for Company

Sligo to Benbulben round trip

The west of Ireland rises like some imaginary kingdom out of the sea, wild mountains pushing up like the heavily ripped deltoid muscles of a green-skinned steroid-abusing giant. Usually they are fringed with dark, messy charcoal smudged skies. Mountains have their own mythology and magic.[1] It's a deeply spiritual – perhaps religious, in the transcendent meaning of the word – experience, climbing a mountain staring down at the green patchwork fields below, the sea, feeling the rain beat your face and the wind clearing your head.

I woke up in my B&B in Sligo and noticed something strange coming through the chink between the curtain and the window frame. On closer inspection my suspicions were confirmed. Sunshine. I realised that on this day I couldn't piss away my time talking shite in pubs with locals. This time it was going to be different. This time I'd taste the sweet Irish air and really deserve my liquid refreshment at the end of the day. This time I really would climb a mountain.

[1]Though not the Paul Daniels kind.

   Benbulben, a mountain immortalised by W. B. Yeats in
one of his mystical poems (Well, aren't they all a bit mystical? But maybe it's the one about death and the horsemen
riding by, what is it . . . 'dum der something something something ride by'), is one of a group of plateaux that loom over
Sligo town to the east, great hunks of rock that look like the
prows of First World War battleships and seem more appropriate to a South American jungle than the soft-aired north-
west coast of Ireland. Like the Venezuelan *tepuis*, giant rock
plateaux straight out of *The Land That Time Forgot*, they're
often covered in cloud, especially the tops, which makes
them seem even more mysterious.

   Yeats spent many of his holidays in Sligo, eventually
settling there in the last years before his death. His grave lies
in a village at the foot of Benbulben.

   I had a crumpled piece of paper on which was written a
map and a vague description of the walk which I'd picked up
at the local tourist centre. I set out for Sligo and headed
North East-ish through the town until I got to the N15. The

streets of Sligo are apparently so full of writers and artists that many ordinary people have been advocating an annual cull. I personally believe that's a bit drastic – some kind of registration and rationing system like they do with cars in Mexico City would probably suffice. Near the N15 round-about I slipped on some water-covered moss on the pave-ment, thanks to the lack of grip on my walking boots. They were cast-offs, given to me by my friend Spizz who'd gone off to live in Canada. I landed on my wrist, exacerbating an old sex-related injury.

For a while I walked along the N15 – a main road with very heavy traffic – away from the town, then stopped at a gate and looked back to do some sketches.

Little Sligo town was ringed by hills, the most prominent of which was Knocknarea, the mountain where the legendary Queen Maeve (the one who was always pinching other people's farm animals) is buried, according to legend.[2] My picture, needless to say, was very unlegendary.

I then trudged the four miles or so to the village of Rathcormac, where I was supposed to turn off the main road. I stood at the sweep of the road as it wound into the village and admired the view of the mountain and the green plain below. The farmland appeared to have only just been re-claimed from some primeval sea, the mountain bursting out of it in a huge cliff. I was hungry by now, after using up lots of energy dodging the articulated lorries and camper vans full of German tourists on the N15, but I hadn't brought any sup-plies with me due to my lack of organisational skills (Moira, my charming landlady, had even left a week's supply of fig rolls next to my bed but I hadn't touched them). At the junc-

---

[2]These graves have never been opened so the mystery still exists. They have, however, found prehistoric sites in this area which are older than the pyramids. While in Sligo I was reading a book called *Celtic Myths and Legends* by an Edwardian writer, T. W. Rolleston, who believed that the indigenous population of Ireland (pre-Celtic) was related to the Egyptians.

tion, between a petrol station and a newish-looking white church, I purchased a soggy egg mayonnaise sandwich on white bread that had been curling up in a glass cabin for a few days. It was the best meal I've ever had. Just as I finished it started to sheet down with vindictive rain. I asked the stern-looking woman behind the counter which was the best route to the foot of the mountain. 'Are you going up on your own?' she asked me, disapprovingly. 'I wouldn't go up if it keeps on raining if I were you,' she said. But she wasn't me – I was a hardened traveller with high-quality walking boots (albeit with no grip) and a chunky waterproof jacket, whereas she was simply a countrywoman addicted to making white bread egg mayonnaise sandwiches. Still she could come in handy later – I thought about carrying her up on my back so she could make me some lunch in a few hours' time. But she stared at me sternly with a 'If-you-get-stuck-up-there-I-won't-be-making-you-a-special-egg-mayonnaise-rescue-sandwich' look, so I headed out into the rain.

Which had stopped. In the neat churchyard I stared at the statue of Christ on the cross for five or ten minutes to see if it moved,[3] really gave it a good hard look. Then it started to rain again. Like those venerable Princes of Piss who stand at a urinal for a while when the flow stops for five minutes or so then starts again as the next pint comes sloshing through their system. Benbulben's sheer cliffs loomed powerfully in front of me. Following the map, I turned off onto a narrow road for about a mile, then turned right at a T-junction and walked for about thirty yards. A wizened old countryman with a long Sligo nose and sad eyes, sitting on a pony-driven trap, suddenly appeared in front of me, reminding me of the

[3]SAFETY NOTE
Stand well back when approaching potential moving statues. Their movements can be very quick and you might be hit by a religious figure as it accelerates out into the road.

scene in *Nosferatu* (the original Murnau silent film, not the seventies remake with Klaus Kinski) where the hero is on a road looking for Dracula's castle. A deathly carriage arrives and he asks for directions, before it moves off silently (obviously) at an amazing speed. The old man looked at me with ancient eyes and asked where I was heading. I said up the mountain. Ah, be careful, the mountain is dangerous, don't go up if the light changes he said. Hah, he continued, but you'll be wanting to go that way. It's a lovely way up the mountain. He pointed back down the road. I hadn't even seen the little path he was talking about but I went back ten yards or so and *there it was* . . . up a beautiful vale with flowers and mad sheep, with the sound of a stream, the wind and children laughing far off in the village, a ruined cottage, rotten gates, long-forgotten crumbling dry stone walls, small flowers in the lush grass, insects – I stopped to do a couple of quick sketches, then it started to rain again.

I wasn't sure whether or not this was a bona fide track – I was following the course of a stream, but ended up having to climb up sheer waterfalls, some seven or eight feet high. If I'd had proper walking boots I might have been able to scramble up the high grassy banks but Spizz's cast-off Caterpillars were letting me down. I edged up one tall, almost sheer, bank then started to slip and had to stick my fingers in the soil for grip as I went back down again. I was on my arse several times. It was slow progress, and by five o'clock I had only done about a quarter of the walk, but kept going anyway, always keeping an eye on the huge black cloud hovering menacingly over the mountain like a monolithic German U Boat.[4]

It's exhilarating but unnerving being up a mountain on your own and I was getting a strange tingling sensation at the

[4]'Nein, you shall have no train tickets today! Ha ha ha and there's nothing you can do about it Tommy!'

base of my spine telling me something – like 'get a move on', 'send a flare' or 'order another egg mayonnaise sandwich'. Usually when you climb or walk there are loads of brightly clothed tourists around screaming, 'Valdereee', and 'Schnell!' at each other, and I could have done with a bit of company. It can get lonely when you don't really know where the fuck you're going. Group walks are OK, as long as there's not some anal retentive who insists on following a map at all times, and I've been on some lovely routes with my parents in various places (my mother is an acolyte of the *Walking with Wainwright* books). But I usually prefer to walk on my own. I see things more. I don't know why this should be – I'm not anti-social or anything like that but when there's someone else there they psychically take up your space. You are aware of them as well as the scenery. I thinks it's part of our primitive make-up – the presence of someone else means that a part of your brain will always unconsciously be thinking about them. Like they're going to hit you on the head with a rock or something whilst you're out hunting. Don't worry mum and dad if you're reading this (and I know you'll buy several thousand copies to help me earn back some of that advance . . .) I never suspected you of wanting to hit me on the head with a rock. My father wouldn't have to pussyfoot around with such underhand methods, anyway. He'd just face up to me, call me a prat and give me a good old Marquis of Queensberry jab in the ribs.

The greyfogged cloud came down for a while and with it the rain. Even though it was very sticky, I had to do up my waterproof. It had been donated by Karen, Spizz's wife, who had also migrated to Canada. And it was only now, as I struggled with the zip and realised that it was broken, that I became aware of the value of good equipment. I thought of the two of them posing on some swanky ski resort in Canada with their new Canadian celebrity friends like, Steve Podborski, Bryan Adams and, er, William Shatner, in all

their shiny new designer sportswear and laughing as if through some echo chamber from the cheap *Dr Who* special effects department. It served me right for being so tight with my money.

Luckily I had my trusty compass. I had to admit, though, that old red-faced beardy from Adare was right – it *would* have been far handier if the woman down at the sandwich shop could now have located *me* using my compass and brought up some lovely fresh (as in two-day-old) sandwiches for my delectation. But I managed to follow the rim of the mountain without falling off and at the top the cloud lifted. I started to walk with a bit more urgency. I had quite a bit of time to make up, I thought.

The top of Benbulben is like being in a huge field, with craters of mud, tufts of thick grass – for a while I didn't feel as though I was up a mountain at all, until I got to the edge and I saw the wonderful views of Donegal Bay to the north and Sligo Bay to the south-west. The dark submarine-like cloud above me was getting bigger. I started my descent. On the way down I slid no end of times,[5] once going about six feet and landing on my dodgy left wrist (the mossy pavement/sex-injury one – also used for holding pints).

I followed a barbed wire fence for what seemed like thirty miles, then wound my way through a gorse bush grove and over some walls onto a muddy track which I knew would take me off the mountain and back to civilisation. The sun was out again, reflecting off every damp surface and glancing off the bay. I eventually turned onto the elusive 'metalled road' and past a ruined stone farm house with no roof. At the side of the building was a lean-to with an old red cart inside that looked as though it hadn't been used for seventy years. Behind it was Benbulben, in front the whole sweep of Sligo Bay. Good *feng shui*. I've always been crap at visualising my future yet for a brief moment I saw myself here. It was all laid out before me. This was my dream house. I stood for a few moments, taking in the vision. Then another vision burst through – me sitting next to a fire in a cosy pub holding a newly poured pint. My dream house got packed away somewhere in my undersized short-term memory tank.

For years Irish friends have been banging on to me about how everyone in Ireland hitches around. Students, farmers, doctors, lawyers, TDs, guards, moving statues of Our Lady – they're all at it. Why anyone would need their own car is beyond me. And – get this – no-one, at least according to the myth – ever drives past if you've got your thumb out. However, I've always suspected that car drivers are like small children and dogs – they can spot a suspect character

---

[5]SAFETY NOTE
Don't wear cast-off walking gear given to you by people who are about to emigrate. It'll end in tears.

instantly through some kind of sixth sense. But I decided to give it a try. I jauntily stuck my thumb out after twiddling it around a while to warm it up (didn't want to pull any sensitive thumb muscles). Almost immediately a young woman in a little red Ford zipped past me in the opposite direction and smiled. I took this as a positive sign. I often do this – read too much into things. I am invariably wrong.

A car then went shooting past on my side of the road – it was a posh-looking bloke. I laughed as he drove past. I pressed on with my Mr Positive persona. A second car went past. A mother with kids. Hey that's cool, I said to myself. A few more cars followed. I smiled jauntily (again). And another car. I kept walking until I passed the church and reached the café, where I went in for another egg mayonnaise sandwich. The woman had sold out, but managed to persuade me that her cheese salad was of the highest quality, having been prepared only at the start of the summer. It was, indeed, delicious. I looked at her with a funny expression as if to say, 'Remember me – I was that bloke you thought you'd never see again, but I've just climbed Benbulben on my own, naked, on my hands, while singing the complete Christy Moore back catalogue.' She looked at me as if to say, 'Sod off back to England, you smug greasy-haired fecker.'

Outside I walked slowly, thumb out, up toward the end of the village, as the cars roared past me. I decided it was because I was walking, so stood still for a while. I stopped near the school at Rathcormac – just before the bend in the road as it wound up the hill perpendicular to Benbulben. The location was good, with enough room for the cars to see me and stop in time, but it was necessary to achieve success quite quickly because there was a group of amused-looking latchkey urchins with big curious grins messing around on bikes around the school yard. I ignored them and haughtily stuck out my thumb. Cars zoomed past, one after the other. What was I thinking about? The mountain, that nice warm pub. I realised that my shades were probably making me look a bit dodgy so reverted to my normal pair of specs. Still no luck. An English car came towards me. I tried to look 'ironic', surmising that he'd give me a lift. After all, that's what sets the English apart, isn't it? – a sense of 'humour' where you say one thing but mean something else ha ha ha. He drove past. Then more cars. It was getting very boring. Then one car indicated and stopped further along the road. Elated I started to move off, casting a triumphant glance at the kids who by now had become bored and looked as though they were about to go home. Someone got out then the car moved off again. Bastard! The kids drifted back, intrigued.

Fifty cars had gone by. I tried to be telepathic about it, saying things like, 'Pick me up pick me up.' I tried changing my thumb shape from an orthodox hitch angle to 'Lincoln-shire half-cocked'. I took off my glasses. I put my shades back on. Took off the shades again. Smiled. Looked serious. I was getting really tired. I tried to grin and be positive. Even the urchins were now starting to feel for me and giving me that 'You can do anything if you really try' look of encouragement.

Eventually I decided that it must be the fact that they couldn't see my eyes properly, couldn't trust me – trust is such an important thing when you're hitching. I realised I must look like a mad tinker, so I smoothed down my wild hair, though I couldn't do anything about the five days' beard.

I tried to smile again. Tried to look 'nice', the pleasant son-in-law look (which I'm not very good at). When you try and look nice and happy but you're not really feeling it, you're going to end up looking sad and confused or (in this case) just plain evil. Then I sort of went into a trance where I could hear the cars going past but all I was thinking was, 'Bastards. Fucking bastards the lot of you. Bastards bastards bastards!!' Finally, after about two hundred cars had gone past, the kids had all gone home and it was starting to get a little dark, I called it a day and chose to walk. Fuck them, I said again. A hundred thousand fucking welcomes my arse! As I walked I started to sing 'Carrickfergus' and 'Whiskey in the Jar' and 'Forty Shades of Green'. I'm crap at remembering lyrics so had to sing mostly dumms and derrs. People in their gardens looked out but I didn't care – if they were worried about a Lincolnshire nasal whine ruining some of their most famous folk songs they should have sorted out some kind of consistent policy on hitching, the fuckers. After a while the singing away to myself made me feel ecstatically happy, and I started reciting spontaneous love poetry[6] in my best Richard Burton voice – if only there'd been someone to hear it. Or write it down.

I eventually got back to real civilisation (defined as 'an area adjacent to working telephone boxes') and rang the landlady, just to let her know I was OK and hadn't been eaten by a mad rabbit up the mountain.

(Phone rings.)
Moira (the landlady): Hello.
Me: Hi, it's Tim. Just ringing to let you know that I'm OK and will be back late.
Moira: Oh Tim, you're wonderful. Oh you really are. Oh *thank you.*

---

[6]My first volume of love poetry will be titled *Nymphomaniac Jazz Chicks.*

It was really lovely to hear her voice. I had this warm vision of a roaring fire and a skipload of fig rolls. After the fifteen-mile round trip I was shagged out, so after facing another Abrakebabra ('Incredible – you've finished yet your stomach feels empty. It's magic!') I decided go and bag a couple of artists and writers to stuff and hang on my living room wall. A few years ago I read an article in the *Irish Independent* about all the writers and artists in Sligo. At the time there were probably only about six or seven, and all were friends or acquaintances of the journalist, I expect. But as soon as other writers and artists see a piece like that they think, I must live in Sligo, that's where all the writers and artists are.[7] And soon it is.

Back in the town, I went straight to a pub, where there was a session on. I started drawing some of the musicians. A woman who bore a striking resemblance to the singer Dolores Keane came up to me and asked what I was doing.

[7]A similar thing has happened in London. Pieces in the *Evening Standard* and *Time Out* about places like Hoxton and Clerkenwell have made everyone move there. Sligo is slightly more pleasant than Hoxton.

Drawing the old fiddle player with the big nose, I said. She says, that's Peter the old fiddle player with the big nose. They often get artists in painting him but they never ask and they make lots of money out of him. I said they should *shoot* artists who do that. I thought of asking Peter if he had a horse and cart and whether he'd been up near Benbulben earlier on in the day. Or had a twin brother with a fetish for German expressionist cinema. I chatted with her for a while then she introduced me to her

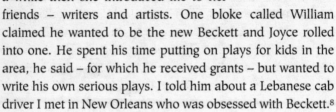

friends – writers and artists. One bloke called William claimed he wanted to be the new Beckett and Joyce rolled into one. He spent his time putting on plays for kids in the area, he said – for which he received grants – but wanted to write his own serious plays. I told him about a Lebanese cab driver I met in New Orleans who was obsessed with Beckett.[8]

---

[8]'I love Ireland. (pause) Do you know Samuel Beckett? I am studying Beckett. (pause) He is my hero. I studied Beckett at university. Drama and literature. (pause) I did one of his plays. He understands the human condition, the condition of existence. (pause) He understood the emptiness of existence, like Kafka – another of my favourite writers (pause).

'What time is your flight? Oh OK. (pause) Theatre of the absurd. *Krapp's Last Tape* is one of my favourites. (pause) Tell me, you have been to Ireland? What is is like? Hmmm. Existence is absurd when you think about it . . . Can we ever know what is the point of things (pause). Hell, man, get in your lane what the hell are you doing? Trying to kill someone? Some people are mad in their cars (pause). Everyone should read Beckett. Especially Americans. Like Beckett said in *Waiting for Godot*. Jewish conspiracy. Hollywood. American culture. The world is being taken over by McDonalds and Coca Cola.

The Americans. (pause) Low in intelligence, shallow people. (pause) Joyce, the shallowness of American culture and the world Zionist conspiracy.'

He was writing a novel about being a Lebanese taxi driver in New Orleans. Aside from Beckett, George Bush was his other hero. I engaged him in pleasantly meaningless (Beckettian?) metaphysical banter for about twenty minutes until he turned and asked something that had been bothering him for some time.

'Is it really true that Beckett married James Joyce's daughter during his stay in Paris?'

Maybe you can turn that into a play, I said. He looked at me as if to say that it was a really crap idea. It was past closing time. Then the landlord of the pub, a little sandy-haired fellow with specs, stomped over and said, straight to my face:

Landlord: Are you German? Or Australian?
Me: No, I'm English.
Landlord: Well, fuck off out of my pub then.
Me: What?
Landlord: Go on, fuck off.

Soon after leaving the pub I began to be followed by a strange-looking, thin white dog. Every time I looked back, the dog would slow down, then I would hear the little pitter patter of its feet as I carried on walking. It followed me all the way out of the town until I was about twenty yards from my B&B. Then it disappeared. The Sligo Dog Spirit Guardian of English People Who've Been Chucked Out of Pubs, I decided to call it.

According to the Dolores Keanish bodhrán player, all these artists and writers, when they can be arsed to get up from the pub and get out and about, sometimes drive to Drumcliffe where Yeats is buried and pay homage, alongside busloads of middlebrow poetry-loving Yanks and Italians who go to have their picture taken at the grave. It's all very nostalgic. Is that all this landscape has to offer, something from a Yeats poem? People stop seeing its real beauty – they 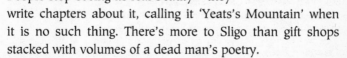 write chapters about it, calling it 'Yeats's Mountain' when it is no such thing. There's more to Sligo than gift shops stacked with volumes of a dead man's poetry.

W. B. Yeats v. Daniel Donnell – a Cultural Conflict

Around Sligo

People have had enough of the pretending, the prevarication and the pussyfooting around the subject. Enough is enough. They want the powers that be – the government, the *Irish Times*, the *Late Late Show*, Ian Paisley, whoever – to announce who Ireland's greatest ever cultural hero is. William Butler Yeats or Daniel O'Donnell?

The dead poet may seem to be the favourite in many people's eyes. He's dead for a start (always a good thing for a hero to be). He also begat a whole artistic movement – nay, a cultural repositioning, placing Celtic folklore once again at the forefront of Irish life. But O'Donnell, too, has his own followers, hordes of middle-aged women with lacquered hairdos who would swear that Daniel is the new Elvis and that they are part of some grander scheme. There are other similarities. Yeats had the haughty bearing and highly strung sensitivities of the Polexfens, his mother's patrician family. O'Donnell, meanwhile, is widely known to be a 'mammy's boy'.

(Scene – B&B on the outskirts of Sligo. I am standing in the hall, being encouraged to go and visit Daniel O'Donnell's hotel in Donegal by Moira. I am not keen, preferring to have a cup of tea and a bath, then head off down to a pub in Sligo Town.

Moira puts herself between me and the tea, rests her head on one side, places her hands on her hips and continues talking in a singsong Mayo accent.)

Moira: Do you like Daniel, Tim? Do you?

Me: I, er, well . . .

Moira: I like Daniel. I like Daniel *a lot*. He's a lovely, lovely voice. Do you like Daniel's voice, Tim?

Me: Ermm . . .

Moira: Oh, it's *lovely*. Wait till I tell yer, Tim, wait till I tell you. People say he's a mammy's boy. Do *you* think Daniel's a mammy's boy, Tim?

Me: Well . . .

Moira: (winking) But you know what they mean when they say he's a mammy's boy? Don't you? Don't you, Tim? They mean that he doesn't like girls *(nods exaggeratedly then winks again)*. It's jealousy, Tim. That's what it is. *Jealousy*. He's got a lovely voice and a lovely hotel and he's popular so they have to make up these stories about him. Like they say that his girlfriend is really his mother.

Me: Eh? . . .

Moira: Have you heard that one, Tim? Have you? Oh it'll *murder* you, it will. They say he's in love with his mother and is pretending to have a girlfriend so he can stay with his mother. No one has seen this girl, but I don't believe it, Tim. Do you believe it?

Me: Gosh, it's . . .

(A middle aged woman comes down the stairs.)

Moira: Oh, here's Mo. Mo's been to Daniel's. Mo, tell Tim about Daniel.

Mo: Oh he's lovely. I went to his hotel yesterday.

Moira: Was he there? Mo? Was he?

Mo: No, he wasn't there. But we had a cup of tea and saw some pictures of him. I'm going to go again tomorrow.

DANIEL'S HOUSE

VIKING HOUSE HOTEL

DANIEL'S FANS

DANIEL'S JUMPER

(A middle-aged man comes down the stairs. It is Mo's husband.)

Moira: Tom. Mo says you're going to see Daniel again tomorrow.

(Mo winces.)

Tom: What? We only went yesterday.

Mo: Ah, but he wasn't there, Tom, was he? He might be there tomorrow.

Tom: Ah, jaysus. And if he's not we'll have to go the next day. Then it'll be Joe Dolan's bar, then God knows who else's place.

Me: Do they all have bars or hotels, these singers?

Moira: Oh no, Tim. There's only Daniel who's got a hotel and Joe Dolan's got a bar in Mullingar.

Me: I've never heard of Joe Dolan.

Moira: *(evidently not keen to talk about Joe Dolan)* Anyway, it's a nice hotel, isn't it, Tom? Isn't it?

Me: So do you like Daniel, Tom?

(Tom looks at me and rolls his eyes.)

Moira: *(laughing)* Tom thinks he's a mammy's boy, don't you, Tom? Don't you?

(Mo ruffles around in her handbag and takes out a sheaf of postcards.)

Mo: Look, I got these at Daniel's. It's a picture of the hotel.

Moira: Oh Mo. It's beautiful. Tim, look at this. Isn't it lovely?

Me: *(looking at picture of very ugly-looking modern hotel)* Mmm, it's er . . .

Mo: Would you like that picture, Tim?

Me: Er, I . . .

Moira: Oh, yes, Tim, that's nice, isn't it? That's very nice of you, Mo. Isn't it, Tim?

After my trip up the mountain, it was time to get some insider information on Yeats.

(Scene – B&B on the outskirts of Sligo. I am standing in the sitting room, searching through all the tourist guides and leaflets for something about Yeats. There's a load of stuff about adventure holidays, fishing, trips on lakes, zoos and restaurants, but nothing about Ireland's No. 1 – or perhaps No. 2 – cultural hero. Moira suddenly appears in the doorway.)

Moira: Oh Tim. How are you?

Me: Great. I was just looking through your stuff here.

Moira: Oh there's some great things to do, Tim. Did you see the one about boat trips? Oh, wait till I tell you. They stop off at all these interesting places. And there's a very nice restaurant in town. I had a nice leaflet but I gave it to that American couple who was in here last night, the ones here when I made your cup of tea and they were having a cup of tea too – do you remember, Tim? And so I gave it to them and they said they'd get me some more leaflets after their meal. Would you like me to get you one? Would you, Tim?

Me: Well, I was really looking for something about Yeats.

Moira: *(frowning and obviously disappointed)* Oh.

Me: Well, I thought I'd like to go to the Yeats museum now I've been up the mountain.

Moira: *(looking puzzled and slightly concerned)* Well, I've never been to either of those, but I'm told the museum is just a load of photographs. Not very interesting at all, Tim.

Me: What about Loch Gar and Innisfree?

Moira: Oh the loch's just down the road. You can get a boat or go fishing. Oh, that's lovely that is, Tim. Lovely.

Me: OK.

Moira: Do you like Yeats, Tim? Do you? I never actually read anything by him, Tim. I only really heard of him about ten years ago. All these French and Italian students started coming and visiting his gravestone. This lovely French girl came to stay once and said she thought Yeats was a lovely man, a beautiful man it was she said. He's a poet, isn't he?

A few days after these conversations the headline on the front page of the Irish *Daily Mirror* read *Mammy's Boy Pretends to Have Girlfriend* (actually it was something like *Daniel's New Love*). A picture of a simpering Daniel staring into the eyes of a not-bad-looking woman who looked like a nurse or primary school teacher. Daniel had taken her along to some awards night and it was big, big news. I went out and bought *Thoughts of Home*, a Daniel O'Donnell CD, to find out what all the fuss was about. If you've ever perused Daniel's work in a record shop you'll see that many of his releases are concept albums. Religion, Classic Songs, Irish Ballads and this one, *Thoughts of Home*, all about wistful sentimental songs based loosely around the idea of loss and alienation.

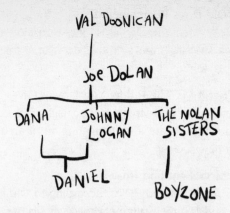

Track 1: 'My Shoes Keep Walking Back to You'
Soft rock beat. Daniel does Roy Orbison, echoey vocal as if recorded in the gents at the Boston Arms in Tufnell Park. Am I right?

Track 2: 'The Mountains of Morne'
Oirishy ballad. Violins. Vocal high in mix. Song about a bloke trying to make it in London town but pining for home back on the mountains of Morne. Mournful, Joy Division meets Joseph Locke.

Track 3: 'London Leaves'
Jauntier arrangement which belies the sad sentiment. Daniel likens love to nature – death and rebirth. 'Like the leaves you'll soon be gone from me,' sings Daniel, plaintively. Like to see Shane MacGowan and Jah Wobble on this one.

Track 4: 'Blue Eyes Crying in the Rain'
Chas 'n' Dave Daniel sings about love dying again. Needs to put a bit more pain into his vocals, but hits the note every time. Sounds like fifties' crooner. Some slide guitar.

Track 5: 'Old Days Remembered'
Waltz. Decay. Memories. What is time? Consciousness. Lots of grannies swaying from side to side with Daniel scarves chanting his name.

Track 6: 'Send Me The Pillow You Dream On'
Heavy metal guitar and screaming vocals, Daniel sings about bringing down the state and instigating an anarchist's template for a new society.

Track 7: 'Moonlight and Roses'
Did the CIA kill Kennedy? Yes, according to Daniel who in this song outlines their attempts to cover up the vast conspiracy. Barrel organ and tuba.

Track 8: 'A Little Piece of Heaven'

Track 9: 'Far, Far from Home'
Drum-and-bass remix of an old classic with Daniel in fine form.

Track 10: 'The Isle of Innisfree'
Moany whiny vocals over meat and potatoes pub band. Fans of Yeats may want to compare Daniel's version with their hero's.

Plus six more great tracks . . .

Track 11: 'My Heart Skips a Beat'

Track 12: 'I Know One'

Track 13: 'I'll Take You Home Again, Kathleen'

Track 14: 'Second Fiddle'

Track 15: 'My Favourite Memory'

Track 16: 'Forty Shades of Green'

It was pissing it down outside. I put on my waterproof and ran out into the wet pattering, turning left towards the black shape of Knocknarea past bungalows and fields. Round down another lane then turned left at some trees at the bottom of a little hill. This took me up to the waterside. The loch was misty and silent. I stood for a while trying to be poet-like, but all I could come up with was I am fucking cold. Brr brr. I then went up to the holy well and stared at the statues to see if they would move. A man arrived with a dog. He stared at me for a while as I stared at Christ. I think he thought I was taking the piss out of Jesus. I wasn't. I was just staring to see if this statue would move. If I'd been taking the piss, I would have stood with my arms outstretched or something against a tree. I turned round and wandered back to the lane, trying to catch the eye of the man with a dog. But he refused, merely staring straight ahead.

I got back into the house. I knew I'd only have about five more minutes to write down my thoughts before my memory switched off and they were gone forever.

(Scene – B&B on the outskirts of Sligo. I am standing in the hall, soaking wet and about to head upstairs to put pen to paper, when Moira appears in front of me, blocking my way to the stairs. She puts her hands together as though about to tell me bad news.)

Moira: Oh, Tim. Wait till I tell yer. You know that leaflet about the restaurant I said to you before, the one I gave to the Americans, well I said they were going to bring me some more so you could have one but, do you know, Tim, they've paid up and gone and they didn't bring me any more leaflets. What do you think of that then, Tim? Oh I don't know.

They're Americans but I think they're strange. They get up very early in the morning and they go out for the day then they come back and go to bed early. Or they go to a restaurant – I told them about that restaurant Tim, they didn't know anything about it until I gave them that leaflet, Tim. Have you been to America, Tim? I'd like to go to America. I've got friends in America. My sister lives in Australia, though. I've been to Australia. Do you like Australians, Tim? They're very loud, aren't they? But Americans, they are polite, aren't they. Those people you met yesterday, the couple I told you about, the ones that didn't want any biscuits and she didn't take milk with her tea, they were very nice. I'd rather have nice people staying here than not nice people. We had some people from the north last year, Catholics they were and I'm a Catholic but I don't really like Catholics from the north they're very rude. I like Protestants from the North they're very nice people, very polite and their children are very well behaved but these Catholics they were very loud and they stayed up late one night in the sitting room and got drunk and my husband had to go downstairs to tell them to be quiet and they had a girl with them and he says you aren't staying here and they says who d'ya think you are, the police, and he says no but the police only lives three doors down I'll get him for yer. They says no thanks and he says I want you out first thing in the morning and I want you out now he says to the girl and I don't know, Tim, about all this politics; my husband does but I don't, Tim, but what do you think about this united Ireland I'm sure I don't know we don't really want them down here to tell you the truth because it's all trouble.

People want their cultural heroes to say something about the society that spawned them. They also want them to have nice haircuts and look good on TV. So who's best, W. B. or Daniel? This is the question that will ping around your brain like a mink in a fishtank that's taken what it thinks is ecstasy but is actually a mixture of rat poison and aspirin, long after you've thrown this book in the bin or given it away to someone at work you don't really like.

Who's closest to his mother?
Yeats not bad but Daniel is the world's best at mother loving.
Yeats 6   Daniel 10

Who's more in touch with Irish culture?
Daniel does a few old Irish ballads but Yeats repositioned high culture in the early years of the century.
Yeats 9   Daniel 5

Who would be best at running a hotel?
Yeats a bit up in the clouds, but Daniel is a successful hotelier as well as one of the world's top singers.
Yeats 4   Daniel 8

Who's better in a blandish country music idiom?
Yeats tended not to stray into this territory. But it's Daniel's favourite genre.
Yeats 3   Daniel 9

Who has reinstated traditional Celtic culture into the fabric of Irish national identity?
This is Yeats's legacy. Daniel has had some swirly Celtic patterns on his album covers now and then.
Yeats 10   Daniel 3

Final score Yeats 32, Daniel 35.
Daniel O'Donnell is Ireland's Number 1 cultural hero.

I sent a message to Daniel to tell him the news.

> Dear Daniel,
> I am currently writing a book based around various journeys I've made in Ireland. My travels around Sligo and Donegal led me inevitably to the work of yourself and the celebrated poet William Butler Yeats. It soon became obvious to me that you are in your way just as important in

terms of Irish culture as Yeats. A further comparison of both of your bodies of work led me to the conclusion that might surprise you – it could be argued that you have probably had more of a lasting impact on Irish life than Yeats himself. Have you ever recorded any of Yeats's poetry in the form of song?

One other thing – could you tell me whether or not the track 'My Shoes Keep Walking Back to You' on your album *Thoughts of Home* was recorded live at the Boston Arms in Tufnell Park, London.

Yours sincerely,

Tim Bradford

PS: Next time I'm up in Donegal I'll pop into your hotel. I've already got one of your postcards.

No reply from Daniel. Undeterred, I recorded a song of my own composition, entitled 'The Singing Leprechaun' (I sent it to a couple of publishers as well).

Ever since the day I was born
For the green hills of Ireland I did mourn
And never will I rest, that I have sworn,
Until I discover the singing leprechaun.

Oh the singing leprechaun
Oh the singing leprechaun
He isn't a real leprechaun at all
And he's only eight inches tall.

Still waiting to hear about this one.

Daniel may be a soft wet blanket who loves his mammy, but I bet he'd have stopped for me when I was hitching on the N15 if he'd heard me killing 'Forty Shades of Green' at the top of my inadequate voice.

The Ian Paisley Impersonators Talk about Weapons

Derry City Walls

For several days in Derry I lay ill with flu, sweating and shivering with just a soft blanket and sheet over me. It felt like prison, the bare walls of the hostel, no TV. I couldn't get hold of any e-mails because the 'net café had recently closed; even most of the phones nearby seemed to have been vandalised. I was cut off. At night I could hear loud club music mixed with rich Northern Irish voices, hallucinations, a nightmare, a new dance record about the Troubles perhaps with cut-ups of McGuinness, Adams, Paisley. I was living solely on the hostel's greasy breakfasts – saturated fat and troubled dreams.

I hadn't really planned to go to the North – it would turn my journey into something else, I feared, something which would mean I'd have to think about politics and history, even though temperamentally I was inclined just to go for walks and hang out with people. It had never really crossed my mind until I was alone on the mountain briefly to leave the cosy confines of the Republic. In Derry, unlike the rest of Ireland, I knew I'd be aware of being English. It somehow felt loaded with meaning. I suppose

I knew my illness was psychosomatic all along.[1]

I'd had that sickly butterflies feeling in my stomach as soon as I arrived. The reputation of a city gets carried around with you subconsciously – I'd read something dodgy about Quito in Ecuador in a guide book so was always watching my back when I was there; New York; New Orleans; parts of Brixton; Caistor in Lincolnshire (a rival town ten miles away from where I was brought up) – all have given me that 'buzz' at some time. From early childhood I'd heard stories on the TV and radio about Derry (or Londonderry as it was always known). Hearing about pubs being blown up, someone being shot by a sniper, the Bogside and, mostly, Bloody Sunday, when thirteen innocent people were shot by the British army while on a peaceful protest march.

On my last night I felt better and ventured out – Derry seemed like a mixture of a smaller version of Leeds or Manchester and the sort of medieval walled city that you'd get in Italy or central France. Derry was in fact the last walled town of its type, the most modern in Europe. The walls themselves are in good condition and have immense symbolism for many of the inhabitants – it was here that the Apprentice Boys locked the gates to Catholic King James II's advancing army in 1692 (one of the reasons why the lads with the bowler hats go marching every year).

It was a warm, slightly sticky evening. The city was quiet, with just a bit of traffic on the ring road down below. Tucked away just near one of the gates was a little craft village, designed for the tourists who don't come – even in high sea-

---

[1] I'd got something like that the year before, on election night in England. I spent the entire evening projectile vomiting. I'd met some friends but after about twenty minutes I had to go home – walking down Tottenham Court Road spewing six feet in front of me. Puked twelve times before I got home. I sat up until six cheering and puking into a bucket. At the defining moment, when Portillo went down all along our street there were cheers and I cheered too then barfed again. My mother – who knows how sensitive I am – had a theory that it was cathartic: after eighteen years I was exorcising those foul Tory spirits.

son, the restaurants were empty. Or maybe it was just me –
everything seemed so much quieter than any other big town
I'd been to. I walked around the walls a few times, occasionally stopping to read the little information plaques on the
wall. At one section the path opened out into a wider cobbled
area with trees, which at one stage was used as a parade
ground and where now all you'd want to do was open a
bottle of wine, have a picnic and run your fingers through
someone's hair. I looked down to the east at the famous *You
Are Now Entering Free Derry* mural painted on an end terrace
wall. A symbol of the Republican struggle, it now stands in
the middle of a dual carriageway, the only remains of the
street from which it sprang – modern life pouring around it
and leaving it looking like a relic. I walked a few hundred
yards to the north and noticed another mural, this time for
King Billy's Flute Band, adorned with Union Jacks. As in all
wars, these people who live virtually side by side must have
so much in common – yet as usual they are the ones, rather
than the masters of rhetoric and politic, whose loved ones
never came back.[2]

You can still see a few remnants of the recent past – barbed
wire, a deserted army command post – and from an older
time too – various cannons dotted around. Even after all my
preconceptions (and I had more cultural and emotional bag-
gage than usual about this visit), all I could see now was
beautiful scenery and a view over to the sweeping river as
the sun began to go down. Tottering fifty yards behind me
I heard a rich Ulster voice nattering away: 'Ah but in the
First World War the Bruttush used Lay Unfailds.' It was a
group of old lads walking round the walls just behind me.
They were talking in foghorn Ian Paisley voices – maybe, I

[2]Maybe this is an old-fashioned analysis. Working-class communities have
nurtured the conflict just as much. Cockneys hate Geordies, Mancs hate
Merseysiders. These rivalries and resentments will always be there but it doesn't
necessitate killing.

thought, it was a branch of the good Reverend's Fan Club, perhaps visiting from Pretoria or Chicago or Sydney, grown men whose hobby is to sound like their hero and repeat his catchphrases. They started chatting about all the different kinds of shells that would have been fired in various wars, particularly World War Two. They were, of course, Irish, on some kind of reunion trip. I imagined them staggering off a big coach on a geriatrics' tour of the province.

'Nay Surranda!' That was his best soundbite. Ian Paisley always came across as a loudmouthed bigot on British TV – though maybe this was just the way his speeches were edited for broadcast, leaving in all the juicy bits – and most people I know held him in contempt for always putting the brakes on any kind of possible peace deal. Yet travelling around in Ireland I'd been surprised by the amount of people who, although disagreeing with his politics, seemed sympathetic towards Paisley, that he was honest and stuck to his principles, and was actually a better man than the caricature on the news broadcasts. This is the trouble when, as an outsider, your views – like mine – are taken entirely from the media, and have already been shaped to some extent by someone else. Yet I'd always had a strange admiration too for one of the leaders of the other side, Gerry Adams, though I thought he was much cleverer and more dangerous than an old blood-and-thunder merchant like Paisley. Weirdly, I got very angry when a journalist friend of mine said she'd met Adams at some function and thought he was 'sex on legs'. I was somehow outraged at this – I don't know why I got so irate. Perhaps it was the fear in the cautious sensible Englishman of the dark dangerous Celt.

I'd been wandering around in a T-shirt, shades, straggly hair and the usual five-day beard. I must have looked like death. My face wasn't quite as white as usual but the eyes were still gone and each step felt as though it was taking up all my energy. A man said something to me, like, 'Oyy rayyy oi you' – one of a pair of middle-aged drunkards sitting on a bench. I turned and walked back towards them. He looked visibly surprised and shocked and I realised it did seem a bit intimidatory. Sorry mate, didn't hear you, what did you say? He smiled. Ah, an Aussie eh? Spare a bit o' change, Aussie? Stuff the English, eh? I handed over a quid and decided not to get into an explanation of my roots.

Most of the shops in the centre of Derry were English, as were the fucked-up phone boxes. I had to keep telling myself that – politically, at any rate – Derry wasn't another country, it was the UK. I certainly didn't feel a part of it, though. Yet it was also so different from the Ireland I'd been travelling around in – the people were harder looking, like Limerick, say, but decked out in what I can only describe as Northern English style, buttoned-up shirts and cropped hair for the blokes, girls in short skirts and tight dresses. You won't get any of your hippy tie-dye mystical Celt bollocks henna tattoos here, Tim, my lad. In the pubs the tensions seemed electric (invented by me, no doubt) where steely-eyed bald old men and their young moustachioed sons sat nursing pints and staring at TV sets on the wall, as blokes do all over the world when there is some kind of football programme on. In Total Jessie Mode, I had a half and glanced at some highlights, not catching people's eye, as loud club music thudded in from the street.

In all of these places it would be either Celtic or Rangers. I've seen Celtic–Rangers games a few times, and still watch it now and again on TV, though I am always put off by the intensity of the fixture. Tribal roar. We are great and you are shit. The Old Firm, the Tims against the Hun, the green against the blue (or orange), us against them, Catholic v. Protestant. No surrender to the IRA (a cry which is heard increasingly at England matches, bizarrely enough). Each time an Old Firm game takes place it's like the Battle of the Boyne being re-fought in front of seventy thousand

Glaswegians. In real life it's crap, but you can just about get away with it in football, it's that sense of theatre that creates what people call atmosphere. If it was all too cuddly the 'edge' would go. Can you tell I'm not convinced?

A few years ago I went round to my friend Mike's house to watch a big cup game on Sky Sport. Mike is a six-foot-three-inch gruff unshaven Scot with dark Connaught genes and on these occasions a Celtic shirt far too small for him which makes his arms pop out straight like a corkscrew. He'd invited me and a few other oddballs for a night of sectarian fun. One of his friends arrived sporting a brand new top – I couldn't take my eyes off the proud figure sitting on the back of a rearing horse, his thick hair (or was it a wig?) blowing in the wind. It was the first fluorescent Rave-influenced William of Orange T-shirt I had ever seen. Splodges of bright orange and grey over a white background with a really badly drawn picture of Billy on horseback, the explanatory words 'King William' above it (which was just as well, because the character depicted could have been anyone from the Duke of Wellington to the Cisco Kid, or even my great-great-grandfather the Horseperson[3]).

'That is the most fantastically coloured sectarian garment I've ever seen,' I said to the owner of the shirt, ever so slightly awe-struck, 'but why is King Billy wearing stockings and suspenders?' (It's true. It really did look as though he was wearing the sort of cheap lingerie you get at jumble sales or pre-Christmas everything-a-pound bargain shops.)

'What?' He looked at me with eighty per-cent pity and twenty per-cent menace. The lad was a Chelsea fan who

---

[3] I really liked the Richard Harris film *A Man Called Horse*, about an Englishman who goes to live with native Americans in the eighteenth century, and thought of my ancestor in a sequel, *A Person Called Horseperson*.

supported Rangers as well because 'It's the British thing, innit. The flag and that. Patriotism.'

And I suppose that's what I have never understood, and still don't. That these people who, ostensibly, share the same religion as me would have a far more defined idea of their nationalism than I do, though I was born and brought up in England. Yet walking the Derry walls on a sunlit evening, although history is thick in the air you have to believe that in years to come the sectarian rituals will have no more real meaning than a village Morris Dance or pan-cake race.

As night fell the hardcore techno noise thudding out from basement clubs was turned up a notch and the loud-voiced lads out and about seemed even more like boisterous squad-dies. Except now I could see Man Utd shirts, Leeds shirts too. I popped into a couple of pubs and found none of the themey Oirish style that I thought might have permeated up from the South. I sat down at a table in one (Mad Relation: 'You're mad. Completely mad!'), a place gradually filling up with groups and couples, and tried to get a handle again on what this place actually was. I thought of the war-torn com-munity I had heard about on TV as a kid. I thought about the kind of ruthlessness that enabled people to kill their own countrymen and neighbours over an Idea About Life, and decided you could drive yourself mad thinking about the waste.

I tried to hold that thought, tried to feel earnest and con-cerned, the sensitive traveller searching for expressive and sympathetic phrases. Then the friendly waitress brought my fish pie.

'Dyay wunt anothor Gunnuss?' she asked as I stuffed my face greedily. I nodded and she scuttled off, my eyes fixed on the game show on the ceiling-mounted TV as the couple next to me started stroking each other's hair and the lads at the table behind discussed which club they should go to that night. Like a goldfish my mind emptied of everything. Perhaps long-term memory is over-rated after all.

Next morning at breakfast I was first down and was tucking into my sausage and egg when I heard what sounded like the leader of the Democratic Unionist Party coming down the corridor. It was the old lads, the weapons experts, but dressed in cycling gear. They cut fine figures. They wolfed down their food and talked about their next journey. I, in my jeans and ever-expanding beer gut, felt slightly embarrassed as they filed out and headed for the open road. I was going back to the comfort and security of the Republic – on the way to the bus station I passed a sports shop full of Celtic paraphernalia and saw the reflection of a confused and uneasy man.

Thinking in Four-part Harmony is a Scary Thing to Contemplate

Mullingar to Moate

I had decided to go to Mullingar because of something I read in the *Rough Guide* about a former mad inhabitant who believed he was a bee. That gives Mullingar a head start over most towns. But don't get too excited about the story because I won't be mentioning it again. Back in Doolin, when Ted had found out where I was going he got excited because, of course, *he* had a musician friend in Mullingar,[1] a guy called Declan, and said he'd get in touch with him to say I was coming.

'No that's all right,' I said.

Ted insisted.

'Really,' I said, Englishly, 'I don't want to be any trouble'. Ted wouldn't have understood that attitude, but he wasn't listening anyway, so went ahead and phoned him up. Declan said they wouldn't be in Mullingar that night but were playing a gig in a town called Moate about twenty miles south west and I was welcome to come along. 'His name's Tim and he's a tallish bioke with long messy blond hair. You can't miss him,' said Ted, pleased.

[1] Some people have a girl in every port. Ted has a backing musician in every prosperous market town.

'Thanks Ted,' I said. Cheers mate.

Mullingar is a grey but prosperous country town where there didn't seem to be that much to do during the day apart from eat toasted sandwiches in dark and empty pubs, stare at the screens in the Internet café, or attend a function at the main hotel full of posh dressed-up people blathering on about fox hunting and fine wine. I decided, after all my living it up, that I was too tired to look for Declan and his mates, so sat in a crappyish restaurant and ordered a meal.

'I'll just see if the chef is still there,' said the pouty waiter.

He phoned the kitchen and said they had a customer. He raised his eyebrows and pursed his lips as he got a rant from the other end.

'No,' he said slowly, 'that's not my problem, it's your problem!' Fantastic, this was dialogue straight from *The Usual Suspects*.

'Don't give me that,' he almost shouted, then slammed the phone down. He was all smiles as he came over. 'Are you ready to order?'

As I was finishing off my meal the moody chef (who obviously thought he was bloody Marco Pierre White) came and stood at the bar to make up with the waiter, and frowned at me. He was like a smaller Sean Penn with a thin black moustache. I wanted to say, 'Your food is shite, you pretentious little git,' but didn't (too English, see, English don't *do* that stuff), so just picked at the overcooked goo feeling sorry for myself. After paying up, at about 11.30 I was about to go into a blues session in one of the nearby pubs when suddenly a vision appeared in the sky, long reddish/yellow beard flowing. It was Ted.

'And lo I say unto you, get ye to Moate, for 'tis written that I might need some backing singers at some time or other so I must need to keep them sweet. You can buy them a pint and say it's from me.' A great vision – I changed my mind and decided to go to Moate after all. As I strolled across to the taxi

rank the vision appeared again, 'Oh, and Tim, if they're coming to Doolin again can you get them to bring some brochures
about bass amplifiers. Ta. Oh, and some bottles of red lemonade. We've run out up here.' Twenty pounds later I stood
outside Into the West, a saloony looking joint in the centre of
Moate, covered in light bulbs. I could already hear sweet
singing. Was it angels? Lord, I'm a comin'.

As I entered and adjusted my eyes to the smoke and booze
haze I saw a crowd of four young blokes in a corner strum-
ming acoustic guitars and singing 'Four Seasons in One Day',
surrounded by a large crowd of drinkers. I stood at the bar
and ordered a pint. When the song was finished I went over
to the musicians and said I was looking for a bloke called
Declan.

'Ah you must be Tim. Great. Sit yourself down! Have you
got a drink?' I was slightly confused. I'd imagined this mate
of Ted's to be a middle-aged, big-bearded guy in his fifties
or sixties (yes, a sort of Ted clone) yet Declan, in his late
twenties–early thirties, looked like a cross between Evan
Dando and Barbra Streisand with long blond curly hair
falling down to his shoulders. He and his mates did another
Crowded House song, 'Whenever I Fall at Your Feet'.
Crowded House are a bit of a wussy band – nice harmonies
and all that but the singing and the lyrics are wimpy, like
some bloke whose heart just breaks every morning when he
looks out the window at the little birdies. For sure, Declan
and his mates sounded better than the original. I was introduced to the band – apart from Declan there was Little
Declan – no relation – who looked like a gone-to-seed fly-
weight boxer; Albert Lee, who in a previous era would have
been a New York cop and Deej, and who was the dead ringer
for Jeff Tweedy from the country band Wilco. I sat and
gabbed away with some of their mates while the band sang
for an hour or so. It was strange for me to hear four friends
with such amazing voices who could sing in harmony

like that. One amongst any particular group is usually rare enough.[2]

And then the beers really started to flow – and a beer in a lock-in is a beautiful thing indeed. Someone foolishly got me a big whiskey and I was on maee wai, chatting too the landlords dorter about all kynds of rubbish and she rote her a dress annumber down yahaay and invited me to stai with her in Dublin then my head started to loll a bitt lollll all kinez ov rubbish she invited me to Dublin you knowm she did what's that a gitar was thrust into my hanz grinning faces all around big grins go on Tim youuu plaaay somethin' you you yoooou, so I concraitid very hard and remembered G major strummm strumm strummitti strummm I like yu C major thingy waiyoorspaklin G major thingy earings C laayy Gagenst yor C skin sooo D major browwwn strummma strumm strumm strrumm etc. yoouuu knoww I wohnlet yoouuu doowwwwn strumm strummm . . . Aficionados will recognise a reedy whiny Lincolnshire version of 'Peaceful Easy Feeling' by the Eagles, thank God that's finished, polite applause you luvlipeepl, and then a bull of a man with glasses called Enda began singing a Tom Waits sing thing in a voyss soooo loooow my bowels startid to rumble and it woke me up a bit where's the bloke who thought he was a bee then I suddenly lose it and find it again and we're on a coach heading back to Mullingar and I'm sitting with

[2]It had never been like that when I tried to sing with my friends – I was in various bands as a kid with friends like Plendy, Scotty and my brother Toby (the letter y is very popular in Lincolnshire – something to do with the Vikings apparently) but none of us could really hit a note.

Little Declan holding a can of some kind of pisswater and we're all singing in close-part harmonies and it's scary because I'm singing too aarrgh they have infected me then head lolls sleep I need sleep then awake again, stone-cold sober, on the early-in-the morning streets of Mullingar, and we're buying thirty-two beers from a nice bloke with glasses who runs a pub.

'Well, I'll be off then,' I say, jauntily, and begin to prance off towards my hotel with my best Pretending To Be Mr Sober grin, but these are strange music sprites who have a spell on me and I am dragged off to Declan's ex-girlfriend's house while she is away (note to editor – maybe change Declan's name so he won't get done for this) and we sit around and drink drunk drink the beer and wine too and as if by further magic two pretty girls arrive – daaa daaahhh – at the door: one a little Irish redhead, one tall blonde and French and it's more singing and I am now even thinking in four-part harmony and that is a scary thing to contemplate:

Thinking in four-part harmony is a scary thing to contemplate Thinking in four-part harmony is a scary thing to contemplate Thinking in four-part harmony is a scary thing to contemplate Thinking in four-part harmony is a scary thing to contemplate Thinking in four-part harmony is a scary thing to contemplate is a scary thing to contemplate Thinking in four-part harmony is a scary thing to contemplate

And Declan has taken some kind of powerful pheromone spray because one girl is on his knee and the other hanging around sitting at his feet so I chat with Arthur Lee about country music and Ted in Doolin who they love very much apparently then I can feel my head lolling loll I am goin agin goin sleep muss sleep piisst as fart pisst its five in th' mornin no don't go they say musss go muss sleep go help help muss escape from evil music sprites evil evil and sleep where you stayin tell hotel you mad expense stay here madman I go bye bye evil music people . . .

Heritage Ireland

The arts centre, or craft shop, is the beating heart of Heritage Ireland, that fictional country that lies somewhere between the Irish Sea and the Atlantic Ocean. These shops contain all the best luxury items that Ireland's pottery, tweed, linen, porcelain and musical-leprechaun craftspeople can throw at you – taking you back to a time before the invention of cars and electricity, when the populace lived on Irish toffee and green Guinness.

Leprechauns in snow domes

Plastic, liquid-filled domes with white flakes and a seated leprechaun, waiting to be shaken up. All over the USA people will have them on their TVs or stuck to their gun cabinets. The legend of the leprechaun in the snow is an ancient one – he went through the back of a drinks cabinet in a little bar in Kilkenny and ended up in Narnia. That's the official version, anyway. He's holding a shamrock, though it looks more like broccoli. It's not snowing. Pick up the dome and shake it around. Now it's snowing! Hey!!

Plasticy Celtic swirly pendants

These pendants, tied to a piece of mouldy bootlace, are based on ancient Newgrange designs that are supposed to represent deep 'stuff'. They're made of some kind of plastic and look like squiggles designed by monkeys let loose on an old spirograph, carved into pieces of the finest kiln-fired dogshit.

Amusing Guinness T-shirts

Badly drawn cartoons of what happens after four pints of Guinness screen-printed onto a black cotton T-shirt. People will pass you in the street, point at you and go 'Ha Ha!' Will give their new owners (rictus-grinning fat-arsed tourists) pleasure for years and years.

Tweed flat caps

Transform yourself into a bookie or former manager of the Irish football team with these classic, timeless hats. Woven from a mixture of Irish grass, cabbage and wood shavings.

'Our Lady' figurines

Ireland's No. 1 female star moulded into a fine statuette by some of the country's leading sculptors.

MARYLAND

South

WATERFORD

BLARNEY

ROSSLARE

BALLINSPITTLE

TRAMORE

HAMMERSMITH

YOUGHAL

MARYLAND

Smelly Stuff, God, Moving Statues and Space Jockeys

Ballinspittle, Co. Cork

Back in 1996 I'd met a poet in a pub at the bottom of Shandon Hill in Cork who told me that his life had meaning because he had decided that God was a fish. You could go snorkelling in the Caribbean and think, wow, one of these fish right in front of me might be God, he said. But which one? You could spend hours looking through the shoal for the God-fish and all the time God would be sucking on a sea anemone about fifty yards away on the ocean floor. Anyway, I said to the poet, what sort of fish? Tuna? Parrot fish? Stickleback? That strange prehistoric fish they found in the Indian Ocean around the end of the 1970s? The poet had no more answers.

How about, I suggested, if God was a beer. Granted, it's not a very original thought. Red-eyed alcos throughout the world must stare at their bevvies and wonder if the Almighty is about to slide down their throat. But if God was a beer, he'd be a pint of Guinness. Ah, said the poet, but there's Guinness and there's Guinness. Any particular pint of Guinness you're talking about here?

'How about that pint in McGann's, a lively little pub on the north side of Doolin, Co. Clare.'

'Fair enough. When though?'

'OK, the *first* pint I had on the 29th of December 1993, at about half-past nine at night. I looked at Him for a couple of seconds, then downed God in one. I'd just met up with some friends and there was a music session going on.'

'Mmm. Can't you be a bit more specific than that?'

When I heard that the statues were on the move again in various places in Ireland I arranged to meet up with Theresa and Molly again and drive down to Ballinspittle. It was here, back in 1984, that Our Lady (the Virgin Mary) had appeared to a group of schoolchildren and told them that there should be world peace, that contraception was bad and everyone should vote for Fianna Fáil. The children's father probably had a hotel chain in the area. So they built the grotto to commemorate this amazing phenomenon. Then a short while afterwards a few local adults said they'd seen the statue move. She raised her arm or something like that, as if waving to someone. Then it all went crazy and the grotto became internationally famous, like the one at Medjugorje in Yugoslavia. I spoke to a couple of people who claimed they had seen 'something' at the grotto. I decided to investigate, in my usual methodical style.

'Why are we going to look at a statue?' asked Molly, with the good sense and intelligence of a child.

'Tim thinks it might move,' said her mother. Molly looked

at me crossly. She was used to chiding me for being silly, so only had to purse her lips and shake her head for me to get the message.

'It'll be great,' I said, sticking both thumbs in the air and smiling stupidly like a lobotomised kids' TV presenter.

The grotto is at the side of a main road about ten miles outside of Kinsale. We sat down on a wet white bench and began to stare at the statue of Our Lady. It was built in realistic colours, lifesize, in a little leafy cave. The hilled garden around it was very well manicured, with flowers and other fancy stuff. At the bottom left of the garden was a smaller, less well-crafted statue, of a woman praying.

After a few minutes, Molly had had enough. 'This is boring,' she huffed, 'the statue isn't going to move.' I smiled and said, 'Sshhhhhh.' Theresa laughed and told me that when she was twelve or thirteen she would have sat and stared as a proper passionate Catholic, all Hail Mary's, fear and belief.

The leaves behind the statue rustled and gave the impression of movement. Then I thought I saw something. It seemed to me that Our Lady was sneering at me. The muscles around her mouth seemed very fluid and she looked at me contemptuously.

'I think she's having a go at me,' I said.

'Nothing's going to move,' said Molly, also looking at me contemptuously. 'Statues don't move.'

We sat for about ten minutes more, Theresa and I still and patient, Molly swinging her little legs and humming to herself. Then it happened. The miracle.

An old man, who had been standing further along the parking area from us with his little 100cc motorbike, chain-smoking while staring at the statue, began to have a coughing fit. As he doubled up and spat phlegm and spume onto the tarmac, *he carried on smoking*, sucking hard on the tobacco. It was incredible. We sat and watched this in awe then turned to each other and smiled, knowing that we had seen something truly remarkable.

Molly was strangely unaffected by this and decided she wanted something to drink. We got to the wall where there was information about the statue and a little cup with holy water. I lifted Molly up and she dipped her fingers in, then made the sign of the cross on her forehead and chest. 'She's started getting into this at school,' said Theresa. 'She came home on the second day praying and blessing herself. I've a feeling it's just a phase she's going through.' I dabbed some water on me but Molly frowned. I hadn't done it properly so she dipped her little hand in again and made the sign of the cross on me.

I did see God once, on a bus between Waterford and Cork. The bus stopped. I looked up and saw a tall thin old man with a long white beard get on. There was something familiar about him and it wasn't until he had sat down in the seat in front of me that I realised who it was. The Almighty was on his way West. I could see His reflection in the window and admired His immense white beard and kindly, loving eyes. Next to Him was his great stick, for smiting sinners and noisy backpackers. I was quite pleased to be sitting at His right hand (albeit one row back). I thought of the Greek myth of the River Styx, and the boatman taking the dead to the underworld. Perhaps God was taking us to the next life on Bus Éireann.

How did I know it was God?

1. He had an immense white beard.

2. He had kindly, loving eyes.

3. He had a great stick, for smiting.

4. He was Very Old.

5. He wore on his head a flat cap shaped like a halo.

6. He wore Old-style clothes.

He didn't stay long on the bus. After about twenty minutes he took hold of his stick and pulled himself up from his seat and got off at a crossroads.

Ireland is a mystical country. Things like the grotto don't seem part of the church but connected to an older tradition of spirits, goddesses, pagan beliefs and faeries (or, of course, out-of-work jockeys) who magically appear and give messages and signs. For some reason, visitations and visions just don't seem to happen to high-flying city workers or politicians – cities make you more cynical, cut you off from older spirituality, which is tied to the land. Thus it tends to be country folk who see visions, people closer to beliefs in fertility, nature and the seasons, people whose life struggle is thus given some kind of meaning. And it's very often children. And why do they see Mary? Perhaps it is because of pagan beliefs in fertility goddesses that Ireland is more preoccupied with the nurturing mother figure rather than the central characters of the official religion, Jesus or the boss man, God.

Maybe Ireland is at heart still a Celtic land, eager for the mysteries of the old religion. Perhaps Catholicism is just a veneer on the surface even after fifteen hundred years, an armour plating of moral correctness. The moving statues are perhaps Catholicism's way of incorporating the old ghosts and beliefs into the new, in the same way it has done with African deities in the voodoo of Haiti and New Orleans. I am not attracted to its dogma, but I do like the imagery of the Catholic church: icons, beads, figurines, smelly stuff – it feels ancient and alive in a way that sometimes makes the hairs on the back of your neck stand on end. A good use of the 'dynamics of mysticism'. Catholic churches in Italy have done this to me, until you see the enormous ugly gold Christ statue – then the intellect kicks in and you're revolted.

I was brought up in the more restrained and prosaic beliefs and ambitions of the Church of England, administered either by an old wrinkly in what to all intents and purposes was a dress that buttoned up at the front, droning on about the gospels while farmers, lawyers, teachers and sweet-shop owners in stiff collars and their wives in thick coats and wavy hair perfected the glazed-eye snooze and thinking longingly about Sunday dinner; or the trying-so-hard-to-be-trendy-and-get-through-to-the-kids-that-it-hurts, Let's-Be-Friends-style acoustic guitar blather that tried to ape the majestic joyful spiritual harmony of gospel, Baptist churches, but ended up sounding like what it was – eager new vicar and twenty-something music teacher pretend to be Sonny and Cher while the congregation gets used to the idea of watching minority broadcasting and Open University on a Sunday morning.

If freedom of choice is the ultimate goal of all human beings (as we are told in our end-of-history market economies) then freedom of religion and the choice of after-life must be a part of that. If 'God' is to survive he has to compete with all the other possible paradises – Hindu, Buddhist, Muslim, Catholic, Baptist, Mormon, Episcopalian, Methodist. And what about the Gods who aren't so popular nowadays, the Celtic, Egyptian, Greek and Roman deities?

Do they still exist in a reduced sort of way or were they victims of market forces, pushed out of business by more modern set-ups?

If there is a God, why would he try to make us realise that He existed by the device of making statues move? And then not move in a naturalistic, expressive way but by winking, twitching or bleeding (or sneering). There might be a case for saying that he created the universe. But after that, why would he intervene in our affairs? I mean, why would he listen to our daily prayers and make a statue move, then let terrible things happen – wars, famine, Boyzone? A friend of mine told me she once prayed to God for some curtains. She had seen them in a shop and didn't want them to go so she prayed to God. But when she got to the shop she realised that the curtains she'd been praying for weren't the best curtains for her after all. There were some much nicer ones. And that was because of God. God showed her that what she wanted wasn't necessarily what was the best thing for her. It's a rather limited brief – He can't stop terrible accidents happening in the world but he can help you buy nice home decoration material.

It does seem far-fetched, but perhaps no more far-fetched than intellectually accepted ideas like black holes or cosmic string (in fact a lot less far-fetched than the cosmic string thing) or the world being controlled by a race of evil Space Jockeys, perhaps via remote control. OK, so that's not an intellectually accepted idea. Yet.

On a perfect evening, with the sun going down, God decided to bathe the southern Irish countryside in a red-lemonade glow. He was everywhere – in pub condom machines, in Roy Keane's right foot, in Sinead O'Connor's priestly robes, in the fold of Daniel O'Donnell's side-parting, in the belly of a singing leprechaun, in the head of a pint of Guinness, in the legs of a Dublin Bay prawn, in the brake pads of a Vauxhall Corsa.

The Art of the Storyteller

Blarney, Co. Cork

Unlike any other of the world's peoples, the Irish have the skill of being able to talk over each other and still understand what's going on. It's like a multi-part harmony. I was brought up to wait until someone had finished speaking before speaking myself (so if one of my family suddenly developed Tourette's Syndrome and wouldn't shut up for days, I'd sit there meekly awaiting my turn). This has meant that sometimes I've been well and truly struck dumb sitting around a dinner table with Irish friends. There is a tradition of the strong silent type in Ireland, but I've never met any.

Another thing is that Irish people do what your mother always told you not to – they talk to strangers. They haven't so much kissed the Blarney Stone as slept with it on a 'no-strings' basis over several years. Anecdotes turn into yarns which then turn into fully fledged official myths. In 1990 I went with Annie to kiss the Blarney Stone. It's on top of a castle. You lie on your back and stick your head out over the battlements until you're nearly upside-down, give the lump of rock a good tonguing then someone pulls you up. The Blarney magic is supposed to last seven years, after which you need a regular top-up, a bit like anti-tetanus booster jabs (except without that painful yet strangely enjoyable 'stiff' feeling for a day or so afterwards).

Before leaving Cork I'd met Theresa's cousin, Connor, who had come over to her house to saw some logs. We stood staring out over the fields leading into the little valley near their home, saying nothing. Sighing occasionally.

'Tim, have you ever been to Phibsboro? That's an interesting place there in Dublin. You should go there. Yes.'

'I don't think I've got time.'

He reverted to silence and carried on cleaning his tools.

Connor looks like a figure from a fairy tale. Big, kindly hooded eyes, goblin big nose, red hair, big beard. Connor is a trucker who, when not working his ass off, likes to sit in his chair and hold forth about Country & Western poet Kinky Friedman. My conversations with Connor usually took a pre-ordained route. We'd chat about all kinds of things for the first couple of hours, then he'd put on some Kinky Friedman. Connor's style is  to sit in wide-eyed reverence and repeat each line of the song, in his lovely lilting Cork/Kerry accent, a fraction of a second after Kinky has sung – the effect of this is that Connor is doing a slightly delayed voice-over. Or an echo chamber in which the echo is Irish. He'll do this for a while until, suddenly, halfway through a sentence, he'll stop. His head jerks back, and he's asleep.

Kinky: You poked fun at my cowboy shoes.
Connor: You poked fun at my cowboy shoes.
Kinky: You said they looked just like big canoes.
Connor: You said they looked just like big canoes.
Kinky: Now it's time for the chosen ones to choose.
Connor: Now it's time for the chosen ones to choose.
Kinky: Before all hell breaks loose.

Connor: Before all hell breaks loose. Listen to this next bit.

Kinky: Turn out the lights, honey, turn on the news.

Connor: Turn out the lights, honey, turn on the news.

Kinky: God save the Queen and the kangaroos.

Connor: God save the Queen and the kangaroos.

Kinky: And what kind of rubbers did Joseph use.

Connor: Ha ha ha listen to this bit and what kind of rubbers did Joseph use.

Kinky: Before all hell broke loose.

Connor: Before all hell broke loose.

Kinky: Time to resign from the human race.

Connor: Time to rsgnn fr hmmmmm . . .

Kinky: Wipe those tears from your lovely face.

Connor: Wmmmm mmmmmmmm . . .

Kinky: Baby, wave to the man in the ol' red caboose.

Connor: Bmmmm . . .

Kinky: Before all hell broke loose.

Connor: Bffffffzzzzzzzzzzzzzzzzzzz Zzzzzzzzzzzzzzzz.

Kinky: Hell on America!

Connor: Zzzzzzzzzzzzzzzzzzzzzzzzzzzzzzzzz . . .

Although I felt shite again, it wouldn't have been too much of a bind to travel around to Blarney to give the old stone another peck. On the radio there was a discussion (there always seems to be a discussion on the radio in Ireland when you're feeling tired and a bit anti-social) about women who have 'social affairs'. I tried to concentrate on the road, watching out for hidden tractors, while half listening to the revelations on the airwaves.

Presenter: (with deep, mellifluously honeyed mid-Atlantic Irish accent) So, Maureen from Tullamore, have *you* been having a social affair?

Woman: (high-pitched and shy voice) I have, yes.

Presenter: Do you want to tell us about it?

Woman: Well, we meet up every week to go dancing and play cards.

Presenter: And is that it?

Woman: Yes.

Presenter: What does your husband think?

Woman: He doesn't mind.

Presenter: Are you attracted to this man?

Woman: I am, yes.

Then a female social-affair guru person comes on and blathers on about Maureen from Tullamore's case. 'I think you should talk to your husband more, really get it out in the open,' she says, or something incredibly brilliant like that.

Presenter: And we have another caller, Jane from Limerick. Hello Jane.

Caller 2: Hello, yes. I'd just like to say that I think it's wrong. I think it's very wrong.

Presenter: (mock concern) What do you think is wrong, Jane?

Caller 2: Well if people are married they should be faithful. I've been married to my husband for seventeen years. We've had our problems all right, doesn't everybody. But we've stuck at it. Young people these days just run off at the first sign of trouble.

Presenter: So do you have a 'special friend' that you want to tell us about?

Caller 2: Er, I do actually.

Presenter: And who's this on the line? It's the singing leprechaun calling from a phone box somewhere near Bantry.

Singing leprechaun: . . .

Presenter: Hello, Mr Leprechaun? Are you there?

Singing leprechaun: . . .

Expert guru person: I understand your pain. But you have to open up, let us know how you feel.

Singing leprechaun: (sings tune to 'When Irish Eyes Are Smiling') Dee doo dee doo dee do doooo dee dee doo dee doo dee doooo.

Expert guru person: I think what you're saying has touched us all. In some ways, all of us at some time in our lives have felt like that.

Presenter: Do you feel that this has become a problem for you?

Singing leprechaun: . . .

Presenter: Have you talked to family and friends about this?

Singing leprechaun: . . .

Expert guru person: What do you think your family would say if you told them?

Singing leprechaun: (sings tune to 'When Irish Eyes Are Smiling') Dee doo dee doo dee do doooo dee dee doo dee doo dee doooo.

Kinky: When I find myself alone in my house and in my head.

Connor: When I find myself alone in my house and in my head.

Kinky: And I blow the candles out and I take myself to bed.

Connor: And I blow the candles out and I take myself to bed.

Kinky: And I'm old enough to realise, ah, young enough to know.

Connor: And I'm old enough to realise, ah, young enough to know.

Kinky: When the Lord closes the door, he opens a little window.

Connor: When the Lord closes the door, he opens a little window.

Kinky: When sleep closes my eyes and sends me searching for you.

Connor: When sleep closes my eyes and sends me searching for you.

Kinky: And I'm feelin' blue as the sky without your love to carry me through.

Connor: And I'm feelin' blue as the sky without your love to carry me through.

Kinky: And I'm weak enough to be afraid but strong enough to let it show.

Connor: And I'm weak enough to be afraid but strong enough to let it show.

Kinky: When the Lord closes the door, he opens a little window.

Connor: Wmmmmmmm mmmmmmmmmmmmmm.

Kinky: Baby I'm a gypsy boy, I'll ride the night until.

Connor: Bbzzzzzzzzzzz zzzzzzzzzzzzzzzzzzzzzzzz.

Kinky: I come to you like moonlight through your raggle-taggle window sill.

Connor: Zzzzzzzzzzzzzzzzzzzzzzzzzzzzzzzzzzzzzzzzzzzzzzzzzzzzzz.

I stopped to buy a paper. I knew there were a few garages worth checking out in Youghal. At Theresa's I'd scribbled down the number of a garage so decided to give them a call. The guy on the other end seemed very friendly. How much are you looking for, he said. Oh, around six I said, noncha-lantly, looking at my dirty fingernails, smoking a panatella and sipping from a chilled martini. Hmm, it's not for me. But I know a fellow who could be interested. I'm sure he'd like to take a look at it. He gave me directions and I hung up, then punched the air in delight. Back in the car I sung along in best out-of-tune style to Nik Kershaw horrendous eighties synth rock for a while and the singing leprechaun hummed a more traditional ballad. Then I took a turning back onto the Cork–Waterford road and the garage of gold at the end of the rainbow.

Kinky: Somethin's wrong with the Beaver.
Connor: Somethin's wrong with the Beaver.
Kinky: Somethin's wrong with the Beaver.
Connor: Smthzzzz zzzzzzzzzzzzzzzzzzz.
Kinky: Somethin's wrong with the Beaver.
Connor: Zzzzzzzzzzzzzzzzzzzzzzzzzzzzzzz.
Kinky: The Beaver I believe-uh is gone.
Connor: Zzzzzzz zzzzzz zzzzzzzzzzzzzzz.

Selling a Car in Potato Town

Youghal

Youghal is a small town in East Cork about half-way between Waterford and Cork City, consisting of a main street, with thousands of interesting looking pubs, an old town gate and the sea. The town dates back to Celtic times and was an important trading centre for the Vikings and the Normans – by the thirteenth century Youghal had become the second largest port in the British Isles after Bristol. Later it became famous as the home of Sir Walter Raleigh, and its reputation as a town of sensual delights springs from this time – as well as being the official First Potato Town of Ireland[1] (an important accolade); the first tobacco to reach this part of the world was probably smoked in Youghal as well. The town was no doubt full of lads with goatees, full bellies and bad coughs then and little seems to have changed on that score. Fifty years later Oliver Cromwell spent the winter of 1649 there, using it as a base to strike out into the rest of southern Ireland. Rather than a legacy of fags and chips, he left only a stone gate in his name.

[1] Raleigh was a terrible businessman by all accounts and eventually sold his land to Sir Robert Boyle, who made his fortune in pig iron. The joke is that they have a potato festival in the town and not a pig iron festival. It's not a great joke, but certain people – fat, farmer-type people – probably find it amusing.

With such a history, it's a pity that Youghal always seems to be the sort of town that I drive through on the way to somewhere else – either racing through from the ferry to reach the intense pleasures of Cork City, or racing back towards Waterford to stay the night before spending several hours in the bar on the ferry eating crisps and breathing in cigarette smoke. With every other building seemingly a pub, it looks like it should be a party town and is the kind of place that I might go for New Year if I lived in West Waterford. But every time I just head straight on through, saying to myself, 'I must stop in Youghal some time.'

The name 'Youghal' derives from the old Irish '*Eochaill*' – meaning 'Yew wood'. Now it's *you would* love to stop there if you weren't in such a hurry. You're supposed to pronounce it *y'all*, as in (puts on big Texan accent) 'How y'all doin'?' or, 'Y'all wanna see mah new pickup truck?' or even, 'Y'all gonna like this next number it's about when ah was a little boy growin' up on a farm outside Austin on the edge of the Texas hill country. Take it away boys 1-2-3-4.' You probably get the idea. I still insist on calling it *yoogerl*, much to the consternation of friends. Getting my teeth around Gaelic words has always proved to be a bit of a problem. I tend to trudge slowly through them like a tractor through a boggy field in November, reading each bit separately rather than observing the whole and thinking about how it should sound. Regretfully, this is (so I'm told) a typical Anglo-Saxon trait.

In terms of car selling, Youghal hadn't originally been high on the agenda. I'd already written it off as the sort of place where I'd have to spend all afternoon in one of the pubs and then end up swapping the car for a couple of greyhounds (but only if I could stick around for a few days because the greyhounds had to be fetched from the bloke's cousin in the midlands). I'd done some research on the area and located two or thee used car garages. But, as I'd already discovered, there is something not quite right about a scruffy, unshaven bloke with bags under his eyes, driving a nice shiny girl's car and looking to offload it quickly.

But although I knew we didn't look good together, I had to make an effort to make a sale. Back in Youghal it was starting to rain. On my little crumpled piece of paper I had the name of a garage on the main road. I parked in the middle of the forecourt, which was full of cars of every description and age, all looking just a little bit worn out. At the end of the forecourt was a little hut with big glass windows. Four people inside were deep in conversation. As I got to the door I could see them more clearly. There was a big bloke with a red face and dark blue blazer, with silver hair and longish sideburns for a man of his age in the late 1990s (they were seventies' leftovers). A skinny guy with scared animal eyes with a 'tache and a Barbour jacket stood to his left. I knocked on the door and walked in. To the left of the door was a fat farmer type with a face that was waiting to laugh in that explosive way that people do when they laugh at anything – 'a ha ha ha ha ha ha ha' – and on the other side a small sandy-haired bloke who looked like he might have been a welterweight boxer, with a denim jacket and a little black woollen hat. As I walked in the farmer was just speaking – 'a ha ha ha ha ha ha!' Then the conversation abruptly stopped and the Blazer, who was behind the desk and therefore ostensibly In Charge, asked what he could do for me.

I'd said this little speech so many times and had so many negative responses that I felt a bit embarrassed – I had this idea of myself as a sharp wheeler-dealer who would convince these country folk of the great deal I was offering, but all that came out was the usual articulation of a Loot advert, interspersed with lots of hesitations '. . . Vauxhall Corsa . . . er . . . not mine . . . er . . . selling it for someone else . . . er . . . one previous lady owner . . . er . . . 36,000 miles . . . er . . . sunroof . . .'

There was a pause as Blazer breathed in sharply, then smiled with his eyes and winked over at Woolly Hat.

'I suppose it's got a condom machine fitted,' he said. There was a brief pause, a sweet silence before Barbour Moustache started a little wheezy heeeh heeeh heeh, Blazer smiled broadly at his joke and Woolly Hat raised his eyebrows. But it was Farmer who really startled me. If Monty Python and Woody Allen had turned up there and then in that room and presented us with their funniest gag that they'd been secretly working on for years, with Seinfeld doing the script editing, Farmer couldn't possibly have exploded with mirth any harder. Tiny droplets of fluid, which I hoped were spittle, flew past my face against the side wall.

And, of course, he *was* the sort of bloke who would laugh at anything. I replied with a rather thin, 'No, I've had a vasectomy so we've just got the basic model,' but like those crap sitcoms with an over-zealous studio audience, in which the actors can't carry on until the laughter from the pissed-uncle-figure-from-the-suburbs-who-doesn't-get-out-much-but-is-in-town-for-the-day had subsided, so I had to wait as the blobs of spittle and orgasmic laughter died down.

'So, what do you think?'

Woolly Hat, whose name was Brian, then knocked me sideways with the magical words that everyone wants to hear. 'Yeah, I might be interested.' A mere chuckle from Farmer indicated that this was indeed a serious answer to my plea. We went outside to check the car. Brian, a really nice gentle bloke (even if he looked like he could punch your lights out if you fibbed about the MOT), looked it up and down as he asked me the usual questions about the car's history. I knew the form. Years ago I'd done some car-looking-up-and-down for a friend in Norwich who was into buying up old Beetles. All you had to do was frown, stroke your chin and occasionally check under the wheel rims, then ask how many miles it had done and what sort of price was wanted. It was a ritual.

When I told him how much I wanted – about six grand – he

didn't look too fazed. Inside I was shouting 'YESSSSSSSS!' but tried to look cool. He'd got a couple of garages further in the town, and gave me directions and a plan of action. I was to drive to it and show the car to a guy called Damon. I did as instructed and met Damon, a youngish lad in his early twenties who immediately started telling me what he thought of the Corsa. The English model had been super-seded by the more recent Irish Opel version, but my 1.4 SRi still had a few features to be proud of and an engine that could give much more powerful cars a run for their money. Apparently.

ALLOY WHEEL

'It'll be great with all the kit, a good pair of speakers, alloy wheels an' that.'

I had visions of money. I'd stay in Yoogerl that night and take Farmer out on the town, challenge him to a laughing competition. 'Did you know, Farmer, that in Mongolia they do circular breathing when they laugh at funny jokes so it sounds like a really deep vacuum cleaner? Can you do that, Farmer? Can you?' Damon informed me that we had to go to yet another garage, where his boss (I was getting confused) was based. Damon hopped in and we drove to the other side of town, with him trying to explain to me exactly why alloy wheels were so desirable. ('They're just really *cool*, like.') When we got there Damon disappeared into the bowels of a greasy smelling workshop, then a couple of minutes later emerged with a small sandy-haired guy in blue overalls, who could have been a welterweight boxer. It was the same guy – Brian – with different clothes on, I was sure of it. And I became more convinced as he started to openly slag the car – it's more a woman's car (don't I bloody know that already pal!), it's too small, its engine's too big, it would cost too much to insure in Ireland because they'd have to put all the kit in like electric windows (ooooh) and alloy wheels (a quick glance at Damon – he was smiling slightly and nodding) and sell it as a sports car to blokes and young blokes would have to pay £1,500 on insurance for a sporty car like that. It was the old 'nice used-car dealer/nasty used-car dealer' routine. One gives you a cigarette and says, 'It's a lovely car,' the other knocks it out of your mouth and scowls, 'You slag – it's in terrible condition you useless bastard!'

'How much do you want for it?' asked Nasty Brian.

'I'm looking for six, what with the exchange rate the way it is at the moment.'

'Ah I can't give you more than four and a half for it.'

Damon bit his lip. He was genuinely disappointed and I felt more upset for him than for myself. He had convinced me that it surely would have looked great with all the kit and alloy wheels and that.

'The trouble is,' I said, 'that that's only about three and a half in Sterling.'

Nasty Brian shook his head and cursed.

'The Punt is fucked, absolutely fucked. Those bastards have managed to wreck a perfectly good economy.'

He made it seem like the collapse of the global free market system. A barrage of insults at various politicians, filling their pockets, feathering their nests while the likes of him just wanted to do an honest day's work.

The pessimism was infectious.

'And,' I said, 'then there's the Import Registration Fee, or whatever it is you call it.'

This was £1,200 that I would, officially, have to pay before I could sell the car.

'Ah we'd get round that. We'd tell them the car was damaged and you sold it as scrap and you'll be fine. But I can still only give you four and a half. You're not interested then?'

I drove Damon back to the other garage. We talked about the different types of engines in cars and the insurance premiums involved for various models, the acceleration/handling/size equation. I rarely had conversations like this.

As he got out he gave me a little, rueful smile. 'Somebody's gonna get a nice deal on that car. I tell you, alloy wheels. Pheeew!' He shook my hand, then he was gone. I thought about continuing west straight away, to go and talk to Nice Brian again. But I knew the garage wouldn't be there anymore. It'd be a sweetshop or newsagents, run by Farmer, who would look at me sternly and deny all knowledge of ever meeting me. Never again would I try to sell a woman's car in a town famous for its celebration of root vegetables.

Youghal Survival Kit

Potato
Cigarette

Music
'Car Wash' – Rose Royce
'Go West' – Village People
'Pull Up to the Bumper' – Grace Jones

Places to visit
Cromwell Arch
Big Blazer's garage
Nice Brian's garage
Nasty Brian's garage

The Beach

Tramore, Co. Waterford

On Tramore High Street I stood in a chipper and stared without expression as a bloke in chip shop gear lifted a bag of sliced potatoes into the deep fat fryer. Cunningham's chipper is the best in all of Ireland, so say the experts on these matters. If the Gaelic Athletic Association held a Fish and Chip shop tournament, Cunningham's would, it is said, walk it. The night before had been an early one, my first proper sleep for over four days. Annie's parents had listened with patience on the phone to my tales of cack-handed car-selling attempts (though I made sure not to tell them about the singing leprechaun – you never know how people will react). Her mother then said that she was thinking of selling her car and would Annie let her have the Corsa for free? I can't do that, I said. I have a duty, a mission, to get the best price possible. Well, why didn't you try to sell it in England? said her father, gently yet rationally. Hmmm. It's the spirit of the thing, I tried to explain, with furrowed eyebrows. It's a quest. It's an excuse to travel around and hang out with your mates for a few days more like, he laughed. I went a bit huffy and quiet and with great precision began to attack my fourth baked potato, pretending I hadn't heard him.

The chips were great but very hot – I walked down to the strand and sat down on a bench to eat them, watching the people stroll by and burning the roof of my mouth, thus combining two of my favourite hobbies. At the edge of the beach, amongst the pebbles and plastic bottles, where in a few months' time fat people would sit baring their hairless shins in the weak sun, a little lad was knocking a football about, dreaming of some future World Cup glory in a green shirt. A small dog of indeterminate breed ran past, its lead dangling, headed for nowhere in particular. Then three well-built old lads swaggered along on a post-pub jaunt, slightly jelly-kneed after a lunchtime pint. Bloated and brilliant faced in their Sunday best, they chattered and laughed away, probably about old timers' business – Jackie Kyle's genius, cars, the war and real drinking days when they would have been hell-raising local boys about town. A little bloke with a black 'tache and insistent beer gut waddled into view down the strand like a baggy bullfrog, his family in tow, parading the latest in tracksuit style. It must have been said before but it seems that the idea of the tracksuit has got lost somewhere along the line. Why does it only seem to be fat-arsed no-hopers with a lard addiction who wear sports gear nowadays? Or is it simply another triumph for aspirational advertising?

Tramore provides old-style holiday entertainment – amusement arcades, shops full of little kids' fishing nets, chippers – and takes you back to the 1950s or 60s, before the days when people could fly away to Spain more cheaply than have a three-course meal in a seaside restaurant back home. The difference down here is that you rarely see the German, Italian and American tourists who swarm all over other more historic or orthodoxly beautiful parts of the country.

At one stage Tramore was regarded as the seaside capital of Ireland, the Blackpool of Erin, the Skegness of the Emerald Isle, the Scarborough of the Old Sod. People would come from all over the country for their annual two-week holiday, then sit out on the pebbles and try and get their hairless shins a bit brown. Like so many Irish places the old Gaelic name is simply an expression of the town's setting which has been misheard or misunderstood by the dozy English at some point in time – *Trá mór* means 'big beach', and the strand here is one of the most immense in the whole of Ireland. A walk along it on a wild day is the best hangover cure going.

The town, originally a fishing village, was set up as a resort in the 1780s by a Waterford merchant called Bartholomew Rivers, who also set up a racecourse near the beach at around the same time. In the 1850s a fellow called Lord Doneraille, who was no doubt attracted to the area by the fact that there is a pub there called The Doneraille (what a coincidence), relaid and improved the course in response to the area's popularity as a tourist destination (helped by the opening of a railway line to the town a year or so earlier). By 1912 the sea had proven too strong and the course became completely submerged into an area of water known locally as the Back Strand. The sea is very powerful here – deceptively so, with rocks hidden at the bay's entrance. Many ships have ended their journeys, mistakenly, in its thrashing waters. In 1816 the *Seahorse*, a troop-carrying ship, came into the bay thinking it was Waterford Harbour, hitting the rocks and going down with all 363 of its passengers and crew. Now on the cliff top there is a beacon called the Metalman, which informs shipping that this is fierce Tramore Bay.

I drove up out of the town along the cliff road and headed for the old segregated swimming area where, the winter before, we had stood to watch seals in the bay. When I first came to Tramore almost ten years ago you were quickly out of town and in real countryside – small gentle hillocks, pastureland, old farmhouses, a dolmen here and there, the sound of foxhounds and hunting horn on a cold crisp winter's day, birdsong in summer. Now there were new houses everywhere, gaudy and expansive and mostly packed into

lucrative estates with small gardens and side windows looking into each other's property.

The Irish may be a beautiful race of artists, poets, writers
and musicians but they've no idea how to build a bloody
house. Up until recently there were two kinds of Irish house:
the trad stone cottage and the trad farmhouse. Cottages are
low and made of stone with whitewash on the front and are
now usually owned by rich American widows or German
artists. Many of them will only be used for about four weeks
of the year, but they were always there for local people to
look at and admire. This must be particularly great fun for
young couples who can't afford to actually buy an old
cottage. They can move to a housing estate and come and
look at the cottage at weekends, perhaps.

Farmhouses are made of brick and have a blocky lay-
out and are inhabited by English hippies or, in very rare
cases, farmers. A farmhouse should by law have bits of old
machinery and cars lying around in the garden, perhaps an
old bathtub as well. The bits of car, if stuck together, should
in no way be able to form an actual vehicle, taken as they are
from many different models of car from different eras. It is
some kind of rural ritual that when people visit they leave a
part of their car in a far-flung part of the garden so that it can
rust. A bit like those modern art sculptures you sometimes
get outside libraries and public buildings.

Now it's all changed and the country is full of bungalows,
chalets, ranches, castlettes, turrets,[1] mini-chateaux that eat
into fields and meadows, taking away the ring of breathing
space that every community needs, so that what was once
rural becomes part of town. There's not even bits of
machinery and stuff out in the gardens anymore, just nice

[1]People in Spain and Portugal managed to build for themselves sturdy and, in
that context, aesthetically pleasing dwellings, but it should be remembered that
what is attractive in old Spanish and Portuguese cities isn't necessarily good looking in Ireland.

shiny new cars. It's not nice to say but the only attractive houses in Irish towns seem to be ones left over from British rule, when perhaps only a certain class and religion would get you an attractive dwelling. Certainly in Dublin for a while there was no love for the fine Georgian buildings in the centre of the city – they were seen as symbols of British oppression and were left to rot for decades. Now the attitude has changed and they are, rightly, regarded as being an integral and beautiful part of Ireland's heritage.

And yet, perhaps this thing about pretty houses is a red herring. It could be just a traditional difference in attitude to life. If Irish people have always been more into community activities, *craic*, drinking, going out and enjoying day-to-day existence than stay-at-home English in their self-styled castles, maybe the need to live in something impressive is not so great.

I went off for a walk for a few hours. Tramore, so gaudy, bright and fish-and-chip noisy in summer, was a different proposition off-season. It was quiet and peeling and so very melancholy, my own bittersweet nostalgia mingling with that of the place itself. On this day, the sea at Tramore sounded like Hammersmith Broadway – no, to be more precise, it was like the Westway. A constant roar, wind driving the banks of water back into the long shore, the acoustics intensified because of the horseshoe bay. Another Quink sky, blue-grey-brown splodges, running at the edges into light grey, smattered with a clumsy brush. The only colour that departed from the greyish was the yellow of a giftshop, closed up for the winter months, a quarter of a mile away. I leaned against a handrail, the old white paint flaking off in my hand, revealing the rust beneath, like scabs. Big houses loomed over the cliff at the Protestant end of town. There was a deathly stench of seaweed.

There were now new apartments down at the edge of the strand, for the busy professionals, a hard style, new iron railings, pink and white with grey roofs. Behind them was a mess – old fridges, plastic toys, mud-puddles. Resting dodgems lay in piles round the back of what had once been the Deluxe Hotel, alongside a faded asteroid wheel – like a tinker's back garden. Other miscellaneous fairground parts were scattered around. A red-faced man with a wild white quiff halfway round the back of his head, green baggy sweater and Wellington boots, with two huge dogs, clomped past me, staring straight ahead at nothing. The Arcade looked as though it had been given an attempted eighties-style corporate makeover, turquoise and cream livery over the buildings and drapes hanging from lamp posts. The wind picked up. It seemed now that I was virtually alone in the town.

The main street winding back up the hill from the sea was silent, except for a radio blaring out of an empty JCB, Eamon Dunphy inviting callers to phone in to gab about something or other. Back up the street I passed a few gnarled old ladies, faces like leather, who stared at me from street corners with pursed lips. More JCBs lurked in the back streets. I walked past the Grand Hotel, where at Christmas in happier times a pianist would play a grand piano, and Annie would meet up with all her fellow emigrants for their once-a-year reunion.

I remembered an evening spent with Annie's father on a reservoir near the town. Annie rowed us out to the middle – as she always used to do as a kid – and he would try to catch supper. He never caught a thing in all the times that Annie or her sister Elaine went out with him. He decided it was some kind of Irish women's curse against fishermen, because whenever he went solo he'd come back with a whole fish shop worth of shiny fresh fish. Out in the middle, with the sun going down slowly, he cast away, while I made a quick sketch. 'Where's the shaggin' fish?' he'd curse, then we'd row around to the next spot. As ever, someone else had all the

The 'Irishwoman's curse' means a trip to the fishmongers

fish – a bloke in a boat about 150 yards away seemed to be doing well so we rowed towards him. But still nothing.

In the minicab office opposite the Hibernian Hotel, the day before, a young woman complains to me about the town. 'I used to live here but I've been in Wales for years. Don't know why I came back – it's just dead in winter. Nothing ever happens.'

I tell her I prefer it off-season, a little sad, as though it's seen better days – like a tree which sheds its brightness in autumn. She sighs. 'Oh why did I come back?' I take her taxi to Waterford and wander around the glass factory and showroom. It's all most people ever seem to know about Waterford. I watch the blowers at their hypnotic and ancient work in teams, engravers bowed and bent over their pieces. It's fascinating, but I hate glassware, unless it's for wine or whiskey. A visit to the factory showroom brings to the surface my long-dormant desire, mixed with my current mood, to create mayhem when surrounded by delicate glass of this sort. Glass objects. *Objets*. Chameleons. Bing Crosby. Celtic crosses. Christmas trees. Angels. Golf balls. Footballs. Fishes. Tennis racquets. A large glass bear. I want to smash them all, but particularly the large glass bear. I picture myself going over to it, caressing it, whacking it, kicking its stupid glass head across the room. I take some deep breaths to calm myself down a bit.

An English woman in front of me complains to her husband about the discount. He smiles but he's somewhere else, perhaps playing golf with Bing Crosby. The staff are Stepford Wives dressed like air hostesses, scarves and grey jackets and skirts, smiling and polite. I feel like I'm in a dream.

There's something terrifying about so much glass. My grandmother used to collect little coloured glass animals. I always wanted to smash them as well. My desire to knock over all the stands and shelves is so strong that soon, I fear, someone will have to help me out of the door. My head is buzzing. I walk right up to the glass bear. Standing next to it I feel intoxicated, or is it like vertigo? I can hear the sound of it breaking into a million pieces. Nearby is some glass 'art' by four of the world's leading glass artists, household names like Hirohi Ramoro and Richard Marquis. 'From East to West', 'Fish on the Earth of Celtic Spirit', 'Angel in Aftermath', 'Waterford Dog Piece', all for ridiculous amounts of money. I see the avenging hammer in my hand. I go to the desk and order a taxi. There hanging up is an absurd picture of a tired and confused-looking man holding a large Waterford Crystal jug to an engraving wheel as if working on it. It is laughably pathetic. I take my picture down from the shelf and pay the five pounds fee to the woman behind the desk. She orders me a taxi. I get out just in time.

I walked back through Tramore, past the faded paint and silent hum of bygone revelries. The mood was infectiously desolate. Feeling very cold and quiet I listlessly hung around the library, reading some William Trevor short stories from a volume well thumbed by insomniac middle-aged women, stories of loss, betrayal and remorse. The place was scattered with old people and kids and me. Then I was outside again and suddenly in tears. It must have been the wind.

Once Annie and I had sat in Powers, a little bar in a Tramore backstreet run by an old lady, one of the last of a dying breed. We'd sat together quietly as the woman told us stories about her family and the people who came in. I didn't really take any of it in. Gradually the place filled up until there were four old men seated at the bar and us, looking out at them. I thought back to when I was in Ireland with her for the first time, when we'd driven about eight hundred miles in a week, getting lost, drinking loads, sitting on mountaintops holding pieces of quartz and planning so many great adventures, listening to music and me all the time being wide-eyed with wonder at her beautiful country.

If you're never going to use a car very much, I've always said, there's no point in having one. I have always been so much into community activities, craic, drinking, going out and enjoying day-to-day existence that I'm never usually sober enough to drive a car in the evenings anyway. It's great for long journeys, granted, but even then I've always felt much more free on a bus or train, when I can jump off at any point like they do in old western movies, with just a bag on my back and a bottle of whiskey in my hand, and search for adventure at the local saloon or public library. Back at the house I made one last, vain attempt to prise six thousand pounds out of Annie's mum ('Come on love, where's your purse?'), then picked up the phone to call a local garage. Even before anyone answered, I'd put the receiver down again. I'd been defeated. I was a failure. London was calling, as Joe Strummer once said. Actually, Joe Strummer said Laarrghlurrrghzz Caaargghghlgghhhh. Whatever, it was time to start thinking of home.

Born to be Wild (Now and Again, if I'm in the Mood)

Irishness to Englishness

Going home from Ireland is always an anti-climax, yet it goes past so quickly. It was in some kind of knackered trance that I drove that cute-but-powerful-with-lots-of-leg-room woman's car through Waterford and Wexford and onto the ferry at Rosslare to do the journey that Viking warriors had done a thousand years earlier in reverse. I sat slumped at one of the restaurant's Formica tables and force-fed myself with greasy cod and chips, alternating between staring at forlorn fellow passengers and the sick grey sea. (If you were ever writing a book about Ireland, this would be a good place for a launch, I thought to myself.) I went to sit in the bar and nursed an orange juice amidst the thick sweet coat of cigarette smoke, as people shouted at each other, desperate, so very desperate to be heard above the din of people shouting at each other. In the gift shop I saw more of the singing leprechaun's captive family and thought about setting them free, like some crazed Singing Leprechaun Liberation Front activist. But where would they go? How would they live? I knew they'd never make it on their own so opted instead for an a capella chorus of 'When Irish Eyes Are Smiling', pressing their little bellies one by one.

One minute I was in West Wales, chugging along behind

a line of slothful lorries, the next I was zipping past everyone on the M4 heading into London, that time obviously spent in quicksilver daydream of *Nicole-Kidman-lookalikes-petrol-Guinness-mountains-hitchers-and-freedom*. The golden rooftops of West London shone like magic eyes as the sun slanted down in the soft evening light. Those roofs sang their beauty, to the city and to me. Back to good old civilisation and shit, tube trains and John B. Keane. I looked down at the bedraggled singing leprechaun and pressed its tummy. Nothing. The battery had gone. It didn't matter. I was feeling great and decided I'd go and get a passport photo of the two of us looking like a pair of great beat generation hobo poets, me stern and moody, him grinning inanely (it's the only expression he's got). As Hammersmith Broadway welcomed me with its carbon monoxide, concrete and tarmac embrace I started to plan a new trip over to Ireland and vowed to spend more time moving from place to place, at a slower pace, to dig a little deeper into the cultural underbelly[1] and maybe sell the car to some madman totally bonkers Celtic druid car dealer over in the West. Man.

Ah but I'm all talk, even to myself. Three days later I sold the car to the smart garage in Chiswick where it had been bought four years earlier, for four and a half grand. I bet that's just what Kerouac would have done too, the big mummy's boy.

A few years ago an English friend of mine once went out briefly with a surly Irish guy. He was good looking but had a chip on his shoulder about something. The first time they slept together he went completely wild, shouting agitprop slogans with every pelvic thrust, in a Gerry Adams accent –

[1] That's 'spend even more time in pubs talking shite' for those who haven't been paying attention.

that's for eight hundred years of repression (ugh ugh ugh ugh), that's for the Protestant plantations (ugh ugh ugh ugh), that's for brutally suppressing the 1916 Uprising (ugh ugh ugh ugh), that's for Bloody Sunday (ugh ugh ugh ugh), that's for, erm, rugby (ugh ugh ugh ugh), that's for Maggie Thatcher (My God oooooooohh yeeeessssssss aahhhhhh). She was, she said, shocked. There were obviously a few of his slogans she was unsure about because very soon she – apparently – wanted to do it all again.

Another close friend, this time an Irish guy, went for years only being able to get sexually aroused by the well-brought-up daughters of former members of the British armed forces. I asked him if he'd ever thought about therapy for his problem but he didn't see it as a problem. 'Just another form of guerrilla warfare,' he mused.

There are probably statistics showing the percentages of people who think about colonialism and oppression while having sex. But this isn't that sort of publication. I'm not into statistics at all. You can get hundreds of textbooks from your local library if you're interested in that kind of thing. And it's also time to let go of the stereotypes that have dogged Anglo-Irish relations for so long – Irish people are just like English people in that their shit smells and they like drinking and shagging and listening to music and fighting and eating and getting a bit nationalistic and reading and walking and sometimes they pray and sometimes they don't and loving and laughing and writing poetry (mmm, maybe not that last one for English people). The only difference is that 92.5% of Irish people's bodies are made up of potatoes.

I'm not singing for the future
I'm not dreaming of the past
I'm not talking of the first time
I never think about the last

Now the song is nearly over
We may not find out what it means
Still there's a light I hold before me
You're the measure of my dreams,
The measure of my dreams.

SHANE MACGOWAN
'A Rainy Night in Soho'

Appendix

IRISH PUB GUIDE

Just so this book can offer a tiny bit of practical advice, here's a handy guide to Irish pubs around London which you can cut out and stick in a shoebox and leave under the stairs.

Hardened Irish pubgoers will no doubt have cottoned on to the fact that most of these pubs are in a very small area of North London. They are actually locals that are within walking distance of my new high-tech underground writing laboratory in the middle of Finsbury Park. If you've got a favourite London Irish pub you want me to check out for a later edition, email tim@jayzus.com.

Thanks to Sarah, Terry, Martyn, Spizz, Tony and Phil for research.

Key

 Over the top Irishness

 Guinness too cold

 Marketing man's idea

 Music pub

 Old men drink here

 Urban trendies drink here

 Hard drinking Irish singer alert!

 Good Guinness

 Huge pub

 Football on TV

 Gaelic sport on TV

 'European' barstaff

 Threat of violence

 They should knock it down

 Maudlin

 Irish colleen barstaff

 Loud city boys

The Arsenal Tavern

Mountgrove Road/Blackstock Road N4

An idiosyncratically rambling old men's play pen or a dark and fist-fight-friendly cavern? Depends on your attitude. It is a shambles though with a few wine-bar style high tables tacked on at some point in the mid 80s to give it style. I like it. Best place to watch Irish sports if you don't want to walk all the way into Finsbury Park. Name allegedly changed in the 30s by Arsenal boss Herbert Chapman when he did for Gillespie Road tube.

The Auld Shillelagh

Stoke Newington Church Street, N16

The dimensions of a canal narrow boat. Fabulous Guinness and a real heavy-duty lock-in. Last time I was here I got so plastered I didn't know who I was so went for a walk at midnight to get some fresh air. They still let me back in afterwards. That's as good a recommendation as you can get for a pub.

The Bank of Friendship

Highbury Park N5

They have a theme tune which is sort of Bryan Adamsish and goes
  'It's the Bank of Friendship,
  The one for me and you.
  The Bank of Friendship,
  We can drink there too.'
Actually, no – that's a complete lie. It is a nice, usually quiet, local, its under-the-counter Irishness only obvious when you spot the Ireland football shirt and picture of Pat Jennings on the wall. There's a crowd of Dubs who sit by the door of one bar who'll probably know you if you went to school in Dublin between 1946 and 1960.

Biddy Mulligan's (the Pride of the Coombe)

Kilburn High Road

Lots of daft slot machines and tacky ballad music. Even stooped to harps on the carpet. Biddy's don't serve normal Guinness, only the extra cold stuff that freezes your insides on its way down. Not the sort of pub to attract a real Irish crowd, you'd think. But you'd be wrong. If you ever get violent urges to sing 'Molly Malone' in public this would be the place to do it.

The Blackstock

Blackstock Road, Finsbury Park

Subtle Irish drinking den. It's only the small well-placed leprechauns that give it away. Guinness good and cheap. Kitchen looks not to have been used since the sixties. Circular bar so you can keep running if someone is trying to kill you. Recently done-up (i.e. painted). When I went to the bog, flies suddenly appeared buzzing round my genitals. It was like a scene from *One Hundred Years of Solitude*.

The Blarney Stone

Lordship Lane, Manor House

Sprawling Irish superpub tucked into a quiet little spot just north of the reservoirs. Clever use of green in the livery. Best place for an Irish-style knees up in the N16 area.

The Boston Arms

Dartmouth Park Hill, Tufnell Park

Mammoth and shabby Irish boozer that seems more like it's in inner-city Dublin than most modern inner-city Dublin pubs. Average age of clientele about sixty-two on a good day – lots of big old blokes with very red faces. Takes ten minutes to walk from one side of pub to the other. More when pub is full. Often traditional music in the side room, which has a separate bar and a stage. Irish football or English Premiership on a big screen. If you're looking for long-lost Irish relatives this is a good place to start.

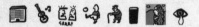

Bodhrán Barneys

Merton Road, SW19

Until very recently this was just a nondescript old South London pub called the White Hart before it caught the Irish disease. The only thing that seems to have changed, apart from the quite terrible name, is the plethora of beer and food information in coloured chalk sub-standard Gaelic lettering. It's in a bloody awful location as well.

Callaghans

Piccadilly

Grossly overpriced beer, pathetic decor – 'while it may be authentic, it's not authentically theirs,' said my Irish companion. Probably designed by computer for the American market. Traditional soft-soap ballads playing – probably a CD called 'Callaghan's Pub Favourites'. Callaghan's even have their own merchandise – T-shirts and baseball caps. It's really just part of a hotel. Not a real pub, more a cultural disease.

Clancys

Holloway

Attractive but expensive take on Irishana. Took me two or three attempts to find it again after my last visit which suggests that it is a state of mind.
NB Went back to this pub recently because I was starving and met a Norwegian opera singer drinking himself into a stupor. He was the only other person there and gave us a quick flick through his repertoire. The Guinness was still too cold but at least it felt like a scene from *The Marriage of O'Figaro*.

Filthy McNastys

Amwell Street, London N1

Shane MacGowan often sits at the bar and his Pogues gold discs are displayed on the walls. Proper Guinness served at decent temperatures for a young mediaish crowd, most of whom wear those modish sub-NHS designer specs. Trad sessions some nights and at weekends in the back bar. Literary evenings too. No TV, just loud music and loud people talking about their jobs.

Finnegan's Wake

Fulham Palace Road, London W6

Huge 1940s building just round from Hammersmith Apollo – get lots of people in DJs before ballets, etc. Used to be a bog standard crappy Fulham Palace Road place before getting the shamrock makeover around '96. Far too Oirishy for real Irish, one would have hoped but, again, not so – gets groups of lads and middle-aged women sitting out the night. They have Irish music live sometimes and it's usually crap – red-faced blokes with moustaches murdering old standards and encouraging singsongs.

Finnegan's Wake

Lambs Conduit Street WC2

Used to be The Sun, a fine smoke-drenched drinking hole with interesting beers, before being Finneganised a few years back. I only went in once and it broke my heart so I've never been back.

The Kingdom

Kilburn High Road

A big long bar on the left and a big long velvety cushioned bench on the right – no wasting of space with silly partitions. Five Guinness taps and one Beamish. Authentically dingy. Mad old Kerrymen, who have set up home at the end of the bar, jump up to take the piss out of any strangers that might accidentally wander in off the street. Judging by the reaction of the barmaid, this is obviously a regular occurrence.

Liam Og's

Walworth Road, Camberwell

Like a little village pub or the sort of thing you get off the main road in the south and west of Ireland. When I last went in (early '94), surrounded by crimson-faced old boys and labourers, I felt like a tourist (which I suppose I was – it's South London for God's sake).

Liberty's

Camden High Street, NW5

Pics of Irish writers on wall suggests tackiness but this is a real Irish pub: great Guinness, football on TV (Celtic are favourites) and very friendly staff. Always seem to be rumours flying about that it will soon be turned into a wine bar but at the time of writing it's hanging in there. There used to be a short story club which met near the front bar every Tuesday evening.

Lord Nelson

Holloway Road

Pistachio green and black monster. Lads at the bar check out racing on the TV from their pints of Guinness (perfect temperature).

Maggie's

Chamberlain Road, Kensal Rise, NW10

Imagine going to visit your great aunt and uncle in a little house on the out-skirts of Macroom. The sitting room is covered in red and cream velvety flock wallpaper and a few of their OAP friends are round sitting on hard chairs nursing halfs of stout and chatting away in accents you can't under-stand. That's what Maggie's is like. Old fellas in crisp suits and creased faces. Seems to have disappeared though.

McGoverns

Kilburn High Road

Like a big canteen, mustard yellow walls. A long empty bar on one side, small bar at the back. Old blokes stand about talking football. The only visible beer tap was Kilkenny – prepared for disappointment but all the others hidden. Good Guinness. High-backed armchairs. You'd come here if you were eighteen looking for beer-fuelled, cheap-perfume-and-aftershave action.

Moll Cutpurse

Stamford Hill Road, N15

Old pub with loads of real ale long handles, none of which are connected up. 'Nah, we stopped doin' that a while back.' Middle-aged blokes sit around doing crosswords. Seen better days but a nice atmosphere all the same. Setanta sport on two screens.

Molly Malone's

Whitecross Street, EC4

Pre-fashionable Irish theme pub just on the edge of the city. I saw David O'Leary score his penalty v. Romania in 1990 World Cup here. 'YEEEEE EEEEEESSSS FUCKIN YEEEEEEEESSSSS!!!!!!!!' said the man next to me. Went back recently and it too has gone. Is there an anti-Molly pub policy in London?

North London Tavern

Kilburn High Road

Old-fashioned, high-ceilinged Edwardian boozer with dark wood fittings. No internal connection between the 'posh' lounge and the more downmarket (and thus appealing) public bar. A crowd of content *owl fellahs* watch the racing on the telly. Barmen smart in white shirts.

O'Hanlons

Tysoe Street, London EC1

Dublin Guinness – seems like a quite genuine old country pub but you know it can't be. Friendly staff, great food and the best beer selection in London (they brew their own). A mixture of people from middle-aged businessmen to the ubiquitous young Clerkenwell trendies. While you're standing around waiting for a table, check out the attractive old mirror.

The Old Bell

Kilburn High Road

Crappo English boozer exterior suggests it's not an Irish pub at all but inside it is a cavernous real Irish drinking den. A stage and at the back a mass-ive mural of an Irish farm labourer. Irish voices echo from all parts of the building. Smells of lock-ins and snooker.

The Ould Triangle

Plimsoll Road , N4

Used to be the Plimsoll, now sports shiny new wood fittings and dense 60s style cigarette smoke that makes it difficult to see the other side of the pub. Sessions some days. Very fine Guinness. The clientele is very small – possibly a jockey family nearby.

O'Neills

Fitzrovia

Fakey two-floored pub for thick men in suits who talk about sport and like shit beer.

O'Neills

Rupert Street

Scary non-Irish Irish pub. Foreign barstaff didn't understand our accents to start with then laughed when we scarpered after a half pint. Could they be deported, perhaps?

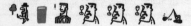

O'Neills

Euston Road

It's near the Barclays cash machine and it also has special music nights. Girls I know like the little barman called Fiachra who looks like Liam Gallagher.

Pelican

All Saints Road, W11

Pool room upstairs and darts. Popular for market traders from nearby Portobello. One of best Paddy's day venues if you like tears, hugs and sentimental music (and let's face it, who doesn't?). Used to have Irish cable sport channel Setanta, but not anymore (a hurling downturn?). There's a colour code system to denote how long people have been drinking there – bright red, more than 15 years, down to pinkish, last couple of months.

Powers

Kilburn High Road

A trendy pub/bar, dark atmosphere, Victorian artefacts scattered about and eclectic art on the black wood walls. More of a thirtysomething urban post club scene crowd than other nearby pubs, does DJ parties and gig nights. Do they run an anti-old-bloke policy?

The Queen

Ferndale Road, SW9

Yes, it's in Brixton, but no, it's not achingly trendy. Far from it; far from everything in fact (somehow it feels like you're in Dresden in the aftermath of Bomber Harris' tender ministries). A solid, sound old London-Irish pub with a generous lock-in policy. Magnus Mills drinks here.

Quins

Hawley Street, Camden

I was very drunk when I came in here after a long session but I remember the Guinness was too cold and I drew a ballpoint-pen tattoo on somebody's cleavage.

The Rose

Snowsfield, Borough

The place to watch hurling and Gaelic football. Big screen at the back for crop-haired young sports fans, small TVs at front for older crowd. Great mural along the back wall of a stylised Irish pub crowd in which all the punters look like film stars. If you like hearing Life Stories, this is the place to come.

Rosie O'Grady's

Camden Road

Smallish North London pub with not too much over-the-top Irishness and a penchant for real music sessions. Rumour has it that Rosie O'Grady is the landlady (and therefore a real person) and not a marketing brand, which is almost unheard of these days.

Scruffy Murphy's

Fleet Street

Ropey boozer cashing in on famous name on the site of older English pub. To begin with there was an old rusty bike outside, but presumably someone pinched that. The 1920sness of it is all a bit much and the beer isn't that great either. They usually have Irish people behind the bar but they're more likely actors than trained staff. Tends to get too full of 'suits'.

Scruffy Murphy's

Piccadilly

For a theme pub it's not bad – small, with OK decor and beer that is marginally cheaper than other pubs in the area (which if you tot it up over several years could be beneficial for your pension plan).

Shannons

Putney High Street

One-off kit pub in a crappy pseudoposh S. London location which, by the time this comes out, will have changed its name to the latest pub fad (McTavish's, Bavarian Sausage Kellar, Ye Olde Worlde Tavernee, etc.).

The Toucan

Soho

Great little bar right on the edge of Soho Square – nice staff, quiet, didn't seem too touristy (which is hard to believe considering the location). Would have stayed for the night but hit it at the end of long afternoon session. Miles better than the WaxyOneilly Murphys in the same area.

The Twelve Pins

Seven Sisters Road, Finsbury Park

Not encouraging from the outside but a spacious light interior is surprisingly present. Impossible to escape the TV sport experience, no matter where you are in the pub a screen looks down on you. Lots of wood and yellow stained-effect paint.

Waxy O'Connors

Rupert Street

Cavernous theme booze in the heart of the West End. A dead tree is the centrepiece. Different styles of bar – a cellar where there's sessions, loud music piped upstairs, Guinness or Murphys and proper barmen (Dublin/Sydney rather than Madrid/Bordeaux) serving in black trousers and white shirts, red-faced twentysomething Irish city type crowd with too much money singing away to the toothbrush and knickers in handbag brigade. Groups of foreign tourists sit at tables with just a mineral water between them – this sort of behaviour should be outlawed.

Winchester Hall Tavern

Archway Road

A huge and very beautiful High Victorian boozer with Irishness running through its veins and not its colour scheme. Ornate glass, high ceilings and two bars – one for youngish blokes and old ladies, the other for sixty-something Irish guys with melancholy faces. The only bad thing is that it's not a lucky pub for the Irish football team.

Irish Crossword

compiled by Terry & Pat

ACROSS

1. Liquid cross in Ireland. (9)
6. One from 1 ac., 2, 5, 14 dn, 15 may be arresting. (5)
9. Fall from Faith (left with part of church). (5)
10. Silver coins scattered about holy man make people dubious about God. (9)
11. Listen to this! Rum trees love Marg! (10)
12. Against Antrim's National Trust Institute for a start. (4)
14. Red Hats confused by famines. (7)
15. Murder Dan, say, in Leinster. (7)
17. Refuse to deal with Cricketing Captain. (7)
19. Internal cast-iron guttering needed by 22! (4,3)
20. One vehicle? Terrible! (4)
22. Obese female with uplifting device needs TV priest. (6,4)
25. American female carpet weaver? (9)
26. See 14 dn. (5)
27. Writer – weird essayist who lost little sister. (5)
28. 'Les Moynes' is wrong – and broke! (9)

DOWN

1. Western drinks found west of England. (5)
2. Faraway place with strange prayer pit? (9)
3. Irish dance No. 1, etc., jigged – let's vote again! (2-8)
4. Orders not the only fruit? (6)
5. Strange land in UK, after first deserted in County Louth. (7)
6. The understanding of 'Soldier Road'. (4)
7. Bad weather, we hear – it's time for a monarch! (5)
8. Not like 22, but still a drunken bent saint. (9)
13. Love-sign with representation unknown used to imitate oil painting. (10)
14, 26. Capital has active youth policy leaders in strength – could make a meal of it. (6,3,5)
16. Annoy a childish horse with artist and container of ecstasy. (9)
18. You won't find 22 in this drink space! (7)
19. Trendy person? That's callous! (7)
21. Part of aria vocals on river. (5)
23. Boardsmen who 7? (5)
24. Love drunken Dubliners – should start the betting! (4)

Irish Crossword

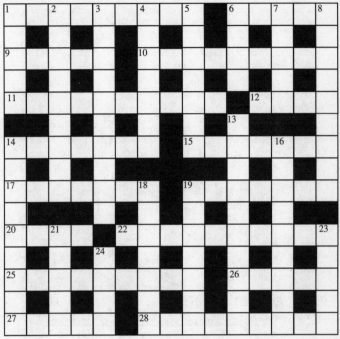

compiled by Terry & Pat

[For the answers – see page 318]

Distribution of tourists in holiday season

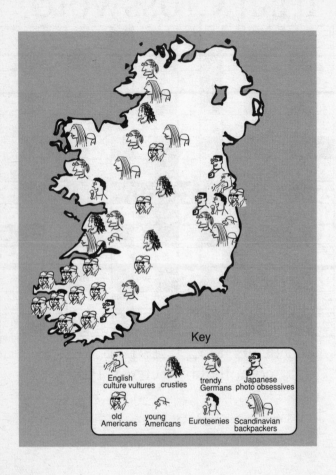

Distribution of rainfall

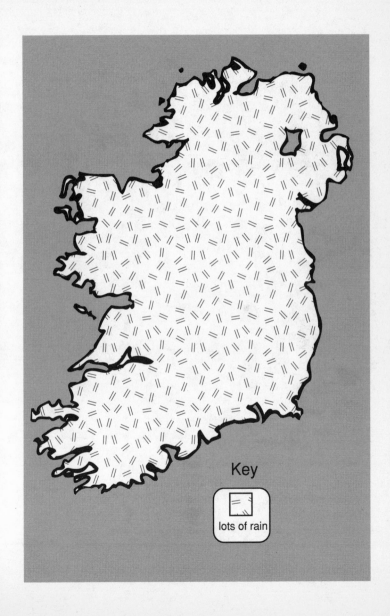

Key

lots of rain

Distribution of conversational topics

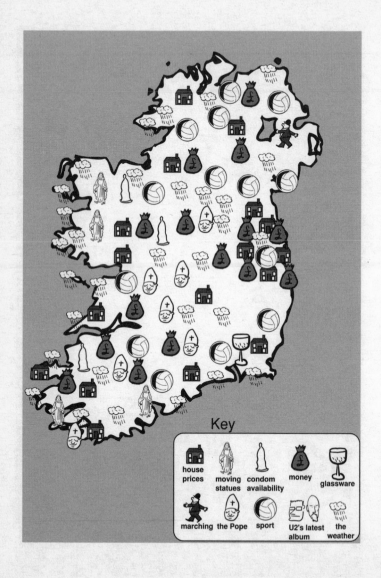

INDEX

SOLUTIONS

ACROSS

1. Waterford
6. Garda
9. Lapse
10. Agnostics
11. Stereogram
12. Anti
14. Dearths
15. Kildare
17. Boycott
19. Iron Gut
20. Ivan
22. Father Jack
25. Broadloom
26. Prawn
27. Yeats
28. Moneyless

DOWN

1. Wales
2. Tipperary
3. Re-election
4. Oranges
5. Dundalk
6. Gist
7. Reign
8. Abstinent
13. Oleography
14. Dublin Bay
16. Aggravate
18. Tearoom
19. Inhuman
21. Avoca
23. Kings
24. Odds